TALAL NIZAMEDDIN

Russia and the Middle East

Towards a New Foreign Policy

ST. MARTIN'S PRESS
NEW YORK

41026427
DLC

33300

RUSSIA AND THE MIDDLE EAST
Copyright © 1999 by Talal Nizameddin

St. Martin's Press, Scholarly and Reference Division,
175 Fifth Avenue, New York, NY 10010

First published in the United States of America in 1999

Printed in India

ISBN: 0-312-22538-5

Library of Congress Cataloging-in-Publication Data

Nizameddin, Talal.
    Russia and the Middle East : towards a new foreign policy / Talal
Nizameddin
        p.   cm.
    Includes bibliographical references and index.
    ISBN 0-312-22538-5 (cloth)
    1. Middle East—Foreign relations—Russia (Federation) 2. Russia
(Federation)—Foreign relations—Middle East. 3. Middle East-
-Foreign relations—Soviet Union.   4. Soviet Union—Foreign
relations—Middle East.   5. Soviet Union—Foreign
relations—1945-1991.   I. Title.
DS63.2.R9N59   1999
327.47056'09'049—dc21   99-14834
                                                            CIP

ACKNOWLEDGEMENTS

There are many people whose help and support I have greatly appreciated, but unfortunately it is impossible to list all of them. However, this work could not have been successfully completed without the assistance of the following: President of the Palestinian National Authority Yasser Arafat; Deputy Director of the Middle East Department at the Russian Foreign Ministry Sergei Kepechenko; and Deputy Director of the Institute of Oriental Studies Vitalii Naumkin, together with the library assistants at the IOS. It is a measure of their generosity that they gave up their precious time to help a student in his research.

In addition, I would like to thank Abdel Magid Farid, who served as Minister for Presidential Affairs under President Gamal Abdel Nasser of Egypt, for his advice and encouragement between 1994 and 1997. I also thank Dr Ahmad Ashraf Marwan, who was chief of national security in the early 1970s under President Anwar Sadat, for providing vital documents of the meetings between the Egyptian and Soviet leaderships from 1971-2; Muhiyaddin Khoja, Saudi ambassador to Russia during the first five years of the Yeltsin leadership, who kindly and candidly answered some difficult questions in the summer of 1996 regarding Saudi foreign policy and its complicated relations with Russia during an uncertain period; Mahmoud Hamoud, Lebanese ambassador to Moscow in the last years under Gorbachev; and Dr Sami Amara, whose knowledge of the diplomatic scene in Moscow made my work there in the autumn of 1996 more fruitful than it otherwise would have been.

Special thanks also to Dr Peter Duncan and Professor Geoffrey Hosking, of the school of Slavonic and East European Studies, University of London, who supervised my doctoral work, for their guidance. Dr Duncan, in addition to offering advice and information, also gave me indispensable technical support. Liza Kolker helped me with Russian texts and materials.

Personal thanks are due to my father Arfan Nizameddin, whose expert knowledge of Middle East politics was made available to me whenever I needed it, and whose help and encouragement were invaluable; also to my mother for lighting the candle when the darkness prevented me from seeing the direction of my endeavour.

Finally, thanks to my sisters Hayat and Rima, and my good friends Herminio Pineiro and Ben Roberts.

Beirut,   T. N.
November 1998

CONTENTS

1

INTRODUCTION
THE MAKING OF A NATIONAL
FOREIGN POLICY

Between 1991 and 1998, Russian foreign policy underwent a quiet revolution. It began with the dreams of a reborn Russia in a new world order where democracy, human rights, free enterprise, co-operation and international law reigned supreme. The new élite in Russia looked to the West as a beacon of hope and salvation. Although Mikhail Gorbachev opened the chapter of co-operation with the West, which brought an end to the Cold War, it was the lowering of the Red Flag over the Kremlin which symbolised the last breath of the once mighty Soviet giant. The psychological reaction appeared to be a sense of anger and bitterness at the past. Those who glorified it were characterised as eccentrics or die-hard extremists. In 1992 and 1993, President Boris Yeltsin and his Foreign Minister Andrei Kozyrev represented the Russia of the future, while those who opposed them were seen as wanting to revive the Communist tyranny which had ruled over them for more than seventy years.

In those early years, those who looked to the future of Russia as being a modern state which saw its fate as closely linked to the West were generally referred to as Atlanticists. Their opponents were known as Eurasianists, partly because of the strong emphasis many members of this group placed on geo-strategic factors. Francis Fukuyama was among the many Western academics who defended Atlanticism and criticised the Eurasianists. He looked back to the disintegration of the Ottoman Empire and the founding of the modern Turkish state as an example of the way a power learns to accept its limitations as a result of internal and external factors.[1] The fluidity of the concept of national interests forms the founding basis of his argument. Thus, from that standpoint, Fukuyama argued that Soviet 'national interests' were not applicable to a new

1

democratic Russia, which must devise a new foreign policy concept based on its allegiance to the democratic West.

Sergei Stankevich represented the view of a growing number of Russian academics, who were not necessarily pro-Soviet, but who maintained that certain unchanging realities existed within the sphere of international relations.[2] Writing in response to Fuku-yama's argument, Stankevich argued that even his Turkish example did not suffice because the once great Ottoman power continued to play a role well outside its national borders, whether in the Balkans, Cyprus, the Middle East, the Caucasus or as far as Central Asia. This was not, he argued, a modern democratic national state but a regional power with neo-imperialist ambitions. Russia was a power on a far larger scale, and for Stankevich and other Eurasianists it would have been naïve to expect it to retreat into its shell and ignore the turbulent events around its borders, par-ticularly in the former Soviet republics.

The Russian Foreign Ministry, under Kozyrev, made a distinct policy change between 1992 and 1993, toning down its pro-Westernism and adopting policies in the Commonwealth of Independent States (CIS) which were more harmonious to those being espoused by the Eurasianists. It was with increasing frequency that Kozyrev and other top government officials began to refer to Russia as a 'great power'. This in itself was a move away from the New Thinking of Soviet Foreign Minister Shevardnadze and the first year under Kozyrev, in which it was tacitly admitted that the internal problems of the country were so great that it was rendered helpless in international affairs. Shevardnadze lamented, in his autobiography, the discrepancy between Soviet 'power' in the world as a leading arms seller, and the 'Third World' condition of many of its citizens.[3]

The development of Moscow's foreign policy resulted in making the 'Atlanticist-Eurasianist' division insufficient for explaining the dynamics of change. From 1992 Russia involved itself in regional affairs – first, in the post-Soviet space with the wars in Georgia, the Azerbaijani-Armenian war, the war in Tajikistan, a dispute with Ukraine over the Black Sea Fleet and other territorial and ethnic issues, and the Baltic states and Kazakhstan over ethnic Russians living there. Kozyrev, a staunch pro-Westerner, himself appeared to be convinced that it was up to Russia to ensure regional stability because nobody else could. The Chechen war added to the belief that if regional conflicts were not controlled, then the tide of chaos could spread inside Russia's own borders. Andranik Migranian, an adviser to President Yeltsin, took this argument further to note that if Russia did not act firmly to promote its interests in the Caucasus and Central Asia, Iran and Turkey were two regional powers which would be able to step into Russia's shoes.[4] In the same way that the Monroe Doctrine outlined the rest of the American continent as a US sphere of influence, the territories of the CIS were viewed as an area for Russian domination.

Kozyrev, while abandoning the idealism of the radical pro-Westerners, did not convert to the neo-imperialist or neo-communist viewpoint. He remained a pro-Westerner, but there was an added pragmatism to his policies. Meanwhile, a large body of media in the West was being discredited for failing to distinguish between those who were hostile to the West in principle, such as Vladimir Zhirinovskii's extreme nationalist Liberal Democratic Party, and pragmatic nationalists, who were suspicious of the West but did not believe a more assertive Russia would necessarily lead to conflict with it. Gennadii Ziuganov and General Aleksandr Lebed were two leading contenders in the 1996 presidential elections who were best categorised as pragmatic nationalists.

Neil Malcolm, Alex Pravda, Margot Light and Roy Allison all agreed that there was a basic left-right-centre division, based on the democratic reformers, neo-communist and centrist outlooks.[5] Others argued that the flux and mutability of Russian internal affairs made it impossible to create a lasting and useful categorisation of foreign policy debates in Russia. However, here I argue that the foreign policy options for Moscow are best analysed in five groups: radical pro-Westerners, pragmatic pro-Westerners, centrist-nationalists, pragmatic nationalists and extreme nationalists. Chapter 4, on the debates and policies in the first five years under Yeltsin, focuses on these arguments in the light of relations with the Middle East.

With the birth of a foreign policy within a 'national' framework, it became more fashionable in Russia to attempt to define the meaning of national interest. One article in *Mirovaia ekonomika i mezhdunarodnye otnosheniia* (1996)[6] noted that the concept of national interests was new to Russia. In tsarist times there was an imperial foreign policy, while under communism it was, in theory at least, underpinned by internationalism. Certainly, Stalin introduced 'socialism in one country', but this was a workers' state and the national divisions within the Soviet Union were not taken into account. The very word 'natsional'nyi' in Russian implied ethnic nationality – whether Jew, Kazakh, Chechen and so on. Thus national interest, since 1991, had to mean not only the interests of Russians within the Russian Federation, but all the 'nationalities' within it. A new problem was created after 1991, when it was noted that many Russians lived in neighbouring countries, such as Kazakhstan, the Ukraine and Estonia. It was asked, not without reason, 'What about their interests?' President Boris Yeltsin immediately affirmed his 'duty' towards the twenty-five million Russians outside the republics: 'But understand me that it is impossible to defend people with tanks. After that their lives would be more complicated. It is necessary to put our relations with those republics on a juridical foundation, one of international rights, which we are presently doing.'[7] This issue remained unresolved, though Moscow insisted that if these Russians were harmed or threatened, then it would be forced to take action to protect them.[8]

Post-Soviet policy under Kozyrev was generally perceived as being confused. His successor, Evgenii Primakov, succeeded in controlling the tide of change after 1991 and channelling it towards a much more clearly defined policy. As one US commentator noted at the end of 1997: 'Seven years ago, Primakov was racing around the Middle East in a futile bid to stop the Persian Gulf war. The Americans regarded him as a meddlesome nuisance. [...] But now, Primakov is finally where he has always thought Russian diplomats should be: at the centre of world attention.'[9]

Soviet interests and the Middle East: competition and co-existence

The West and China posed the most serious direct military threat to the USSR and in this sense at least the Middle East was a minor factor. But the Middle East was a key battleground on which the superpowers had played their Cold War game ever since the British and French began evacuating the region in the 1950s. It is useful to place a high degree of importance on history because without it there would be no reference point from which to compare, contrast or chart the course of Russia's Middle East policy.

The Middle East, in this context, refers to Turkey, Iran, the Arab Gulf states, Israel and its neighbours. The omission from this work of Oman, Kuwait, the United Arab Emirates, Bahrain, Qatar and Yemen (North and South in the Soviet era) is partly due to practical factors; looking at a country such as Qatar, for example, would take up too much space for the sake of making a minor point. On the whole, Saudi policy dictated the general thrust of the policies of its fellow Gulf Co-operation member-states, although since the dissolution of the USSR there were more visible signs of intra-GCC differences. Relations with the Yemens, particularly South Yemen, were very close during the Cold War. However, they were regarded as being on the periphery of the Middle East. From the Soviet viewpoint, they did not relate to the three key features which were of interest to Moscow: the Arab-Israeli conflict, US-Soviet rivalry for influence and control in the Gulf, and relations with the bordering states of Iran and Turkey. These three aspects shape the most important framework for conducting this research regarding Russian foreign policy and the Middle East. Until the early 1970s Egypt formed the cornerstone of Soviet policy in the region by enabling it to rival the United States. Yet once President Anwar Sadat signed a peace treaty with Israel and made his country a US ally, Moscow chose to ignore it. As Egypt did not fit into the three areas of concern listed above, it has been omitted from the post-Soviet period of research.

Stalin's secretive nature superimposed itself on the Soviet system and this did not exclude foreign policy making. This ambivalence during the Cold War era fuelled the Western political and academic debate between left and right, with both sides deftly using the vagueness from the Kremlin to put forward their own interpretations. Although the divisions were far more complex than that of 'pro-establishment' and 'anti-establishment' academics in the West, there was in broad terms a basic conflict in attitude regarding Moscow's intentions. On the one hand there were those, mainly in the United States, who argued that the USSR was an aggressive, expansionist 'evil empire' (to quote President Ronald Reagan) seeking to destabilise the world order for the purpose of extending its own influence. This was countered, on the other hand, by the view that Moscow was generally a 'cautious bear', to borrow the term used by Efraim Karsh.[10] According to this argument, the Soviet Union possessed all the means (including military ones) of a superpower, yet deliberately avoided any actions which could have forced it to use them in a direct clash with its chief adversary, the United States. To elaborate on Karsh's metaphor, the Russian bear did not hesitate to extend its claws when it was necessary to defend itself but it was careful not to use them lest it lead to a life-threatening confrontation.

It was widely agreed, as Robert O. Freedman pointed out in *Moscow and the Middle East: Soviet Policy Since the Invasion of Afghanistan*, that both superpowers, and the leaderships in the capitals of the Middle East, were all locked in the two-camp mentality which was set by President Harry S. Truman and John Foster Dulles on the one hand and Joseph Stalin and Viacheslav Molotov on the other.[11] Khrushchev continued to believe in the epic battle between capitalism and communism, but his policies were based on existing realities at the time, which included the need to divert the Cold War from direct confrontation to the Third World. Alexei Vassiliev, in *Russian Policy in the Middle East: From Messianism to Pragmatism*, supported the view that Khrushchev's reign provided the basis of Soviet foreign policy until 1985: 'After the fall of Nikita Khrushchev, there was no change in Soviet policies in the Middle East region.'[12] George W. Breslauer, in his editorial role in *Soviet Strategy in the Middle East*, was in agreement with Vassiliev about Soviet intentions, which 'sought to protect a radical new ally by pushing for Arab unity and Egyptian mobilisation as a means of deterring US or Israeli intervention, while simultaneously seeking to avoid escalation into a full-scale war'.[13] According to Vassiliev: 'As far as the Soviet Union supported the Arab confrontation with the West (though without pushing things to the point where it might itself have become involved in a conflict) ...Soviet policy had clear-cut parameters and was rather fruitful.'[14]

In the following chapter, describing Soviet-Middle East relations from 1945-85, important documents are presented which outline top-level meetings between the Egyptian and Soviet leaderships before the former suddenly announced it would break off relations with the latter. The Egyptian minutes of the meetings in October 1971 and April 1972, which were classified and remain unpublished but to which I was given access, detailed the growing suspicions between the two sides. Cairo feared that Moscow wanted to maintain a balance of power in the region by preventing an Arab victory over Israel which might have resulted in direct US intervention to defend the Jewish state. The Russian leadership suspected that Sadat was secretly negotiating with Washington in order to get the best deal available for Egypt. As it turned out, both sets of suspicions were founded on a firm measure of reality.

For similar reasons, during the 1970s and 1980s there was growing friction between Syria and the USSR, as highlighted by Dennis Ross, in 'Soviet Behaviour toward the Lebanon War 1982-1984' (Chapter 4 of Breslauer's book). Moscow had failed to dissuade Syria from invading Lebanon (fighting against the Palestine Liberation Army and other leftist forces in Lebanon), and to persuade President Hafez Asad to co-operate with long-time rival Saddam Hussein of Iraq. The Soviet Union was also pressurising Syria to take part in peace negotiations which would raise Moscow's profile in the region. In other words, Moscow's chief objective was to become 'a recognised arbiter of events in the area'.[15] With regard to the Iran-Iraq war, Moscow also found it a strain to maintain a key ally (Iraq), which was in many ways uncontrollable, partly because of Iraq's ability to buy arms with petro-dollars. Russia found it equally difficult to win over a strategically much more useful potential ally – Iran. Ross and James Clay Moltz, in 'The Soviet Union and the Iran-Iraq War 1980-1988', argued that 'what the Iran-Iraq war highlights most of all are the sheer limits of Soviet influence in the region'.[16]

The most popular explanation for Soviet retreat from international affairs, including the Middle East, was economic disintegration at home, blamed largely on the stagnation during the Brezhnev era. *Gorbachev's 'New Thinking' and Third World Conflicts*, edited by Jiri Valenta and Frank Cibulka, studied Soviet foreign policy reforms from that premise. The chapter by Vernon Aspaturian, 'Gorbachev's "New Political Thinking" and Foreign Policy', argued that Moscow's global expansionism and adventures led to the downfall of the system: 'The most serious and crippling price that the Soviet Union has paid for its immense military growth and globalist ambitions was the disorientation, dislocation, and deformation of the Soviet economy, which entered into a period of stagnation and decline.'[17]

This point was repeated in *Soviet Foreign Policy in Transition*, edited by Roger Kanet, Deborah Nutter Miner and Tamara J.

Resler. Under Gorbachev, wrote Kanet and Garth Katner, 'the Soviet leadership recognised its basic inability to mould the international environment to meet its own objectives', blaming the cause on domestic shortcomings. So while some observers such as Aspaturian argued that international demands sucked out resources from the Soviet system, Kanet and Katner pointed out that dwindling resources from within weakened Moscow's international standing: 'The primary objectives of Gorbachev's campaign of perestroika and glasnost were based on the recognition that the position of the USSR in the world depended upon a dramatic improvement in the functioning of the Soviet economy.'[18] Gorbachev's New Thinking totally rejected the role of ideology in foreign policy making; conflict was to be replaced with harmony and the hand of friendship was extended to all willing to share Moscow's new vision. The courting of Israel was among the most notable consequences of New Thinking. Robert Freedman's *Soviet Policy Toward Israel under Gorbachev* argued that this began in 1987. As well as rebuffing Asad, Gorbachev also told PLO Chairman Yasser Arafat in 1988 that 'Israel's interests had to be considered in any peace settlement'.[19] Considering that Moscow had severed all ties with Israel in 1967, and the Jewish state's existence was a key card in Arab opposition, such remarks portrayed a clear reversal in perspective.

The severest test for Gorbachev's new strategy in a crisis situation in the Middle East was the Gulf War. The Soviet position against the old ally Iraq and with the old enemy the United States raised an important question for Gad Barzilai in his book, *The Gulf Crisis and its Global Aftermath*: 'Have economics, interdependence and functional co-operation really come to supersede geopolitical preoccupations like national identity, territory and security which traditionally have ranked at the top of international concerns?'[20] From that premise, it thus raised the suggestion that Gorbachev had replaced one ideologically internationalist outlook – communism – with another vision of humanitarian harmony. This may have had universally noble intentions but it failed to recognise 'primitive' and traditional national interests and security problems. Under Yelstin, the discrediting of Gorbachev's idealism was in part used by the anti-Westernisers to make their point that the realities of the present did not permit illusions of a new world which did not exist.

Russia and the Middle East: setting the parameters

The general aim of this work is to provide a better understanding of Russian policy toward the Middle East since 1991. Chapters 2 and 3 provide a historical setting: the period 1945-85 shows that despite intense efforts, Soviet policy was confronted with serious limitations which brought about the radical policies introduced by Gorbachev and Eduard Shevardnadze. In Chapter 4 an examination of the political and academic debates revolving around Russia's policy will show that the ideals of New Thinking and the radical pro-Westernism met their own limitations, forcing Moscow to face existing realities in international politics. Yeltsin himself announced the need for his country to reassert itself on the world stage: 'It is now particularly important to draw a distinction between partnership (with the West) and attempts to dominate or to foist on us their own actions which run counter to Russia's interests. It [domination] is unacceptable to Russia.'[21]

However, this 'realisation' by Moscow that a new policy was necessary relates to the more specific aims of this work: to refute arguments that Russia would have, out of some kind of nostalgia for the Cold War, resorted to the competitiveness of the past and that out of disappointment with the West, Moscow's élite (and public opinion) would have sheltered in its 'Eastern' or Eurasian roots. In both cases, using the Middle East as an example, the evidence proved insufficient to make such claims- credible. The suggestion regarding the Eurasianist outlook of Russia proved to be particularly erroneous because it was unrealistic for a country with such unique features in such unusual circumstances to place itself in any single 'box'. From this standpoint, I aim to take the argument further and show that Russia was seeking to formulate a new policy from a pragmatic 'national' perspective, which very often collided with past prejudices and accepted norms. As one Russian view contended:

'We are abandoning old friends', charge the critics of this approach, but those now responsible for Russian foreign policy reply: 'We are becoming a civilised state, and are respecting international law in action and not only in words.' New standards and new behaviour brings new friends; the old friends remain friends, as long as close involvement with them does not contradict the new values.[22]

The study of Russia's policies with the key countries of the Middle East in the first five year period fits neatly with this comment.

Up till 1994, it was widely suggested in Russia and the West that there was confusion in Moscow about who was in charge of foreign policy making. *RFE/RL Research Report* published in February an article by Jan Adams titled 'Who Will Make Russia's Foreign Policy in 1994?' She stated categorically that the new constitution gave the decision-making powers to the president and took it away from parliament, which was dominated by opponents of the radical and pragmatic pro-Westerners. The nomination of Primakov as foreign minister on 9 January 1996 added strength to the central decision-making bodies of Russia and made it easier for the new balanced and centrist-nationalist policy to be implemented.

The Western media generally misunderstood this shift in policy. Moscow's developing policy towards one guided by national interests was perhaps seen as being too dull to sell newspapers. Instead, it was implied that Yeltsin was conceding ground to the extreme nationalists (Zhirinovskii was given much more public attention than his real political influence) and that Russia was heading towards a new confrontation with the West. The nomination of Primakov was seen as another step in this direction, as one headline in the *Guardian* asserted: 'Russia selects trouble-maker.'[23] The developing Russian policy was best reflected in the increasing attention that was being redirected towards the Middle East. Yeltsin's special envoy to the region, Viktor Posuvaliuk, who later became deputy foreign minister, stressed in an interview that 'Russia, as a great power, has two key roles with regard to the Middle East. Firstly, it is a close neighbour, a major power with very broad interests, economic, political, spiritual, religious and of course military. Second, is co-sponsorship of the peace talks.'[24] This point was backed up by former Russian Foreign Minister Andrei Kozyrev, who said, 'Russia has serious and long term interest in the Near East.'[25]

In the context of the peace process, Russia did not want to steal the US thunder (and it could not even if it wanted to), but simply re-emphasised that as co-sponsor it could play a positive role. Relations with Israel (Chapter 5) took on a particularly significant feature because this enhanced Moscow's position as an 'honest broker'. Russia's open criticisms of Israel after 1993, which

became more direct in 1996, did not mean that the leade\
was returning to the anti-Israeli anti-Jewish traditions of the So\
era. The criticisms were simply a consequence of the view in\
Moscow that certain actions, such as the bombing of civilian
targets in Lebanon, the building of settlements on disputed territories
while negotiations with the Palestinians were taking place, or the
refusal to discuss the status of Jerusalem, were not conducive to
peace in the region. This was not a radical view, but one that
was actually very similar to the policies of most European capitals.
It was Washington's staunch support for Israel which was out of
line with the international community. Russia was arguably taking
a moderate line.

Moscow's insistence that sanctions against Iraq (Chapter 7) be
eased was similarly misunderstood. While Russia had economic
interests there worth at least $20 billion, the Kremlin acted according
to all UN measures and in full co-operation with the United
States. However, it was increasingly being argued by the political
leadership that it had a right to declare its interests in the region
and to promote its view that sanctions against Iraq should be
gradually eased in accordance with Baghdad's full co-operation
with various UN demands. Kozyrev's attendance in Baghdad of
Iraq's recognition of Kuwaiti borders in November 1994 (achieved
for the first time) was presented as a shining example that Moscow
could play a positive role in the Gulf.

It was likewise with Iran. The dispute over Russia's participation
in the building of a nuclear reactor was perceived as a diversion
from the facts, and suggestions that Tehran's ambition to become
a nuclear power was being aided by Moscow were flatly rejected.
Moscow's argument that it was not in Russia's interest to have
close to its borders an unstable government with nuclear weapons
was totally reasonable. However, the leadership in Moscow stressed
the need to co-operate with Iran because it was a regional power
which carried influence in the Caucasus, Central Asia and the
Gulf; three key areas for Moscow's national interests. For similar
reasons Turkey was given high priority and relations with the
two countries are looked at in greater detail in Chapter 8. The
economic potential in the Middle East of countries such as Turkey,
Iran, Iraq and Saudi Arabia (Chapter 7) in particular was too
great to be ignored. Since 1993, the 'great power' claim that was
becoming more widely heard in Russia, was natural; as a new

nation-state with considerable international standing, it needed to regain the prestige lost in the twilight years of the Soviet era and to build a new basis for national pride. Such sentiments were acceptable for Britain, France, Germany, Japan and the United States and others to have, and did not mean that these countries were belligerent towards others. Moscow was requesting its rightful place as a 'great power' in the Middle East, and the world.

Note on sources

Russian and Arab journals proved highly valuable in the writing of this work. *Nezavisimaia gazeta, Segodnia, Moskovskie novosti* were but a few newspapers which included regular coverage of Russian policies towards the Middle East. *Pravda* was interesting in that it provided the view of the opposition, stubbornly clinging on to old ideas. From the Arab press, *Al-Hayat* was best for its neutrality (most Arab newspapers were directly affiliated to their party or government). *Al-Hayat* also included fairly extensive articles by Viktor Posuvaliuk, Deputy Foreign Minister, who used the opportunity to encourage more trade between Russia and Saudi Arabia (*Al-Hayat* was a Saudi-funded paper), as well as other leading officials from the Russian Foreign Ministry. Other journals, such as *Mezhdunarodnaia zhizn'*, were useful in having a finger on the pulse of Moscow's foreign policy outlook. The Royal United Services Institute for Defence Studies *Journal*, published in London, regularly included relevant articles from authoritative sources. In 1993, it published a presentation by Israeli Prime Minister Yitzhak Rabin to the institute which included interesting observations regarding the end of the Cold War.[26] Its relevance to the Middle East, he wrote, was that 'no Arab leader, be he Saddam Hussein – and he learnt the hard way – President Assad or Qadhafi, can rely anymore on the Soviet umbrella under which he has sheltered for 31 years'.[27]

In addition to contemporary written sources, direct meetings and interviews with individuals closely connected to the subject further enhanced the research basis of this work. Following a field trip to Moscow in October 1996, meetings with several academics and journalists added to the 'insider' dimension. Furthermore, it was possible to meet with officials from the Russian Ministry of Foreign Affairs, most notably Sergei Kepechenko, who was deputy director of the Middle East Desk. The long discussion with Professor Vitalii Naumkin, deputy director of the Institute of Oriental Studies, was positively enriching for this work. From the Arab side, meeting the president of the Palestine National Authority was a particularly productive experience. Yasser Arafat was keen to reiterate the close relations which continued to exist with the élite in Moscow, particularly Evgenii Primakov. Abdel Magid Farid and Dr Ahmad Ashraf Marwan, senior figures in Cairo during the final years under President Nasser and early years under Sadat, provided an insight into Soviet–Egyptian relations at the time and their ultimate breakdown. Saudi Ambassador Muhiyaddin Khoja and Lebanese Ambassador Mahmoud Hamoud both were present in Moscow during the crucial phase of transition, and their co-operation in this research enabled a better understanding of the last years under Gorbachev and early years under Yeltsin.

The approach of this book, in the context of the two choices presented by Celeste A. Wallander, opts for the 'description and documentation of Russian policy', and avoids the 'explicitly and self-consciously theoretical'.[28] The conclusion of that author, who professed a theoretical emphasis, was that 'on the whole Russian foreign policy has become more assertive and confrontational'.[29] By contrast, I hope to show that there exists a difference between defending national interests and adopting behaviour which is 'confrontational', though of course it is possible for the first to lead to the second situation. There was little proof that between 1991 and 1998 Russian policy in the Middle East was characterised by the latter.

Mark Webber reflected on the relevance of the theoretical schism between the schools of Neo-realism and Pluralism/Interdependence on post-Soviet Russia:

> Is it a state which seeks to maximise and assert its power *à la* realism – a course likely to bring it into competition with its erstwhile adversary the US and its new neighbours in the USSR? Or is it a state, now freed of communist ideology, more willing to co-operate with the states of the West, with international organisations and with the other successor states?[30]

Neo-realism, which focuses on the international system rather than internal factors,[31] fits in with this book and the view of

Primakov that multipolarism was the most likely outcome to emerge from the rubble of the bipolarism of the Cold War. However, its leading proponents argued with pessimism that this trend leads to a 'more complicated, more uncertain, and ultimately more dangerous'[32] world.

This book shares the optimism of the pluralist school that the growing role for international institutions and co-operation between the great power centres, a policy of balancing various interests which was repeatedly espoused by Primakov, means a more stable international climate. Russia's behaviour in the Middle East between 1991 and 1998, as I hope I have demonstrated, was generally responsible and rational, giving greater hope for the new millennium.

NOTES

1. Francis Fukuyama, 'The Ambiguity of "National Interests"', in Stephen Sestanovich (ed.), *Rethinking Russia's National Interests*, Washington, DC, 1994.
2. Sergei Stankevich, 'Towards a New Nationalist Idea', in Sestanovich, *op. cit.*
3. Eduard Shevardnadze, *The Future Belongs to Freedom*, London, 1991, p.54.
4. Andranik Migranian, 'Rossiia i blizhnee zarubezh'e' (Russia and the Near Abroad), *Nezavisimaia gazeta*, no.9 (685), 18 January 1994, pp.4-5 and 8.
5. Neil Malcolm, Alex Pravda, Margot Light and Roy Allison, *Internal Factors in Russian Foreign Policy*, Oxford, 1996.
6. Professor A.A. Galkin (from the Gorbachev Foundation), 'Kontseptsiia natsional'nykh interesov: obshchie parametry i Rossiiskaia spetsifika' (The concept of national interests: general parameters and the Russian case), *Mirovaia ekonomika i mezhdunarodnye otnosheniia*, no.8, 1996.
7. John B. Dunlop, 'Russia: Confronting a Loss of Empire 1987-1991', *Political Science Quarterly*, winter 1993-4, p.615.
8. Charles Dick, 'The Military Doctrine of the Russian Federation', *Jane's Intelligence Review*, Special Report no.1, January 1994, p.1.
9. Michael Gordon, 'With Primakov Russia is Again Centre of Attention', New York Times News Service, Moscow, 20 November 1997.
10. Efraim Karsh, *The Cautious Bear: Soviet Military Engagement in Middle East Wars in the Post-1967 Era*, Jerusalem, 1985.
11. Robert O. Freedman, *Moscow and the Middle East: Soviet Policy Since the Invasion of Afghanistan*, New York, 1991, p.16.
12. Alexei Vassiliev, *Russian Policy in the Middle East: from Messianism to Pragmatism*, Reading, 1993, p.62.
13. George W. Breslauer, 'Introduction', in George W. Breslauer (ed.), *Soviet Strategy in the Middle East*, Boston, MA, 1990, p.5.
14. Vassiliev, *op. cit.*, p.64.

15. Dennis Ross, 'Soviet Behaviour Toward the Lebanon War 1982-84' in Breslauer, *op cit.*, p.99.

16. James Clay Moltz and Dennis Ross, 'The Soviet Union and the Iran-Iraq War 1980-88' in Breslauer, *op cit.*, p.123.

17. Vernon Aspaturian, 'Gorbachev's "New Political Thinking" and Foreign Policy', in Jiri Valenta and Frank Cibulka (eds), *Gorbachev's 'New Thinking' and Third World Conflicts*, London, 1990, p.3.

18. Roger Kanet with Garth Katner, 'From New Thinking to the Fragmentation of Consensus in Soviet Foreign Policy' in Roger E. Kanet, Deborah Nutter Miner, Tamara J. Resler (eds), *Soviet Foreign Policy in Transition*, Cambridge, 1992, p.125.

19. Robert O. Freedman, *Soviet Policy Toward Israel under Gorbachev*, New York, 1991, p.xiii.

20. Gad Barzilai, Aharon Klieman and Gil Shidlo, *The Gulf Crisis and its Global Aftermath*, London and New York, 1993, p.11.

21. *BBC SWB*, 29/4/94.

22. Dmitri Riurikov, 'How it all Began: An Essay on New Russia's Foreign Policy' in Teresa Pelton Johnson and Steven E. Miller (eds), *Russian Security After the Cold War: Seven Views from Moscow*, Cambridge, MA, 1994, p.162.

23. *Guardian*, 10 January 1996, p.5.

24. *BBC SWB*, 26 Apr. 1994.

25. *BBC SWB*, 29 Apr. 1994.

26. Yitzhak Rabin, 'Prospects for Peace and Security in the Middle East', *Royal United Services Institute for Defence Studies Journal*, February 1993. p.1.

27. *Ibid.*

28. Celeste A. Wallander, 'The Sources of Russian Conduct: Theories, Framework, and Approaches' in Celeste A. Wallander (ed.), *The Sources of Russian Foreign Policy after the Cold War*, Oxford, 1996, p.1.

29. *Ibid.*, p.2.

30. Mark Webber, *The International Politics of Russia and the Successor States*, Manchester, 1996, p.13.

31. Fred Halliday, *Rethinking International Relations*, London, 1994, p.32.

32. Webber, *op. cit.*, p.340.

2

THE SOVIET UNION AND THE
MIDDLE EAST, 1945-1985:
OPPORTUNITIES AND LIMITATIONS

It would be impossible to understand Russia's relations with the countries of the Middle East without a broader look at Soviet policies towards the region from 1945 to 1985. This forty-year period witnessed the entrenchment of Soviet interests in the Middle East, but it was also accompanied by thwarted expectations and the realisation by Moscow that in many cases the price was too high to justify making a deeper commitment. The split with Egypt in the early 1970s typified the suspicions which both sides harboured. The conclusions drawn from such experiences were to play a noticeable part in the formulation of Russian policy in the Middle East.

There were three distinct phases of Soviet policy towards the Middle East between 1945 and 1985. First 1945-55 when Europe and the United States were the overwhelming preoccupation of the Kremlin; second 1955-67, when Soviet interests in the Middle East reached their peak in terms of success and priorities; and finally 1967-85, when a more calculated approach balanced between aggressive pursuit of low-risk opportunities and cautious manoeuvring in high-risk or complicated situations. These time spans were congruent with the three dominant leaderships between 1945 and 1985: those of Stalin, Khrushchev and Brezhnev. Undoubtedly certain policies, or key aspects of policies, often overlapped as failures and successes passed from one leadership to another. For example, Khrushchev's idea of peaceful co-existence was basically left intact under Brezhnev because it was useful in diverting the superpower conflict to Third World countries where battles could be fought with conventional arms through surrogate armies. Such conflicts, those of the Middle East being a prime example, put the Soviet Union on a par with the United States and forced the two superpowers to negotiate, either publicly or secretly, in order to let the other side know what the limits of their involvement were.

Over this forty-year time span, Moscow had invested heavily in military, economic and political terms in the Middle East, a fact that suggests the region was highly valued by Moscow's top foreign policy makers. But each leadership held its own distinct perception of the region: Stalin paid little concern to the region as a whole though Turkey and Iran were regarded as a high priority because they bordered the Soviet Union. Khrushchev's much broader vision, however, included all countries from the Maghreb to Iran as useful in terms of enhancing Soviet prestige and limiting US influence. This new internationalist outlook also laid emphasis on international institutions such as the United Nations and others created by US-Soviet summits and agreements. Brezhnev's policy was more restrained, in that it dealt only with countries which were either highly reliable or highly strategic. Iraq and Iran, for example, were placed at the top of both categories.

Stalin and the bipolar world

Stalin's immediate priority after the Second World War was to secure the borders of the Soviet Union, particularly to the west, and, as has been fully documented, Europe was eventually divided by Churchill's symbolic 'iron curtain'. Under Stalin, the Soviet Union had become a continental power in both Europe and Asia as its territories straddled both land masses. The Arabs were of little interest to the ageing dictator. But Turkey and Iran, by contrast, were of high geo-strategic value, particularly as they bordered the Soviet Union.

Turkey was of particular interest to Moscow and had been perceived as the chief cause of centuries-old rivalries between the two powers. At the end of the Second World War Stalin pushed forth claims for territories from the Turks, including the Eastern Anatolian provinces of Kars and Ardahan, which were Russian-controlled until the civil war just after the revolution of 1917. But Stalin's more precious jewel was control over the Dardanelles and the Bosphorus Straits. The former would fortify entry into the Black Sea while the latter could be an outlet to the Mediterranean. Anti-Turkish propaganda was intensified and Soviet troops were amassed on the border with the former Ottoman Sultanate so that 'by the spring of 1947 Ankara genuinely feared a Soviet invasion'.[1] But the Turks did not give in to their historic enemy to the north, partly due to strong US backing against the Soviets. Stalin backed down and the troop concentration on the border was nothing more than a bluff. The consequence of this venture was to push the previously neutral Turkey into the arms of the anti-Soviet camp. 'The half-million Turkish army, that helped form NATO, brought the East-West confrontation directly to the USSR's southern border.'[2]

Further east, Iran was seen as another potential buffer to the Soviet Union's southern border. Under the Molotov-Ribbentrop pact Moscow demanded that Iran be in the Soviet sphere of influence. During the war, Soviet troops were stationed in northern Iran while British troops occupied the south in order to prevent the Persians from forming an alliance with the Germans. But an agreement requesting both powers to withdraw at the end of the war was ignored by Moscow, which actually strengthened its military position there in October 1945. Tehran's authority in Soviet-occupied areas was transferred to the Red Army, under the guise of the creation of autonomous Azeri and Kurdish republics.[3] But once again US pressure forced a Soviet retreat; the incident did however create unnecessary hostility from Tehran. A compromise reached between the Iranian leadership and Moscow to establish a Soviet-Iranian oil company and incorporate communists into the government prior to Soviet withdrawal in May 1946, was annulled by Tehran in 1947 when the Red Army had departed.

Beyond the southern border, Moscow's activities in the Middle East were propelled by the motive of expelling the British from the area, which led to its rapid recognition of the Jewish state of Israel. The Arab leaderships were viewed by Moscow as being too dependent on the British, as they consisted of the traditional Arab Hashemite monarchies south of Turkey, British installed Sheikhdoms in the Arabian peninsula and King Faroukh in Egypt. But the Soviet Union under Stalin hastened to show vocal support for Arab struggles for independence from colonial rule, being the first power to support Syria in 1944. It also supported Egyptian demands for British troop withdrawal in 1947. In a speech by Andrei Gromyko to the UN Security Council in August 1947, the Soviet representative said: 'The USSR understands and sympathises with these national aspirations on the part of Egypt and its people towards an independent existence on the basis of sovereign equality with other states and people.'[4] These words were the seeds of a policy that was to be refined and systemised by Khrushchev in later years.

Stalin's recognition of Israel and support for it in the 1948-9 war by sending weapons via Czechoslovakia enraged Arab public opinion, but soon afterwards Moscow cooled relations with Israel. Hence within the very short period of two years, between 1948 and 1950, Stalin's policies had successfully antagonised every single country in the Middle East, though that could have hardly been the real intention. In fact many were puzzled by Soviet policies in the region, particularly the reversal with regard to the creation of Israel. Walter Laqueur argued that the decision to recognise Israel may not have even been made at top level, but 'by some Foreign Ministry advisers and approved by Stalin in a fit of absent-mindedness'.[5] Such a scenario was dismissed by Avigdor Dagan: 'What brought the Soviet Union to the support of the state of Israel were not Russian sympathies but Moscow's assessment that there was a coincidence of interests which the Soviets could use to foster their own aims.'[6] There was no accident or sentiment in Moscow's foreign policy making but design, which foresaw the potential for conflict. Stalin may have hoped that such conflicts could open new possibilities for the USSR, which at the time was completely excluded from the region.

The West's response to Moscow's activities in the region led to the formation on 11 November 1951 of the Middle East Command comprising the United States, Britain, France and Turkey. This bloc was a precursor to the Baghdad Pact. When three months later Greece and Turkey joined NATO, Moscow feared that it was under siege.[7] But the United States found it difficult to foster a broader alliance against the Soviets. John Foster Dulles, US Secretary of State and Stalin's political arch-rival, actually held a very similar outlook of a world divided into two camps that were incompatible. Dulles toured the Middle East in May 1953 to co-ordinate anti-Soviet support. On 1 June, back in Washington, Dulles shared his conclusions:

A Middle East Defense Organization is a future rather than an immediate possibility. Many of the Arab League countries are so engrossed with their quarrels with Israel or with Great Britain or France that they pay little heed to the menace of Soviet Communism. [...] In general, the northern tier of nations shows awareness of the danger.[8]

The Middle East Command was viewed by Moscow as a threat which extended the Cold War arena beyond Europe. The USSR's response on 24 November 1951 to the governments of the United States, France, Britain and Turkey on the issue of the Middle East Command was that such plans 'are nothing other than an attempt to involve the countries of the Middle East in the military measures of the aggressive Atlantic bloc [NATO]'.[9] The statement, probably dictated by Stalin, was prophetic in pointing out that the Middle East would become a local playground for the superpowers, where the game was war.

Khrushchev broadens Moscow's horizons

The power struggle that followed Stalin's death in 1953 was resolved by 1955, and this was reflected in changes to Soviet foreign policy. Nikita Khrushchev's critics described him as poorly educated and unsophisticated, but he was undeniably ambitious and a visionary. His far-reaching domestic endeavours to reform agriculture, modernise industry and place his country at the forefront of space travel and research were matched by an equally enterprising plan for foreign policy. According to such a policy the Soviet Union would no longer be on the defensive as it was under Stalin when the perception was that the world was against the Soviet Union. Instead, Khrushchev's foreign policy sought to attack, seeking new areas as fertile ground for expanding Soviet influence, and this was amply provided in the newly liberated countries of Africa and Asia. It was thus logical that the problem of having Turkey and Iran as a barrier to Soviet expansion could be solved by hurdling over them straight into the heart of the Middle East.

Khrushchev elevated his country from a continental superpower into a world superpower. He believed that the Soviet Union was ready to compete with the United States in every sphere and in every part of the world, but without a need for a direct military confrontation. These aspirations were ideologised by Khrushchev and new slogans were created: peaceful co-existence, peaceful co-operation, the non-capitalist path to development were but a few. Most countries in and around the Middle East were home to US military bases (Morocco, Libya, Turkey, Pakistan and the Arabian Gulf), while British bases in Iraq, Libya, Egypt, Sudan and Jordan underlined Western domination. Moreover, the Baghdad Pact, signed on 24 February 1955, grouped Iran, Iraq, Turkey and Pakistan under a British umbrella in an anti-Soviet alliance. Such 'alliances had therefore to be undermined'.[10] Khrushchev's reasoning was based on the Marxian assumption that 'if the USSR was helping the Middle Eastern countries to win and then to consolidate their independence, it would accelerate the "dying" of the capitalist West inasmuch as the West could not survive without sources of raw materials, without markets and without cheap labour'.[11] Beyond ideological considerations, the Baghdad Pact also provided a large and menacing launching-ground from the USSR's soft underbelly.

A ready ally for the Soviet Union was Egypt's Gamal Abdel Nasser, who vehemently opposed the Baghdad Pact because it directly challenged his pan-Arabist dream, and his ambition to realise it. Khrushchev recognised that it would be necessary to invest heavily in allies in the Middle East in order to find openings which would counterbalance US inroads there.[12] In September 1955 a $250 million Czechoslovak-Egyptian arms deal opened the door for a flood of Soviet supplies and investments. The 1955 agreement included the supply of 100 MiG-15 fighters, 45 Il-28 jet bombers and 150 T-34 tanks as the core of the deal. A new phase in Soviet involvement began in the Middle East, characterised by a high level of political, economic and military commitment.

The Anglo-French conspiracy with Israel against Egypt over the Suez Canal in 1956 was to draw the Soviet Union to the heart of Middle East politics. The Egyptian leader's announcement that he would nationalise the canal was met with a vitriolic response from London and Paris. Nasser's attempt to defuse the crisis by offering compensation to shareholders and to adhere to the 1888 Constantinople Convention on the freedom of navigation was rejected and Operation Musketeer was executed. On 30 October Israel invaded the Sinai peninsula while Britain and France demanded that both Israeli and Egyptian troops withdraw from the canal zone, as had already been agreed in the secret plan. On 31 October British and French jets attacked the canal zone as well as Cairo and Alexandria. The unsophisticated London-Paris conspiracy led to international outrage and it gave the USSR the opportunity to castigate the 'imperialist ambitions' of Britain and France, and of course to move attention away from the Soviet tanks which had been sent into Hungary to crush a disobedient leadership.

Nikolai Bulganin, Soviet Prime Minister under Khrushchev, wrote to US President Eisenhower asking for a joint stand against the aggressors: 'The Soviet Union and the United States of America bear a special responsibility for stopping the war and restoring peace and tranquillity in the area of the Near and Middle East.'[13] These events marked the end of an era for Britain and France in the Middle East, and the beginning of a new one for the United States and the USSR. Whereas in 1955 Soviet support to Egypt passed indirectly through Czechoslovakia, Moscow began to play a direct role. Khrushchev routinised the Soviet view of Israel as a Western puppet with the purpose of causing instability in the Arab world. Bulganin's message to Israeli Prime Minister David Ben-Gurion during the Suez fiasco clearly highlighted this:

> The government of Israel, acting as an instrument of outside imperialist forces, is continuing the reckless adventure, challenging all the peoples of the east who are fighting against colonialism for their freedom and independence ... fulfilling the will of others, acting on instructions from abroad, the Israeli government is criminally and irresponsibly playing with the fate of peace. [...] It is sowing a hatred for the state of Israel among the peoples of the east such as cannot but make itself felt with regard to the future of Israel and which puts in jeopardy the very existence of Israel as a state.[14]

As a measure of Soviet protest, the Ambassador was immediately recalled from Tel Aviv, though diplomatic relations at embassy level continued. A few weeks after the Suez War, on 18 November, Khrushchev said in a speech to fellow communists, 'What is Israel? A country without any great importance in the world, whose only task is to play the role of provocateur before an aggression. If the Israelis did not feel that they had the support of the Great Powers, they would be sitting quietly like little boys.'[15] Such remarks reflected the growing affinity between Moscow and the Arabs, who began to view the Soviet Union in a more positive light: 'The prestige which the Russians gained during the Suez crisis was of great consequence. [...] The USSR was now unambiguously acknowledged by the great majority of Arabs as their protector against Western imperialism.'[16]

One of the side-effects of the British and French actions in Egypt was to dent the moral and political justification of the Baghdad Pact among Arabs still further. Syria, which did not join, felt threatened by Iraq and Turkey, which were core countries in the Western-led alliance. Between September and October 1957 Moscow interpreted Turkish mobilisation and exercises on the Syrian frontier as a prelude to a Turkish-American assault on Syria to prevent it from becoming communist.[17] Again, the Soviet Union stepped in to warn the West, and simultaneously economic and military deals were struck with Damascus. In less than two years from the first deal in autumn 1955 Syria was estimated to have purchased more than £100 million worth of Eastern bloc weapons.[18] To further consolidate the bond in the face of more Turkish pressure, on 29 October 1957 Syria and the Soviet Union signed an economic and technical agreement worth $579 million.[19]

In the following year, a revolution in Iraq disposed of the pro-Western monarchy and put into power the radical Abdul-Karim Kassim. In 1959 he withdrew Iraq from the Baghdad Pact, dealing another blow to Western influence. Though Moscow was not directly responsible for converting the three major centres of the Arab world (Baghdad, Cairo and Damascus) into friendly states that were hostile to the West, this apparently positive development began to create new problems for the leaders in the Kremlin. Iraq and Egypt were rivals since the beginning of civilisation itself. Later in history under the glory days of the Islamic empire which stretched from Spain to India, Baghdad and Cairo wrestled with each other to hold the seat of the Caliph; in other words, leadership. Nasser's aspirations to lead the Arab world were not looked upon with any sympathy by the military government in Baghdad.

Moscow faced a dilemma. Egypt was a key ally, a point confirmed in January 1958 when the Soviet Union provided Egypt with a $175 million loan, as well as $100 million for the building of the Aswan dam.[20] Arms shipments continued to flow and contacts between Nasser and Khrushchev were regular. But the Soviet Union did not encourage Arab unification because it weakened its hand and made Nasser too strong. The Egyptian leader was above all else a nationalist. The United Arab Republic was used by Nasser to crush the communist parties of both Egypt and Syria, where they were gaining influence. By contrast, the Iraqi regime seemed to be influenced by communists and was generally more left-leaning than Nasser's government. In 1959 the Soviet Union pledged $137 million towards Iraqi economic aid.[21]

Moscow's dilemma eventually resolved itself. The union between Syria and Egypt collapsed in 1961, and the radical leadership in Iraq turned against the local communist party, whose support was no longer needed after power had been gained. Khrushchev was also encouraged by Nasser's centralisation and nationalisation of the economy. The Egyptian leader was forced to do this because of increasing economic difficulties, but Moscow regarded the measures as more evidence of conformity with the Socialist camp. Between 1955-60 Egypt received over $500 million of military aid, making it the largest Third World recipient of Soviet aid at the time. Syria and Iraq received over $200 million in that same period. Khrushchev increased this aid so that between 1961-4 Egypt received $700 million worth of military aid. Iraq and Syria received $100 million each.[22] The Soviet Union had been transformed by Khrushchev into a major patron for the Third World, and for none more so than the Middle East. Economic and military aid was also backed up with diplomatic support at the United Nations and *vis-à-vis* the United States, giving it prestige as a champion of the weak states against the stronger 'imperialist powers'.

Despite this, the last years of the Khrushchev era were marked by international developments that were to force an alteration of Soviet policy. The main event was the Cuban missile crisis in 1962. Khrushchev had the sense to back down but the limits of Soviet power and the need for greater superpower co-ordination were clearly elucidated by the crisis. Also in 1962, the United States introduced the Polaris nuclear submarine (SSBM) into the Mediterranean Sea, and later the Poseidon in the Indian Ocean which targeted Soviet cities. US strategic advantage made Soviet Middle East successes appear less valuable than in the middle to late fifties. President Kennedy could afford to be more choosy about friends and allies in the region: 'By 1962 American intermediate range ballistic missiles (IRBM) were withdrawn from Turkey. [...] Conventional military bases near an adversary's border became less valuable' with the development of intercontinental ballistic missiles (ICBM) and the SSBMs.[23] When the Shah of Iran told Moscow on 15 September 1962 'that it will not grant any foreign nation the right of possessing any kind of rocket bases on Iranian soil',[24] it may have appeared as an advantage gained by the Soviets. But in reality the Persian ruler had wisely concluded that the United States had probably no interest nor need for missile bases on his territory and he was offering an empty gift-wrapped assurance to the Soviets.

Khrushchev's energetic policy had the down-side of requiring a huge amount of resources, at a level that was unrealistic to maintain in the long term: 'In adopting "forward policy", Khrushchev overrode his opponents...and plunged the Soviet Union into the thick of regional politics lying far beyond Moscow's traditional security belt.'[25] All of Khrushchev's successors until 1998 appeared to take the view that this mistake would not be repeated; that Moscow would not be drawn heavily into areas which did not produce a tangible return. 'We value trade least for economic reasons and most for political purposes', Khrushchev boasted in 1955.[26] Following the downfall of the ideologically driven Soviet leader, such boasts were to be seen as a source of embarrassment among Moscow's élite.

While the leading countries of the Middle East such as Iraq and Egypt wanted a strong military and made much noise about their antipathy towards Israel, the reality was that Nasser and the Ba'athists of Iraq essentially wanted to drag their countries into the economic forefront. Ba'ath ('renaissance' in Arabic) was an ideology seeking to modernise the Arab society it ruled. Moreover, Nasser and his Arab counterparts were well aware that Soviet support was not, as the Egyptian leader once sarcastically remarked, 'for the blackness of my eyes' (for Arabs black eyes are a motif of beauty), but because of their own needs and interests. Thus even before Khrushchev was toppled, there seemed to be a growing recognition that there was a distinct lack of realism in Soviet policy towards the Middle East.

Brezhnev: consolidation leads to stagnation

The Khrushchev era was followed by collective rule aiming to provide a more balanced government that would not give too much power to one man. The triumvirate was in fact a two man leadership as the President, Nikolai Podgorny, held a ceremonial role. Prime Minister Aleksei Kosygin and General Secretary Leonid Brezhnev were the real power-brokers, at least for the first decade, as the latter was to supersede his former political partners as the most dominant figure of that era.

A number of academics held the view that there was 'no change in Soviet policies' towards the Middle East after the fall of Khrushchev.[27] There was some truth in this in the sense that support for 'anti-imperialist' countries with 'socialist orientation' was the official framework for policy. However, there were major changes under Brezhnev with regard to the nature of relations and some aspects of policy such as economic factors were raised on the list of priorities. The Soviet Union also began to look for military bases to counter the strong US presence in the Mediterranean. This ran against Khrushchev's official strategy of encouraging non-alignment so that members of that movement would refuse military bases for either superpower, partly because of the conclusion drawn in Moscow that the Soviet Union held a disadvantageous position *vis-à-vis* the United States.

Up until 1967, Soviet support for the Arabs was evident, 'though without pushing things to the point where it might itself have become involved in a conflict...Soviet policy had clear-cut parameters and was rather fruitful.'[28] Egypt remained the principal ally and the two countries seemed to be moving closer together. In a speech to the Egyptian parliament, Kosygin, who in the early years played a prominent role in Soviet policy towards the Middle East, highlighted the nature of the relationship of the two countries as it stood on 17 May 1966: 'The proclamation by the United Arab Republic that its national aim is the building of socialism brings our countries still more closely together.'[29] He then described the institution he was addressing as 'the most representative Parliament the country has had throughout its entire history',[30] despite his knowledge that the communists had recently been forcefully excluded from Egypt's political institutions.

A little over a year later relations between the Soviet Union and the Arab world in general and Egypt in particular were put under great strain as a result of the 1967 Arab-Israeli war. Moscow's assumption that Israel was too weak to launch a pre-emptive strike was proved wrong and Soviet policy was then dictated by what one author termed 'collaborative competition'.[31] In effect, this was that competition with the United States would be balanced by co-ordination and compromise to avoid a major confrontation. Soviet statements and signals leading up to the June War mis-represented Moscow's real strategy in the region. On 11 May 1967, Soviet President Podgorny received an Egyptian parliamen-tary delegation headed by Anwar Sadat, who was informed by his host that Israel was concentrating forces on the Syrian border and planned an attack between 18 and 22 May 1967. The Israelis denied the report and the Soviet ambassador in Damascus refused an offer from Tel Aviv to view the border area for himself. On 14 May Nasser sent Egyptian Chief-of-Staff General Mohammed Fawzi to Syria to check the Soviet claims for himself and he reported, in consultation with Damascus, that there were no Israeli concentrations. Having ascertained that Moscow's information was false Nasser may therefore have interpreted the report to mean Soviet encouragement of an Egyptian move against Israel.[32] The Egyptian leader ordered his troops into Sinai on 14 May and two days later asked the UN peace-keeping forces to withdraw its forces from the border with Israel. On 22 May Egypt blockaded Israeli shipping through the Strait of Tiran. These steps were met with criticism from the West but Moscow's response to Cairo, through Kosygin, was that 'we will stand by you'.[33] On 5 June Israel attacked and wiped out the Egyptian and Syrian air defences within forty-eight hours, and in six days achieved total victory, adding more territory and more importantly confirming its absolute military supremacy in the area.

The Soviet Union sought credit for stopping Israel after only six days by warning the United States that it would intervene if Damascus or Cairo were invaded, but in reality Israel stopped because it had achieved its main objectives and was content to complete the war with the little losses it had incurred. The Arabs were furious with Moscow: where was their support? After the war, the Soviet leadership insisted that 'we will stand by you' meant that they would have supported the Arabs if the United States had taken part in the war to help Israel. Moreover, Soviet weaponry had proved to be inferior to the US-made jets and heavy armour supplied to Israel.

The Soviet leadership in turn blamed the defeat on the Arabs for their incompetence. Brezhnev told Arab representatives in Moscow immediately after the war: 'We feel deeply hurt when we hear Israeli officers say that our tanks and aircraft that you abandoned are the best kinds of weapons.'[34] But if Brezhnev and his colleagues were so concerned about war breaking out in the region, why did they give out false information about the Israeli build-up on the Syrian border? The most plausible explanation relates to Syria's domestic political scene, where the pro-Soviet regime was close to being toppled because of economic difficulties and political opposition which included sections of the army. By airing news of an impending threat by its chief enemy Israel, Brezhnev and his comrades thought that public and military support would rally around the government. If that was indeed the intention, then the consequences were disastrous for the Arabs and the Soviet Union itself. To save face, Moscow severed all diplomatic relations with Israel, and launched a huge effort to rearm its Arab partners. On the diplomatic front the Warsaw Pact countries, in addition to Yugoslavia but excluding Romania, began their offensive on 9 June by issuing an ultimatum to Israel to cease hostilities:

> Israel's aggression...is the outcome of a conspiracy against the Arab countries by certain imperialist forces, above all the United States. [...] If the government of Israel does not stop the aggression and withdraw its troops behind the truce lines the socialist states which signed this statement will do everything necessary to help the peoples of the Arab countries administer a resolute rebuff to the aggressor.[35]

Soviet weapons were transported to the defeated Arabs almost immediately after the fighting had stopped. Some 300 modern SAM-3s (Surface to Air Missiles) and up to 20,000 'technicians' were sent by Moscow to the defeated Arab countries by 1971, while 150 MiG-21s were also sent to provide cover for the SAM batteries.[36] The intensified Soviet military involvement, which included military and naval bases in Egypt and Syria as a concession, had obvious benefits for Moscow, but it also had its pitfalls. Nasser wanted the Soviet Union to be directly responsible for Arab air defences, but this would inevitably have involved the United States in any future conflict, and by that stage Soviet leaders were well aware that neither they nor the United States could secure peace in the volatile and often unpredictable Middle East.

Some analysts suggested that the Soviets were happy with a 'no war, no peace' situation in the Middle East because it sustained

Arab dependency upon them, yet such arguments placed a heavy responsibility on Moscow for the continued tension in the area. Breslauer was among a group of writers on the subject who rejected this view, saying that since 1967 there was 'intense Soviet interest in a political settlement that would remove the escalatory potential from the conflict – but not at any price; and neither the United States nor Israel was willing to pay the Soviet price'.[37]

After 1967 the Soviet leadership wanted to initiate a Middle East peace process in order to enhance their country's international standing, and to refine a system of communication and understanding with Washington so that both superpowers would have an immediate understanding and anticipation of the other's reaction should another regional crisis erupt. The superpowers embarked on difficult negotiations following the 1967 war, mainly through the United Nations, until they devised an agreed charter for peace which took the form of Security Council Resolutions 242 and 338. These called for Israeli withdrawal from territories it occupied during the June 1967 war in return for Arab recognition of the Jewish state. The guiding principle of the Resolutions was land in exchange for peace. When Nasser visited Moscow in July 1968, he was to be disappointed by a Soviet stance that appeared to change in emphasis:

> Soviet leaders were unambiguous in conveying to Nasser the following points; 1, The USSR placed highest priority on avoiding a direct clash with the United States in the Middle East; 2, Nasser was engaging in 'daydreams' if he thought that a military solution was possible in the foreseeable future; 3, The Soviet Union would not meet Nasser's request for a long list of the most advanced offensive military weapons; 4, Nasser would be better advised to moderate his demands and seek a political solution to the conflict.[38]

More broadly, these points were the fundamental framework which characterised Moscow's approach to the Arab-Israel conflict until the demise of the Soviet Union and for the years under President Yeltsin.

The death of Egypt's charismatic President Nasser in 1970 was to affect the balance of power in the Middle East psychologically. Few Arabs had dared question his aspiration of reviving national and pan-Arab greatness. His policies and speeches were always aimed at audiences far beyond the borders of Egypt, and that was a major reason why Soviet leaders regarded him as being of such value. In his memoirs, former Soviet ambassador Vladimir Vinogradov wrote a telling tribute on Nasser:

> The feelings of Abdul Nasser towards the Soviet people were not exclusively of respect, but also of warmth. He knew well what our men endured in extraordinary circumstances, because it was what Egypt was going through in her military forces but also in the field of industry, construction and development.[39]

Nasser's successor, Anwar Sadat, was more pragmatic, composing policy solely from a national, that is to say, Egyptian point of view. The Soviet leadership was rather suspicious of Sadat, and in Syria too they were faced with a less ideological and more pragmatic Asad, who led a coup within the Ba'ath that ended the reign of the radical socialist, Salah Jadid. Despite these changes, Soviet power in the early seventies seemed to be at its zenith, rivalling the United States on a global level. There were favourable relations in the Middle East with all the local powers, from Iran and Turkey to Iraq and Egypt as well as Syria. The exceptions were Israel and Saudi Arabia, who were at that time unshakeably pro-Western. When Sadat went ahead with the signing of a treaty of friendship and co-operation with Moscow on 15 May 1971, it seemed to be further confirmation of this trend. Meanwhile, the United States was bogged down in Vietnam and seemed to be paralysed against stemming Soviet influence in the Middle East. So, it came as some shock to the Soviet leadership when Sadat sent a message to Moscow on 7 July 1972, demanding that 15,000 'technical advisers' leave by 17 July.

Since coming to power Sadat had made several visits to the USSR, and on the last visit at the end of April 1972, there was no hint of such a course of action in the joint Soviet-Egyptian communiqué of 30 April. It said that as a result of the dangerous situation that existed in the Middle East, the two sides 'considered it necessary again...to review the measures to defend...the Arab peoples, in particular through raising the military potential of the Arab Republic of Egypt. The Parties agreed to further strengthen military co-operation between them.'[40]

But according to transcripts of conversations between Sadat and the Soviet leadership in October 1971 and April 1972 (these were previously unpublished documents which were made available to me) there was an evident lack of trust on both sides. This was to be a deciding factor in the split between the two countries because it highlighted the basic flaw in bilateral relations, and the differences reflected a more significant turning point in the relations between Moscow and the rest of the Arab world. For Cairo, there was disappointment with Moscow at the limit of its economic capabilities in providing technological and financial assistance. Moreover, Moscow appeared to hold back in providing the most advanced attack weapons which would create military parity between Egypt and Israel. In all the meetings between Sadat and Brezhnev that took place in 1971 and 1972, Egypt's concern with Washington's role in modernising the Israeli military machine was made clear. In April 1972, three months before Soviet specialists were suddenly ejected from Egypt, Sadat expressed his concerns to Brezhnev in their meeting in Moscow. He told the Soviet leader that the latest Phantom jets as well as other advanced weapons were being 'extended' to Israel; that the United States was to set up advanced weapons plants in the Jewish state; and that President Nixon and his administration were making comments which cast doubts over Soviet commitments to Egypt and the rest of the Arab world.[41]

Sadat was in effect probing to test the Soviet response, but the suspicious nature of the relationship was not all one way. Moscow also questioned Cairo's motives in the light of meetings between top Egyptian and US officials in which reports were circulated that an agreement behind the back of the Soviet Union was a distinct possibility. In the meeting of 12 October 1971, Brezhnev's opening remark to Sadat was that 'we [the Soviet side] hope to find with you a spirit of trust and honesty'.[42] This was more than a polite diplomatic opener because in all subsequent meetings this point was to be stressed over and over again by both sides. The US-brokered Egyptian-Israeli peace treaty signed in the late 1970s showed that Soviet suspicions were not unfounded.

The shrewd Sadat told Brezhnev in the October meeting that he believed, from his communications with the United States, that Washington had three aims: (1) an end to the Soviet presence in the area, through sowing the seeds of mistrust between Arabs and the Soviet Union; (2) to remove Egypt from its position as the main centre of the Arab world; (3) the destruction of progressive movements, which after Egypt was subdued would become easy in the rest of the Arab world.[43] Sadat also told the Soviet leaders that Washington was arming Jordan with the aim of increasing its military capacity from 50,000 to 100,000 troops armed with the latest US weapons as a reward for its new neutral policy towards Israel and its friendship with the West.

Sadat told Brezhnev that from Presidents Truman to Nixon, the United States had made it a clear policy to preserve Israel's military advantage. 'I seek a specific request that the Soviet Union stands up to this vile American policy. [...] I want a resolution with the USSR that gives me parity with Israel and one that is carried out.'[44] But Brezhnev was reluctant, fearing that a strong Egypt would wage war against Israel which in turn would result in a superpower conflict because of Washington's commitment to Israel. He encouraged a peaceful resolution to the conflict. More subtly, Brezhnev also pointed out that Soviet debts to its friends had amounted to 14 billion rubles. In other words Moscow was concerned about financial considerations and was not prepared to provide large-scale Soviet aid, as in the days of Khrushchev.

In the meeting of April 1972 between the two leaders relations were quickly spiralling downwards. Sadat warned Brezhnev that the 'United States controls everything. [...] It manoeuvres in the region – politically and militarily – as it pleases, and it encourages Israel to do as it wants.' Following Sadat's impassioned plea for more Soviet help Brezhnev, in his dry manner, responded with the following: 'The President has spoken much and has given the impression that the Americans are all heroes. Sadat: Only in the Middle East and not in other areas. Brezhnev: And the President suggests that we are frightened.'[45] This final remark highlighted the tension that became prevalent in relations between the two leaderships. Brezhnev, whose words were usually carefully chosen, had become uncontrollably irritated at Sadat's constant reminders of Soviet inadequacies in the region. The wording of Sadat's demands suggested that Soviet inaction would appear as betrayal or cowardice, two of the most detestable traits for the Russian character.

When Sadat did not get the desired response he ordered the evacuation of all Soviet personnel from his country. The Soviet advisers packed their bags in an orderly fashion and hastily departed Egypt; gladly, according to observers' conclusions, as it was believed that Moscow had decided it was more involved in Sadat's Egypt than it really wanted to be.

Reorientation after split with Egypt

With relations worsening with Egypt the Soviet Union upgraded its relations with Baghdad, leading to the signing of a treaty of friendship with Iraq in April 1972. Iraq was the natural alternative to Egypt as a great Arab power. Moreover, there were growing reasons unrelated to the split with Egypt which made Baghdad ever more important to Brezhnev's foreign policy chiefs. The Gulf region in general was growing in value as a result of the oil factor and its geo-strategic position. Iraq, unlike Egypt, was able to pay for its supplies with hard currency or with oil which was resold by the Soviet Union to the West for dollars. This led to large-scale military shipments; by mid-1971, the USSR supplied Iraq with '110 MiG-21 and Su-7 fighters, over 20 helicopters and trainers, 100-150 tanks, some 300 armoured personnel carriers, and about 500 field guns and artillery rockets'.[46] After the Soviet-Iraqi treaty of friendship,

> Baghdad also took delivery of SA-3 surface-to-air (SAM) missiles, Tu-22 medium range bombers (the first and at the time the only deployment of this type of aircraft outside the Soviet Union or Eastern Europe), Scud surface-to-surface missiles armed with conventional warheads, and MiG-23 fighters, then the most advanced model available to the USSR.[47]

By way of repayment, the USSR imported 4 million tons of Iraqi crude by 1973, the year of the energy crisis. 'After 1973 the USSR continued to receive Iraqi petroleum at the pre-increase price of below $3.00 per barrel and, given the oil shortage in the West, proceeded to make a killing.'[48] It should be noted, however, that this Soviet practice greatly angered many Arab countries because, first, it undercut OPEC oil quotas and prices, and, secondly, it undermined the Arab embargo of oil sales to Western nations supporting Israel, a move wholeheartedly encouraged by Brezhnev as part of the great struggle against imperialist forces!

Brezhnevite pragmatism, or its double-standards, was also revealed in the way Arab communists were dealt with by Moscow. For example, the Syrian Communist Party, under veteran leader

Khaled Bakdash, had been the most pro-Soviet party in the Middle East. He had spent much of his time in Warsaw Pact as well as other Arab countries, exiled by the various anti-communist military dictators that came and went in Syria. He returned under the Ba'ath party rule of Salah Jadid but a faction within the party in 1969 criticised Bakdash's staunch pro-Soviet line, including his acceptance of the 1947 resolution on the partition of Palestine. Bakdash rejected his opponents' call for the liquidation of the state of Israel as 'non-proletarian' because 'it disregarded the established fact of the Jewish presence in Palestine, [and] the potentially positive role of the Jewish masses...'[49] Despite his opposition to the idea that the transition to socialism could take place through petty bourgeois 'revolutionary democracies' such as Ba'ath party rule, Bakdash finally accepted terms for joining Asad's National Progressive Front under Soviet persuasion and pressure. This caused his party to split and even Bakdash's majority faction was to disappear into political oblivion in Syrian politics, a consequence of Moscow's undermining of one of its most loyal and long-standing communist allies.

Asad meanwhile was sending out co-operative signals to the United States as he embarked on negotiations with Washington on the Arab-Israeli dispute, leaving Moscow worried that it might be left out of any peace deal that might affect the region. Brezhnev and his Foreign Minister Andrei Gromyko also became frustrated at their inability to bring Asad together with Iraq's Saddam Hussein. The reasons for their animosity were closely tied to the history of the Ba'ath movement and the different strands within it, Asad being regarded as a deviator from the mainstream. But a simple explanation why Moscow could not get them to reconcile their past differences for the common good was that there existed a mutual personal dislike. The style of the flamboyant and unpredictable Iraqi leader was incompatible with that of the shrewd and calculating Asad. Such features of regional politics could not be neglected by Moscow as they illustrated the limits of the Soviet superpower, as well as the United States, in guaranteeing influence in the Middle East.

Asad's rule created many problems in bilateral relations between the USSR and Syria. During the 1970s, the USSR modernised and expanded its Mediterranean naval fleet, including the construction of aircraft carriers, yet Syria was the only friendly base in that region. Asad took advantage of his strong position in 1976 and his forces entered Lebanon in 1976 to fight the PLO and other leftist forces seeking the overthrow of the pro-Western government. The Syrian leader was strongly advised by the men in the Kremlin that it would not help the Arab cause to fight against their PLO allies and other 'progressive' Arab groups, but he clearly felt confident enough to ignore it. This was one of many developments during the 1970s in which Moscow discovered that its political influence in Damascus was minimal.

Syria had taken part in the Egyptian-led Arab attack on Israel in October 1973 which was intended to make up for the defeat of 1967. Early Arab success in the war, largely as a result of an element of surprise as the attack took place on the Jew's most holy day, was eventually redressed due to massive US assistance to Israel. Soviet intervention was timed to preserve its credibility as a superpower and to prevent an Arab defeat.[50] While the Soviet Union had expressed its disapproval to the Arabs about initiating the war, it had the positive consequence of setting in motion 'a process of negotiations between Israel and its Arab neighbours which had long been advocated by the USSR'.[51]

Yet as a result of the war Washington grew in stature as the most likely peace-maker, in the eyes of both Israelis and Arabs. Moscow became concerned that Asad would follow the Egyptian example and break off links with the Soviet Union. Fortunately for Moscow, angry Arab opposition to Egypt's peace moves led Syria to delay any similar considerations. Between 1970 and 1974 Syria emerged as the largest recipient of Soviet aid, worth over $2.5 billion. Egypt received a similar amount but this withered dramatically after 1972. Iraq's figure was around $2 billion and Iran's was $600 million.[52] With Egypt forging ahead with the Camp David peace agreement alongside Israel under US guidance, Syria's role at the core of an anti-peace Arab alliance helped the Soviet Union maintain influence in the region. It came in the form of an anti-Egyptian alliance called the Arab Front of Stead-fastness and Confrontation. This temporarily brought together Iraq and Syria as well as Libya, the PLO and other Arab countries to announce that they were still committed to an armed struggle against Israel. They were supported by Saudi Arabia, whose conservative monarchy had been under increasing pressure since 1975 to prove that it was not a Western puppet. Egypt had become the new pariah because of its peace moves towards Israel and the nail in the coffin came when Cairo abrogated the treaty of friendship with Moscow on 5 May 1975.

Iran during that period was dextrously playing the two super-powers against each other by heightening fears about Moscow's growing military support to Syria and Iraq. As a consequence of the Iraqi-Soviet friendship treaty in 1972, President Richard Nixon smoothed the way for the sale of F-14 and F-15 jets to Iran. 'During the years 1972-8 Iran ordered about $20 billion worth of US arms.'[53] Iran was at this time competing with Saudi Arabia as Washington's most important ally in the Gulf. This tussle was to favour the United States which at that time was seeking to secure the oil-rich region by means of a military presence. The two-pronged strategy of the United States was to protect the flow of oil supplies from disruption as a result of Soviet adventurism, and also to consolidate conservative pro-Western regimes with the aim of eventually pushing them to reach an agreement, as Egypt did, with Israel. According to Evgenii Primakov, a top Soviet expert on the Middle East at that time, the US had placed the 'Indian Ocean and the Gulf on a par with Western Europe'.[54] US involvement had grown rapidly in the region during the 1970s, so that by 1977 American military and civilian specialists in Iran and Saudi Arabia had reached 80,000.[55]

While Iran strengthened ties with Moscow, with trade in 1977 between the two exceeding $1 billion,[56] Saudi Arabia continued to shun Soviet attempts to re-establish diplomatic relations and stuck firmly in the Western camp. US arms sales to Saudi Arabia rose 'from under $200 million in 1970 to $4.2 billion in 1978 (a 21-fold increase). The high point for the period was reached in 1976 when sales amounted to $5.8 billion', before returning to $4.2 billion in 1978. 'The latter figure was doubled in 1981 by one arms agreement alone...the $8.5 billion combined airborne warning and control planes (Awacs) and F-15 enhancement package (missiles, extra fuel tanks, and tanker aircraft, all of which enhanced the capabilities of the F-15s).'[57] The motive for signing such an astronomically expensive deal was the revolution in Iran, which saw the toppling of the Shah and the coming to power of the Shi'ite Ayatollah Ruhollah Khomeini. The violently anti-Western nature of the regime seemed to be a gain for Moscow, but the old grey men in the Kremlin were to discover that the Islamic fundamentalist revolutionaries were equally anti-communist.

Because in 1980 the United States had no diplomatic links with Iran – nor with Iraq until 1984 – the Soviet Union tried to end the war that had started between the two countries in the hope that it could strengthen its position in the Gulf. When it became clear that the war had opened up a Pandora's box of regional contradictions Moscow seemed to have decided that Iran was worth backing, even at the price of losing Iraq, though this was delicately done so that not all the proverbial eggs were placed in one basket. But this policy was to backfire because by 1985 the Iranians were referring to the Soviet Union and the United States in the same breath and both were depicted as Satan, further underlining the limits of Soviet influence in the region.[58]

The invasion of Afghanistan did not help change the anti-Soviet outlook from Tehran. In reality, the Brezhnev leadership's involvement in Afghanistan was to prove characteristic in its short-sightedness. Moscow also failed to match the foresight of Saddam Hussein with regard to the Khomeini regime: that its existence was dependent on foreign adventures and influence over Muslims in Central Asia and the Middle East, which was in fact one of the main reasons why Iraq attacked the Iranian Republic almost as soon as it was established.

The oil-rich Gulf states, which were backing Iraq in its war against Iran, were fearful of communist expansion and the destabilising effect of the invasion of Afghanistan. They utilised their oil-wealth to mobilise Arab opposition to the invasion, including severe criticisms of the Soviet action from Baghdad. Saudi Arabia was the first country to announce its boycott of the Moscow Olympic games in 1980. Only Syria obliged by refraining from making attacks on Soviet military action in Afghanistan. In fact Syria signed the Treaty of Friendship and Co-operation with the Soviet Union in 1980 following ten years of evasion and reluctance. Asad finally agreed to sign because of his isolation in the Arab world, dominated then by his arch-rival Saddam Hussein. In addition to this he faced growing internal opposition from within Ba'ath party ranks and uprisings that were suppressed by force.

Asad's hatred of Saddam Hussein actually drove him to take sides with non-Arab Iran in its war against Iraq during the 1980s. Tehran found the Syrian hand of friendship useful, but it clearly felt it could afford to reject similar Soviet efforts. The Iranian delegation to Brezhnev's funeral in November 1982 was made up of junior Foreign Ministry officials, which was not in accordance with protocol for such occasions.

> In December 1982, Iranian authorities permitted a demonstration by Afghan refugees at the Soviet Embassy in Tehran. The crack-down on the Tudeh (communist) Party which had been underway for well over a year culminated in February 1983 with the arrest of the Party's general secretary, Nureddin Kianuri, and other prominent Party members on the charge of spying for the Soviet Union.[59]

The troubled relations continued until the death of Khomeini.

The military dimension

By 1985, the USSR had arguably been transformed into a hollow superpower. As one author pointed out, the Soviet Union 'is a superpower in one dimension only, that of military power'.[60] Under Brezhnev, particularly during his twilight years, inefficiency, decay and stagnation were the typical stereotypes. It had been overtaken by Japan in terms of industrial output and was well down the list in terms of living standards. In the last eight years under Brezhnev, 'the Soviet Union ranked eleventh as a world trader behind the United States, West Germany, Japan, France, Britain, Italy, the Netherlands, Saudi Arabia, Canada and Belgium'.[61] The military aspect of international relations had become primary as it enhanced the Soviet Union's image as a world power. The usefulness of arms sales was that they could be activated quickly, especially in a crisis, whereas economic assistance often requires lengthy preparations.

Soviet economic aid in the Middle East between 1954-85 was as follows: Turkey $3.3 billion, Iran $1.2 billion, Syria $1.9 billion.[62] Turkey was the biggest recipient of economic aid, whereas the emphasis with the Arab countries was on military hardware. Syria and Iraq, the largest recipients of military aid under Brezhnev, bought or were supplied with $19.1 billion and $19.4 billion worth of arms respectively between 1974 and 1985.[63] In overall terms the Middle East was the largest benefactor of Soviet arms (see table).

SOVIET MILITARY DELIVERIES TO THIRD WORLD REGIONS, 1977-86
(billions of 1987 US dollars)[64]

	1977-81	1982-6	1977-86
Africa	18.5	18.9	37.4
East Asia	8.8	9.6	18.4
Latin America	5.0	8.2	13.2
Middle East	21.7	29.5	51.2
South Asia	5.0	9.3	14.3

But US-made weaponry given to Israel consistently proved to be superior to Soviet arms, despite Soviet propaganda which suggested the opposite. Soviet military leaders insisted on attributing the loss of their Arab allies to direct American support to Israel. As one military spokesman wrote in 1982: 'The effectiveness of the air raids carried out by Israel on June 5, 1967 was ensured, at least partially, due to information about the location of Egyptian airfields and planes received from American sources.'[65] He suggested that having received SAM missiles and ATGMs (anti-tank guided missiles), the Arabs were able to mount a much better defence in 1973. 'The Israeli Command underestimated the effectiveness of the Soviet-made Egyptian missiles', he argued.[66]

Moscow's massive militarisation of the Middle East was defended by its leaders as a means of countering similar US actions in the Gulf, and the huge naval presence in the Mediterranean in the form of the US 6th Fleet. Soviet leaders, particularly those with military connections, referred to the 6th Fleet as 'the big stick of US imperialism' in the Middle East.[67] Soviet military experts said a fleet comprising fifty warships including two atom-powered aircraft carriers, *America* and *Saratoga*, operating more than 200 jet fighter-bombers and fighters and with personnel numbering 25,000 officers and ratings with its central base in Naples, Italy, was far more than necessary for a simply defensive task force. 'It seems as though the United States is trying to turn the Mediterranean into a giant launching site', one Soviet military commentator wrote.[68]

Indeed, growing US military power led one Arab specialist on the subject to conclude that 'at least from the mid-seventies onwards, Soviet aims in the Middle East were to a large extent defensive', and were generally directed towards the United States.[69] Soviet military support to the Arabs was intended to 'maintain strong defensive capabilities for Arab forces confronting Israel (particularly

Egypt and Syria), in order to repel any Israeli attack…and to show the Soviet Union clearly as a world power able and willing to uphold Arab national security', but not to the extent that the Arabs could launch a decisive attack of their own.[70] Moscow acted so because it did not want to antagonise the United States, thus reaffirming the point that the Arab-Israeli dispute was never a matter of vital importance for the Soviet Union, nor post-Soviet Russia for that matter.

Conclusion: failure outweighs success

Brezhnev's speech to the Indian Parliament in Delhi in 1980 provided a telling illumination of his leadership's aims and failures in their policies in the Middle East. The ageing Soviet leader proposed a series of measures regarding the Gulf:

> Foreign bases should not be established in the Gulf area and its adjacent islands, no nuclear weapons should be deployed there, force should be neither applied nor threatened against the countries of the Gulf area, there should be no interference in their internal affairs, their non-aligned status should be respected, and the 'normal commercial exchange and the use of maritime communications linking the Gulf states with other countries of the world' should not be impeded.[71]

By 1991, if the nuclear potential of Iran and Iraq could have been taken into account as well as the sanctions imposed on the latter, there was substantial evidence to suggest that each of these objectives ended in failure.

By the time Gorbachev had come to power in 1985, Moscow had no trustworthy ally in the Middle East. The balance sheet under Khrushchev and the early Brezhnev period could be judged as tipping towards favourable for Moscow in the sense that the Soviet Union grabbed the headlines, particularly during the Khrushchev era, in a way which seemed to be positive for most countries of the region. Turkey and Iran were neutralised, the Arabs were given ample political, financial and military support and the United States and Israel were forced to acknowledge that Moscow was a political player that demanded the utmost respect. It was under Brezhnev that things appeared to become more problematic for the USSR. By the late 1970s the Soviet Union did not have the material resources to compete with the United States, yet Moscow believed it was necessary to maintain the pretence.

The loss of Egypt, the unreliability of local allies and events all amounted to a loss of substantial investments but the lessons were not learned. As one author pointed out, 'long before the scale of Third World indebtedness to the Soviet Union became public knowledge it must have been clear to Soviet officials that the USSR was deriving scant economic benefit from its relations with the Third World'.[72] The stagnation and corruption of the Brezhnev era not only sustained untenable policies in the Middle East, but also committed the superpower to a new adventure in Afghanistan which eventually crippled the once mighty Soviet military machine.

Brezhnev's policy was that if control could not be achieved over a given area, then stability would be the next best thing. In the words of one specialist, 'because the USSR's fundamental interest in the Middle East was the stabilisation of the area (albeit according to its own image), a solution to the Arab-Israeli conflict became a pressing necessity'.[73] The Soviet Union wanted stability and peace, but not at the expense of overwhelming US domination over the Middle East. Here was the dilemma for Moscow: how to compete with Washington without antagonising it or destabilising a region which shared its very same borders. Clearly, Gorbachev and Moscow failed to get the right balance.

NOTES

1. Galia Golan, *Soviet Policies in the Middle East: From World War II to Gorbachev,* Cambridge, 1990, p.33.
2. Alexei Vassiliev, *Russian Policy in the Middle East: From Messianism to Pragmatism,* Reading, 1993, p.17.
3. Golan, *op. cit*, p.29.
4. Gromyko speech (translated, together with the speeches of other Soviet leaders, by Progress Publishers), *The Policy of the Soviet Union in the Arab World,* Moscow, 1975, p.39.
5. Avigdor Dagan, *Moscow and Jerusalem,* London, 1970, p.21.
6. *Ibid.*, p.24.
7. Peter Mooney, *The Soviet Superpower: The Soviet Union 1945-1980,* London, 1982, p.97.
8. Dagan, *op. cit.*, p.81.
9. Gromyko, *op. cit.*, p.44.
10. Vassiliev, *op. cit.*, p.29.
11. *Ibid.*

12. Golan, *op. cit.*, p.45.
13. H. Hanak, *Soviet Foreign Policy since the Death of Stalin*, London and Boston, MA, 1972, p.311.
14. *Ibid.*, p.312.
15. Dagan, *op. cit.*, p.114.
16. Charles McLane, *Soviet-Middle East Relations*, London, 1973, p.8.
17. Mooney, *op. cit.*, p.112.
18. Efraim Karsh, *The Soviet Union and Syria*, London, 1988, p.3.
19. *Ibid.*, p.4.
20. Golan, *op. cit.*, p.54.
21. Oleg and Bettie Smolansky, *The USSR and Iraq: The Soviet Quest for Influence*, Durham, N.C. and London, 1991, p.16.
22. Stephen Hormer and Thomas Wolfe, *Soviet Policy and Practice toward Third World Conflict*, Toronto, 1983, pp.17-23.
23. Aryeh Yodfat, *The Soviet Union and Revolutionary Iran*, London, 1984, p.28.
24. RK Ramazani, 'Soviet Foreign Policy and Revolutionary Iran, Continuity and Change' in Hafeez Malik (ed.), *Domestic Determinants of Soviet Foreign Policy*, London, 1990, p.227.
25. Alvin Z. Rubenstein, 'Soviet Strategic Interests in the Middle East' in Hafeez Malik (ed.), *op. cit.*, p.220.
26. *Ibid.*, p.221.
27. Vassiliev, *op. cit.*, p.62.
28. *Ibid.*, p.64.
29. Hanak, *op. cit.*, p.314.
30. *Ibid.*, p.315.
31. George Breslauer, 'Introduction' in George Breslauer (ed.), *Soviet Strategy in the Middle East*, Boston, MA, 1990, p.5.
32. Golan, *op. cit.*, p.58.
33. *Ibid.*, p.59.
34. Abdel Magid Farid, *Nasser: The Final Years*, Reading, 1994, p.24.
35. Hanak, *op. cit.*, p.330.
36. Mooney, *op. cit.*, p.142.
37. Breslauer, *op. cit.*, p.24.
38. *Ibid.*, p.29.
39. Nikolai Novikov and Vladimir Vinogradov, *Yomiat diplomassiya fi bilad al-arab* (Daily Diplomacy in Arab Countries), Cairo, 1990, p.353.
40. Gromyko, *op. cit.*, p.183.
41. These are top secret Arabic transcripts made available to me of minutes of the meetings between President Sadat of Egypt (and his foreign and defence ministers) with members of the Soviet élite, including Brezhnev, Kosygin, Podgorny, Gromyko, Grechko (Defence Minister), Ponomarev and others. The meetings between Sadat and the Soviet leadership took place in October 1971 and April 1972. A meeting at foreign minister level took place in July 1972. The transcripts were kept by the Egyptian President's information secretariat. Transcript of Moscow meeting of 12 October 1971, p.1.
42. *Ibid.*, 25 April 1972.
43. *Ibid.*, p.9.
44. *Ibid.*, p.18.

45. *Ibid.*, 25 April 1972.
46. Smolansky and Smolansky, *op. cit.*, p.18.
47. *Ibid.*
48. *Ibid.*, p.21.
49. Dina Kehat, 'Dilemmas of Arab Communism' in Yaacov Ro'i (ed.), *The USSR and the Muslim World*, London, 1984, p. 275.
50. Golan, *op. cit.*, p.21.
51. Efraim Karsh, 'Soviet-Syrian Relations: the Troubled Partnership' in Margot Light (ed.), *Troubled Friendships: Moscow's Third World Ventures*, London, 1993, p.142.
52. Hormer and Wolfe, *op. cit.*, p.43.
53. Yodfat, *op. cit.*, p.35.
54. Herbert L. Sawyer, *Soviet Perceptions of the Oil Factor in U.S. Foreign Policy: the Middle East – Gulf Region*, Boulder, CO, 1983, p.8.
55. *Ibid.*, p.11.
56. *Ibid.*
57. *Ibid.*, p.96.
58. James Clay, James Moltz, and Dennis Ross, 'The Soviet Union and the Iran-Iraq War 1980-88' in Breslauer (ed.), *op. cit.*, p.123.
59. Muriel Atkin, 'Moscow's Disenchantment with Iran', *Survey*, vol.27 (118/119), autumn/winter 1983, p.251.
60. Paul Dibb, *The Soviet Union: The Incomplete Superpower*, Hong Kong, 1986, p.23.
61. *Ibid.*, p.220. Figures taken from 'Direction of Trade Statistics, 1976-82', Washington, DC, IMF, 1983.
62. Margot Light, 'Conclusion: Continuity and Change in Soviet Policy' in Light (ed.), *op. cit.*, p.195.
63. Mark Kramer, 'Soviet Arms Transfers and Military Aid to the Third World' in K. Campbell and S. Neil Macfarlane (eds), *Gorbachev's Third World Dilemmas*, London, 1989, p.75. Source of figures: CIA in Congress, Joint Economic Committee, 1985/6.
64. *Ibid.* Source for tabular figures: US Arms Control and Disarmaments Agency, 'World Military Expenditures and Arms Transfers', 1987, ACDA Publication 128, March 1988, pp.131-3.
65. Major-General V. Matsulenko, 'Lessons of Imperialist Local Wars', *Soviet Military Review*, no.1, January 1982, p.45.
66. *Ibid.*
67. Vladimir Ukraintsev, 'Tools of Provocations and Aggression', *Soviet Military Review*, no.11, November 1967, p.58.
68. *Ibid.*
69. Mohamad Ja'far Kassem, *Souryia wal itihad al-sofieti* (Syria and the Soviet Union), London, 1987, p.16.
70. *Ibid.*, p.28.
71. Robin Edmonds, *Soviet Foreign Policy: the Brezhnev Years*, Oxford, 1983, p.188.
72. Light, *op. cit.*, p.198.
73. Karsh, 'Soviet-Syrian Relations', *op. cit.*, p.141.

3

GORBACHEV'S NEW THINKING: THE TRANSITION PERIOD

Gorbachev's foreign policy reforms in the context of the Middle East usefully illustrate the break from the past while simultaneously pointing to the foundations laid for the policies of post-Soviet Russia. In ideas and ideology Gorbachev's reforms in foreign policy were unquestionably revolutionary. However, in practical policies the Middle East presented many political realities which prevented such ideas from being smoothly converted into tangible results. Nonetheless, events such as the Gulf War showed that the theory of New Thinking was being successfully put into practice despite strong domestic and external criticisms.

Brezhnev's legacy, generally unaffected by his weak successors (Iuri Andropov and Konstantin Chernenko), was entanglement in Afghanistan, tension with China and Japan, as well as the prospect of a new dimension to the arms race with the United States in the form of the Strategic Defense Initiative (Star Wars). The world order in the year Mikhail Gorbachev came to power, 1985, had become dangerously unstable, with a confrontationalist administration in Washington and a stagnating counterpart in Moscow. Added to this was growing discontent in the Warsaw Pact countries, particularly Poland and Hungary, and involvement in almost every major regional conflict: be it Central America (Nicaragua and El Salvador), or Angola in Africa.

Change was imperative: the Soviet Union's economic situation had become so dire that it simply did not have the resources nor the capability to compete with the United States. The last Soviet leader's overriding aim was to resuscitate the faltering economy, leading to the introduction of *perestroika* (restructuring) in the internal workings of the Soviet system. At the 27th Congress in 1986 (the first under Gorbachev), his speech hardly mentioned the Third World and virtually ignored the Arab-Israeli conflict.

44

'Indeed, Gorbachev's was the first report of a General Secretary since...1952 not to express itself explicitly to the problems of the Third World.'[1]

Gorbachev recognised that in terms of foreign policy, as in other aspects of the Soviet system, there would have to be a change not only in policy, but in the policy making process itself. That there was an unavoidable correlation between domestic priorities and the country's relations with the outside world was an obvious point for Gorbachev; principally, that there would have to be a reduction of the huge Soviet military machine and arsenal, and the need to ease the burden of subsidising an extensive network of client states, particularly in the Third World, as well as its Warsaw Pact 'partners'. As early as 1986 Gorbachev was openly stating: 'Yes, we need peace; we appeal again and again for a halt to the arms race.'[2] Gorbachev's vision went beyond the idea of just downgrading the level of conflict or, as it were, taking a temporary breather before re-embarking on what had hitherto been viewed in Moscow and Washington as an historic battle of ideologies, with each side seeking to emerge victorious at the other's expense. The new Soviet leader wanted to conduct affairs with the outside world on the basis of a new message stressing common human values and the need for survival as the pillars of a new era of co-operation.

The promotion of Gorbachev to the position of general secretary was followed by the appointment of younger and more energetic people to senior positions. This paved the way for a more dynamic style of presenting policy. In July 1985 the post of foreign minister of the USSR was accepted by Eduard Shevardnadze despite his negligible experience in the field of international diplomacy. Yet Gorbachev's decision did have a measure of logic because he did not want someone shackled by old habits. Shevardnadze's ideas were well suited to reform, and he expressed his wish to change the way national security and strength were understood:

> We have captured first place in the world weapons trade (28 per cent of the entire sales total), and have made the Kalashnikov machine gun the hallmark of our advanced technology. But we occupy about sixtieth place in standard of living, thirty-second in average life expectancy, and fiftieth in infant mortality.[3]

Among the foremost challenges for Shevardnadze was to redefine the role of the Foreign Ministry. Although the Ministry of Foreign Affairs was ostensibly the official foreign policy making body, it was subservient to the Politburo and International Department, and had far less influence than the Defence Ministry. In effect, Shevardnadze had to convince the Communist Party élite to relinquish its power over a field it highly cherished to enable his Ministry to see the reforms through. It was therefore unsurprising that from the very first year of taking office there was a clash of interests. But, for the first four years, the reformers enjoyed a high level of success thanks to the immense power Gorbachev wielded and his skilful ability to manipulate it. One commentator went so far as to say of the General Secretary that 'his control of foreign policy was perhaps greater than that enjoyed by any individual Soviet leader since Stalin'.[4]

With Gorbachev's support, Shevardnadze oversaw sweeping changes within the Ministry. 'Between 1986 and 1989 all nine deputy ministers and three out of four senior officials in the Foreign Ministry were replaced. New functional departments were created for disarmament, humanitarian issues, the non-aligned movement, and international economic relations.'[5] With regard to regional issues, including the Middle East, there was a major reassessment in thinking. There was continuity with the past in that the top priority for foreign policy was clearly the United States, but unlike Brezhnev, Khrushchev *et al.*, Gorbachev acknowledged that relations with Washington were closely interlinked with co-operation over regional issues.

In the words of one Gorbachev adviser, the re-evaluation of Soviet thinking was based upon the acceptance of distinct factors, based on the realisation that by the mid-1980s the Soviet Union was no longer a superpower equal to the United States. 'Its allies were primarily underdeveloped countries in the Third World whose interests were purely mercenary...[Moreover,] the idea of achieving strategic parity was totally unrealistic.'[6] Gorbachev's high moral tone initiated a wave of popular support in Europe and even in the United States which was further enhanced by his obvious charm, wit and seeming approachability to ordinary people. But in the cut-and-thrust world of *realpolitik* his preaching about reforms and change required backing-up with action because there undoubtedly remained a great amount of suspicion among Western political élites about Gorbachev's intentions.

Redefining alliances and threats

New Thinking had a profound impact on the nature of Soviet-Middle East relations, which substantially altered the balance of power in the region. However, this did not mean that Gorbachev's concessions towards Washington meant that the region had suddenly lost all of its strategic-economic value: 'Moscow definitely indicated that it would not abandon its investment of over thirty years in the Arab world.'[7] Moscow's traditional allies in the Middle East did not support Gorbachev's aims of transforming the guiding principle of foreign policy from the geo-strategic to one emphasising international institutions, democracy, human rights and free trade.

Gorbachev and Shevardnadze set out to broaden the base of the Soviet Union in the Middle East, despite their acknowledgement that it would be at the expense of long-standing allies in the region traditionally regarded as 'progressive' regimes. In reality this was a confrontationalist and totalitarian bloc of nations led by Syria's Hafez Asad, Moscow's closest ally during the early 1980s. By placing greater emphasis on new factors such as trade and interdependence and abandoning the idea of international class struggle, Moscow's traditional foes in the region such as Israel and Saudi Arabia became acceptable as friends. The post-1985 leadership called on the superpowers to disengage from regional conflicts and encouraged international institutions such as the United Nations to take over in a peace-making role. This was also an acknowledgement that the Arab-Israeli conflict was too deeply-rooted and historic for it to end as soon as there was complete US-Soviet disengagement. Shevardnadze made a clear distinction between Khrushchev's 'peaceful co-existence', which 'applied only to our relations with potential adversaries', and his new 'universal principle of partnership, co-operation, mutual understanding, and joint action'.[8]

Israel and New Thinking

One of the most significant consequences of the Gorbachev period in the Middle East was the forging of diplomatic relations with Israel. This was an integral branch of New Thinking. It was also perceived as a diplomatic slap in the face for the Syrian leadership:

When Syria's President Hafez Asad travelled to the Soviet Union in April 1987, he was told by Gorbachev that the absence of relations between Tel Aviv and Moscow was 'not normal'. A year later, at a Kremlin reception, Gorbachev lectured visiting PLO chief Yasser Arafat that Israel was also concerned about its security and borders.[9]

Israel was keen to establish links with the Soviet Union because of the highly advantageous rewards it promised. First, Tel Aviv could use these ties to create differences between Moscow and Damascus, but more importantly they could open the door to massive Jewish emigration from the Soviet Union. To a large extent both these objectives were attained by Israel, particularly with regard to the latter. Gorbachev, though, must have realised that his open door policy to Jewish emigration would entail the wrath of Arab public opinion and their governments. But there was a plus side to the equation: Soviet concessions on the Jewish emigration issue would ease political pressure from the United States. In this sense, earlier Soviet accusations about the extraordinary influence of the American Jewish lobby and Israel on the political scene in Washington were proved correct because Soviet acquiescence on this issue certainly sped the path towards better relations with both the United States and Israel. Most experts agreed that 'by 1989, the issue of Soviet-Jewish emigration was to become a major factor in Soviet-Israeli relations. [...] By the start of 1989, despite the outbreak of the *intifada*, Soviet-Israeli relations had markedly improved.'[10] Diplomatic relations were established at consular level, with a Soviet consular team having arrived in Israel in July 1987 and an Israeli team in Moscow a year later. The number of Soviet Jews allowed to leave increased year by year: 'In 1987 over eight thousand Soviet Jews were allowed to leave compared with under a thousand the year before. In 1988 almost 20,000 Soviet Jews left the Soviet Union, and in 1989, the number of Jewish emigrants exceeded 70,000.'[11] The figures provide an indication of the rapid development of relations despite the turbulent events in the region in that period.

Soviet and Israeli officials met for the first time in twenty years in Helsinki, in August 1986. The following month, Shevardnadze and then Israeli Prime Minister Shimon Peres met at the United Nations in what was the highest-level meeting of Soviet and Israeli officials since 1967.[12] Meanwhile, the Soviet press and media noticeably reduced the vitriolic attacks against Israel to a more balanced view. One periodical specialising in the observation of the Soviet press suggested that 'the silence about restoring relations with Israel was broken when *Izvestiia* (25 Jan. 1990) political observer Aleksander Bovin analysed the letters received on the subject' and found that 'nine out of ten wanted relations restored and criticised Brezhnev's 1967 decision to sever them'.[13]

The economic aspects of bilateral relations eventually began to bear fruit. In late November 1990, Israeli Agriculture Minister Avraham Katz-Oz reached an agreement with Moscow whereby Israel would sell $30 million in agricultural produce to the USSR as well as providing assistance in water planning, cotton production and the establishment of dairies and chicken coops.[14] Moscow was understandably very interested in gaining access to Israel's successful agricultural schemes, but the Soviet Union's other goal was to acquire technical expertise, ranging from medical equipment to sophisticated military hardware.

However, the road to restoring full diplomatic relations with Israel, which was finally achieved in the dying months of the Soviet state, was fraught with many hazards and potentially insurmountable obstacles. After Moscow had persuaded the PLO to recognise the right of the state of Israel to exist and to renounce terrorism as a necessary precondition to any peace process in December 1988, there was an uneasy feeling by policy makers in the Kremlin that the United States would exploit its new dialogue with the Palestinians. In fact, the opposite happened, with Israel and the United States taking a more intransigent line which severely undervalued the compromise undertaken not only by the PLO, but also by the Soviet Union. Israel's proposal was a plan for Palestinian elections for local representatives that in effect opposed any form of Palestinian state and excluded Arafat from the peace process. Soviet Foreign Ministry spokesman Gennadii Gerasimov bluntly responded that 'elections without the PLO's participation were not elections but a sham aimed at setting up puppet representative bodies with which Israel could reach a peace'.[15]

Also in that year Moscow made vociferous criticisms of Israeli policy in Lebanon, particularly the abduction of Hezbollah leader Sheikh Obeid in July. The Soviet response to that action was direct and unambiguous: 'The act of violence performed by Israel is unquestionably a flagrant violation of Lebanon's sovereignty and no motives can justify it. It constitutes an act of international terrorism.'[16] Despite that particularly tense phase of Soviet-Israeli relations, little action was taken to correspond to the extent of Moscow's displeasure. For example, looking at the rate of Jewish emigration in the summer of that year, which under Brezhnev was sometimes used as a thermometer of Cold War temperature, the rate actually increased rather than decreased: April, 4,557; May, 3,779; June, 4,354; July, 4,537; August, 6,756.[17]

Despite his peace initiatives, Gorbachev could justifiably feel aggrieved at the little gratitude shown from any side in the Middle East as, on the contrary, there was constant pressure and criticism, particularly from the Arab states. Simultaneously, the level of US demands on Israel's behalf was also intensifying, and these included: '1) the re-establishment of full diplomatic relations; 2) the abrogation of the UN "Zionism is Racism" Resolution, which Moscow had helped to pass in 1975; and 3) the finalization of the agreement on direct flights between the USSR and Israel'.[18] Virtually every Arab country had publicly expressed its dismay at the influx of Russian-Jewish immigrants to Israel. To rub salt into the wound, there was growing evidence to support suspicion that the hard-line Likud government in Israel, led by Yitzhak Shamir, was deliberately deploying tens of thousands of these latest additions to the Israeli population to settlements in occupied Arab territories. The motive behind such a move was hardly subtle: to tilt the demographic status of these areas so heavily in the favour of Jews – the Israeli army was active in removing Arabs from their homes whenever they obstructed the growth of Jewish settlements – that the outcome of any potential Arab-Israeli peace negotiations would be distinctly in favour of Israel. That the Soviet Union was seen to be directly contributing to this plan greatly affected Moscow's standing in the Arab world. Ironically, it was the United States, through the tough-talking Secretary of State James Baker, who, in a diplomatic aphorism, twisted the arm of Shamir by threatening to withdraw US loan guarantees worth $10 billion to aid Jewish settlements if he continued to house Jews on disputed territory. This episode further confirmed the growing belief that Washington was the only effectively acting superpower in the Middle East while the Soviet Union was seemingly struggling to rediscover itself.

A further blow to Moscow were moves by Israel which dis-couraged Soviet participation in the proposed Middle East peace process. In 1990 the Likud was clearly dragging its feet over an international peace conference, insisting as it had done in the past on direct country-to-country negotiations with its Arab foes. In December of that year Israel's Foreign Minister Moshe Arens openly undervalued the Soviet role: 'After events in Europe (in reference to the collapse of the Soviet-backed regimes), the idea of viewing the Soviet Union as a superpower equal to the U.S. needs examination.'[19]

As a result of the rapidly diminishing status of the Soviet Union in the Middle East, and the rest of the world, Gorbachev seemed briefly to slow down the advances made with regard to Israel. There was also pressure from internal conservative forces who were arguing with increased confidence that the Gorbachev-Shevardnadze policy was not paying any dividends, with the latter bearing the brunt of most of the criticisms. On 24 May 1990 Gorbachev retreated from his efforts to push through an emigration bill on the Supreme Soviet's legislative agenda. The bill, which would have placed a legal stamp on the *de facto* emigration of Soviet Jews, had been long promised to President George Bush. The fact that the United States had linked the emigration law with Moscow's much sought-after Most Favoured Nation trade status added to the significance of this retreat.

In retrospect, Gorbachev's hardened stand was a counter-measure to the growing strength of the anti-reform conservatives made up from the military-industrial complex and the Communist Party *apparatchiki* who felt most undermined by the changes. Following the failure of the leaders of these groupings to oust Gorbachev in August 1991 in that infamous televised fiasco, Moscow was quick to make up for lost time in its relations with Israel. One month after the unsuccessful *putsch* Moscow reversed its position on the UN Declaration that Zionism Equals Racism, and soon afterwards the Soviet national airline, Aeroflot, signed an agreement with Israel establishing direct emigrant flights from Moscow and St Petersburg to Tel Aviv. Eventually, full diplomatic relations were agreed upon just before the international peace conference was held in Madrid on 30 October 1991.

The Soviet Union and its Arab 'allies'

Earlier in October the new Foreign Minister Boris Pankin visited

Syria to explain Moscow's decision to establish diplomatic relations with Israel. He was given a hostile reception by his Syrian counterpart Farouk Shara. 'The spate of exclamations and rhetorical questions, expressed in a language not suited to diplomacy, let alone to Middle Eastern courtesy, did not let up until I ⸴proposed half-seriously to my colleague that I should go back to the airport', Pankin recalled in his memoirs.[20] For Pankin this behaviour was ironic because it left the impression that it had been Syria which supported the Soviet Union for all those years. 'This stupidity dated back to Khrushchev's time, when it sufficed for a leader or regime to call themselves "socialist" and they automatically became our bosom friends.'[21] In his remark, Pankin expressed the genuine change in attitude that had became prevalent in Moscow under Gorbachev.

Pankin recalled that on the first day of taking office he was given a clear view of the new priorities held by Gorbachev. This was particularly relevant in the light of the failure of the coup in 1991. Pankin was told:

> Talk to Primakov, he has good contacts with the Saudis. Their king is a strong supporter of our democracy. We must change priorities, get rid of prejudices. Yasser Arafat, Gaddafi – they call themselves our friends, but only because they dream of our returning to the past. Enough double standards.[22]

Soviet-Arab differences due to New Thinking were initially kept private, but in November 1989 the USSR ambassador to Damascus, Aleksander Zotov, publicly suggested that Moscow no longer supported Syria's goal of achieving military–strategic parity with Israel. The Gorbachev-Shevardnadze plan was to steer Syria in the direction of a negotiated settlement with Israel but with a greater commitment than ever before. In the words of one observer, 'the idea of holding some kind of conference was not new; it had been a key element in the joint statement on the Middle East made by Gromyko and [United States] Secretary Cyrus Vance in October 1977. From 1987, however, it became central to Moscow's agenda.'[23]

Moscow's new diplomatic efforts appeared to be accompanied by a reduction in military supplies to the region. In Syria's case 'actual arms deliveries fell from the previous average of $2.3 billion per year to no more than $1 billion per year in the period 1985-9.

Moscow also delayed deliveries of Syrian-requested MiG-29 aircraft, providing them first to India and Iraq (which was at war with Iran).'[24]

Other factors placed a heavy burden on Syrian-Soviet relations after Gorbachev assumed power. While the Damascus regime was the most closely associated with Moscow, it was largely isolated in the Arab world. Moreover, Asad was facing growing internal unrest due to chronic economic difficulties which had resulted in food and goods shortages and a growing gap between the élite and the poor. Syria was also shunned by the West because of its alleged links with international terrorism. When in 1986 the United States launched extensive air raids against Libya, killing among others Colonel Qaddafi's adopted baby daughter, Washington warned Syria that it could receive similar retaliation if it persisted in its support of various terrorist groups.

Soviet foreign policy makers sought to take advantage of Asad's weakness to force him to step in line with Moscow's new objectives. The Kremlin demanded that Asad's neo-Ba'athist party make a truce with the Ba'athist regime in Iraq and scale down its support for Tehran. The bitter feud between Asad and Iraq's Hussein meant that Syria was among the few Arab states supporting Iran in its war with Iraq. Moscow also wanted Asad to lessen his support for the Shi'ite Amal militia in Lebanon and to make his peace with Arafat. The PLO position in Lebanon had been seriously weakened as a result of Amal's Syrian-backed military offensives against Palestinian camps.

During Asad's visit of 23-5 April 1988 to Moscow there was evidence to suggest that the Syrian leader had agreed to concede to most of the Soviet demands. A positive outcome of this were agreements amounting to new economic and technical co-operation for the development of Syria's phosphate and oil industries as well as the construction of the hydro-electric Tishrin Dam on the Euphrates.[25] Both sides agreed to reschedule Syria's $15 billion debt and to send a new shipment of arms including the sought-after MiG-29s, which were suddenly arriving more promptly than when they had been requested before. In another sphere, a Syrian cosmonaut took part in the Soyuz TM-3 space mission on 22 July 1987 with Gorbachev describing the event as 'a striking page in the annals of development and strengthening of Soviet-Syrian friendship'.[26]

But sources of tension remained, mainly because as soon as Asad had secured his economic and military agreements, he reverted to his old policies towards his neighbours, particularly Iraq and Lebanon. In February and March 1989, visits by Shevardnadze and Defence Minister Dmitrii Yazov (the latter the first of its kind since Andrei Grechko's visit in 1972) were aimed at reminding Asad of his obligations. In particular, Moscow was concerned about Syrian attacks on the Lebanese Christian leader General Michel Aoun, who had launched a war of liberation aimed at ousting all foreign armies from the Lebanon. The Soviet position on Lebanon had conflicted with that of Syria because Moscow wanted to maintain independent and direct channels to the various political and ethnic groupings. Until 1987, the official line of the Soviet media had not shown any signs of difference on the Lebanese question. Thus, when in February of that year Syrian troops were deployed in west Beirut, it was described as a 'mission of maintaining peace and security'[27] at the invitation of the Speaker of the Lebanese Parliament, the Shi'ite Hussein Husseini, who was known for implementing many of Syria's political objectives in the small war-torn country. Perhaps there was a touch of irony when the report spoke of 'maintaining peace and security' as some of the worse fighting in Lebanon's history had just been taking place.

The PLO, too, was prodded and nudged towards finding an acceptable agreement with Israel, and whatever Moscow regarded as being an unhelpful element of Arafat's position was firmly frowned upon. In the words of one commentary, 'Soviet diplomacy played a significant, if unadvertised, role in bringing about a more moderate Palestinian position on the Middle Eastern settlement', by stressing in all its contacts with its Arab counterparts the importance of a political rather than military solution to the Arab-Israeli conflict.[28] Arafat's public renunciation of terrorism was to a large extent a credit to New Thinking and the unambiguous explanations by both Gorbachev and Shevardnadze to the Palestinian leadership that terrorist acts against innocent civilians would only serve to undermine Moscow's support for their cause. This highlighted a qualitative transformation from the Brezhnev era when terrorism was often justified as part of what Moscow categorised as a national liberation struggle. Many Arab groups and governments were irritated by Moscow's new position because in their view it took attention away from Israeli violations of international law, such as the assassinations of PLO activists who were often unconnected with the military (or paramilitary) wing of the organisation. However, Moscow attempted to adopt a balanced view by strongly condemning such Israeli violations and by supporting the *intifada* as a legitimate popular uprising against military occupation. There was also advice by senior Foreign Ministry and International Department officials to the PLO leadership that it should avoid antagonising US and Israeli opinion by such actions as unilaterally declaring a state or forming a government-in-exile.[29]

There were at times mild personal criticisms of Arafat and his leadership of the PLO. In a diplomatic snub he did not receive an invitation to Moscow while he was trying to generate support for a Jordanian and Western-backed peace plan among his own organisation. The disagreements among the PLO leadership regarding the Arafat-King Hussein peace plan became so sharp that they threatened to rupture the organisation, with the leftist Popular Front for the Liberation of Palestine, the second largest PLO faction after Arafat's Fatah led by hard-line Leninist George Habash, withdrawing altogether. Ironically, a compromise between the various factions was eventually reached with extensive mediation efforts by the Soviet Union so that all the parties returned to the fold, once again under the chairmanship of Arafat. The PLO leader publicly thanked the Soviet Union for effectively providing him with a political lifeline since a fractured organisation would have seriously undermined his international standing.

As a signal that tensions between Arafat and Moscow were eased, the Palestinian leader was finally able to travel to Moscow in November 1987 as head of an official PLO delegation. Once more, public pressure on Arafat to recognise Israel's security needs all seemed to indicate Gorbachev's eagerness 'to participate in a resolution of the Arab-Israeli conflict, and, therefore, greater willingness to meet certain US-Israeli demands'.[30] Moscow's role in convincing the Arabs to recognise the existing political reality was influential in changing the whole landscape of the Middle East and setting the scene for the peace agreements in the 1990s.

Gorbachev and pro-Western states

The *rapprochement* with Egypt signalled Moscow's changed attitude towards pro-Western states in the region. The watershed year was 1987 when the former Soviet ally had become re-integrated into the Arab ranks, partly as a result of Egypt's high profile support for Iraq in its ongoing war with Iran. Gorbachev felt it necessary to end the state of no-contact with Cairo, particularly since there remained outstanding Egyptian debts to the Soviet Union. Diplomatic contacts between the two countries increased until the spring of 1990 when Gorbachev played host to President Hosni Mubarak at the Kremlin. A breakthrough was achieved 'with the Soviet agreement, more than 15 years after the original Egyptian request, to reschedule Egypt's military debts (believed to total approximately $3 billion, to be repaid over a 25-year period)'.[31] The occasional criticisms of Egyptian policy in the media under Gorbachev tended to be more balanced than the outbursts against the murdered Sadat. For example, in 1990 a report in *Pravda* criticised 'the brutal repression of strikes allegedly plotted by religious organisations and communists, but it quoted President Mubarak as saying that he opposed such use of force'.[32]

Jordan's King Hussein, long regarded as staunchly pro-Western, was given full diplomatic honours on his official visit to Moscow in December 1987. Shevardnadze returned the visit in February 1989 as part of his Middle Eastern diplomatic tour, one unprecedented by a Soviet foreign minister. The improvement in relations, which Moscow under Gorbachev valued highly, led to a Joint Soviet-Jordanian Economic Commission which met in the summer of 1989 and agreed to expand trade to a level of $50 million annually.[33] In February 1990 an agreement was reached to stretch out repayment on a $168 million loan to Jordan and to accept most of the balance in goods.[34]

The economic aspect of Soviet foreign policy was a major pillar in Moscow's vision of a new international order. For this reason, the opening up of relations with Saudi Arabia, which by virtue of being the Middle East's wealthiest nation carried substantial political weight, was an obvious target for Gorbachev. There were however major obstacles to Soviet ambitions, not least of which was the occupation of Afghanistan, regarded as a serious threat to Gulf security. Saudi Arabia's King Fahd deliberately made a point of changing his title from His Majesty to Custodian of the Two Holy Mosques (of Mecca and Medina) to underline his commitment to Muslims far beyond his national realm.

From Moscow's point of view a positive step had been made

in 1985, when ties were re-established with Oman, the United Arab Emirates and Qatar, which belonged to the Gulf Co-operation Council (GCC). Kuwait, also a member, had already established diplomatic ties with Moscow. From the Soviet perspective, the jewel in the GCC crown was without question Saudi Arabia. According to one observer Gorbachev hoped to establish full diplomatic relations with Riyadh 'in order to exploit Saudi resentment of American support for Israel. (The Saudis in turn would probably like Soviet help with Iran.)'[35] While the latter statement was accurate, with regard to the former Moscow hoped to exploit this resentment, born particularly from Washington's preference for Israel in the sale of advanced weapons despite Saudi Arabia's leading role in combating communist and Soviet influence in the Muslim world and in moderating the general Arab stand against Israel. For example, with regard to Afghanistan, Riyadh was the first and most generous supporter of the Mujahedeen in their resistance to Soviet occupation.

With each announcement by Gorbachev that he intended to halt the Soviet adventure in Afghanistan, relations between the two countries moved to a higher and more co-operative sphere. In January 1987 Saudi Petroleum Minister Hisham Nazer paid a visit to Moscow as part of an Organisation of Petroleum Exporting Countries delegation. One year later, in January 1988, Saudi Foreign Minister Prince Sa'ud Al-Faisal visited the USSR as head of a GCC delegation. In February of that year, Soviet envoy Vladimir Poliakov, in the first such visit in fifty years, was an official guest in Riyadh. When the Soviet withdrawal of Afghanistan had been completed, Saudi Foreign Minister Sa'ud Al-Faisal went to Moscow in September 1990 to resume diplomatic ties. 'Two months later, the de-ideologization of Soviet policy paid off, in the form of a Saudi loan of almost $4 billion.'[36]

The development of Soviet-Turkish relations showed a similar pattern of improvement, though, as was the case with Egypt, there continued to be occasional outbursts against the treatment of communists and leftists in Turkey. A report in *Pravda* in September 1987 welcomed a referendum that month which allowed for greater individual rights for the Turks, but it noted that 'the Communist Party, other leftist political organisations and democratic trade unions…are still illegal…[and] political prisoners continue to languish in Turkish prisons'.[37] Nonetheless, Turgut

Özal, who dominated the Turkish political scene for much of the 1980s, was highly supportive of Gorbachev's reforms. He made his first visit as prime minister to Moscow in 1986, when his accommodating diplomatic intentions were reflected by his willingness to consider legalising the Turkish Communist Party following decades of Soviet pressure.

In reality, Turkey's biggest source of concern, or perhaps irritation, came from the south of its border in the form of Syria. Among the many issues of contention was the long-standing dispute with Turkey over the Sanjak of Alexandretta, with Syrian maps continuing to show the area as part of its territory. In addition, its 'proximity to the important Nato and Turkish installations of Iskenderum, Lucirlik, and Mersin' left them vulnerable to Syrian missile attacks. 'Syria is also known to train and arm PKK (Kurdish Workers' Party) terrorists who continually infiltrate into Turkey and cause havoc.'[38] Ankara recognised that forging a good relationship with the Soviet Union could help curb the activities of its principal Middle Eastern 'client', Syria. The next visit by Özal to the USSR was as president, taking with him a trade delegation which helped reach an agreement between the two countries to increase the volume of trade to $9 billion by the year 2000.[39]

Moscow and the Iran-Iraq dilemma

A major dilemma for Gorbachev in 1985 was whether to support Iran or Iraq in their bloody war that had already been raging for five years. Iraq was a more co-operative and traditional ally but Iran was potentially more important in geo-strategic and political terms. The Soviet Union dithered until February 1986 when an Iranian military breakthrough placed its army within reach of the major city of Basra and not too far away from Kuwait. Moscow quickly responded to provide necessary military assistance to Iraq. But to the annoyance of most Arab regimes, Moscow procrastinated on the idea of imposing an international arms embargo on Iran; and while the Soviet Union was denouncing Iranian military advances in 1986, in February of that same year Moscow envoy Georgi Kornienko travelled to Tehran on a mission to improve bilateral economic relations.

Despite religious outbursts in Iran about the 'evil atheism' of communism, bilateral relations steadily increased until February

1987 when Iranian Foreign Minister Ali Akbar Velayati travelled to Moscow in what was the highest ranking visit by an Iranian since the revolution. The fact that Iraq's President Hussein had been to Moscow at the end of 1985 and received assurances of support was not a contradiction but only strengthened the USSR's potential role of mediator between the two warring parties. The US Defense Secretary Caspar Weinberger wrote at the end of the war that Moscow's

.... long-term objectives in the region are to establish and broaden its hitherto generally weak relations and influence with the Gulf States and, more generally, to counter the U.S. position in the region. The Soviets also seek to maintain their position with both Iran and Iraq and to emerge as a major extra-regional power in the post–Gulf war period.[40]

By continuing to dwell on the competitive aspect of relations, Weinberger's comments suggested that there was a failure in Washington to understand the changing developments in the Soviet Union.

In the early Gorbachev years there were strident criticisms of Washington's role in the Iran-Iraq war. The disclosure that Iran had received US weapons in the Irangate scandal and the Iranian offensive in which troops captured the strategic Fao peninsula also placed great strain on relations between Tehran and Moscow, leading to Soviet suspicion about US intentions in the Gulf. The USSR's reaction to the Iranian interception of a Soviet ship bound for Kuwait added a new dimension: 'In this new flexing of Moscow's power projection capability, [Gorbachev] has emulated Washington, which informally started escorting some of its ships in early 1986; he is determined not to be outbid or outmanoeuvred by Washington in the high-stake great game in the Gulf.'[41] However, it was debatable whether or not Gorbachev was competing for regional dominance and the naval engagement in the Gulf was most likely simply trying to protect Soviet shipping, not necessarily at Washington's expense.

Towards the final stages of the Iran-Iraq war, Moscow was repeatedly calling for a cease-fire which was in effect a subtle tilt in favour of Iraq because Iran was the party rejecting mediation efforts. The official Soviet position, as it had been before Gorbachev, was for 'both sides to show political will, prudence and a desire for mutually acceptable accords that take the legitimate interests of both Iraq and Iran into account'.[42] But the Soviet press during Gorbachev's office seemed less sympathetic towards the Iranian position: 'Teheran continues to reject these [Iraqi] calls, just as it has rejected efforts at mediation on the part of the UN...insisting instead on "war until victory".'[43] A few articles also cast doubt on Iran's real motives in the light of Irangate, in which the Islamic republic, supposedly violently opposed to the 'Great Satan' (the United States) received weapons from that country which enabled it to carry out successful offensives against Iraq. It was also recalled that the Khomeini regime's most decisive internal action was to obliterate the Iranian Communist Party (the Tudeh), which boasted the largest membership in the Middle East, in the first years of his rule. The fact that Khomeini was allowed to leave from France (i.e. the West) to oust the dying Shah had puzzled many international observers. The implication of this was that the United States hoped Khomeini would be a better alternative than a communist take-over in Iran. In 1987 *Pravda* reported complaints by T. Ramadan, first deputy to the Iraqi prime minister, on his visit to Moscow that Washington provided Iraq with false information about Iranian offensives: 'The Americans' real aim was to drag out the war and use the Iranian threat to put pressure on the Arab countries', *Pravda* quoted Ramadan as saying.[44] And when the Iranian foreign minister visited Moscow, *Tass* quoted Gromyko telling Velayati: 'Our assessment of that war and your view of it do not coincide. [...] We repeat what we have told the Iranian leadership more than once: even one day of war is worse than five years of negotiations.'[45]

When the Soviet Union was due to begin protecting Kuwaiti oil tankers by sailing them under the Soviet flag, it felt compelled to deflect Iranian criticisms that it was taking sides in the war. I.S. Osminin, general director of Sovkomflot (Soviet merchant fleet) told *Izvestiia*: 'The case at hand has to do with the leasing of available Soviet tankers by a Kuwaiti company for the purpose of shipping petroleum. In concluding this agreement, Soviet ship owners have pursued purely commercial interests.'[46] This terse response was in keeping with the principles of New Thinking; that commercial priorities should supersede ideologically motivated policies. It was also in line with a general shift in Soviet policy under Gorbachev which, on balance, seemed to favour Iraq.

As the nationalities issue began to acquire more urgency in Soviet political life, some members of the Soviet élite began to accuse Tehran of stirring up ethnic tension and Islamic fundamentalism in the Muslim territories of the Soviet Union. For example, a report by the influential Igor Beliaev in *Literaturnaia gazeta* reflected 'Moscow's concern that Iran was behind Islamic unrest in the USSR in a warning [by Beliaev] that Moscow could support the Azerbaijanis who make up more than one third of the Iranian population'.[47] (Although there has not been a reliable census of Iranian population trends in recent times, it was highly unlikely that the Azerbaijanis made up a third of the Iranian population.) However, Iran showed similar concern about ethnic violence on its borders by urging both Azeris and Armenians to resolve their differences in order not to give 'Moscow a pretext to keep troops on the Iranian border'.[48]

Although the more militant Imams in Iran were vociferously supporting an Islamic rebellion against the communist system of the Soviet Union, their actual control over the Azeri groups was minimal. Although 75 per cent of Soviet Azerbaijanis were, as the majority of Iranians, Imami (twelver) Shias, this did not guarantee their loyalty to Iranian religious leaders.[49] In 1989 Iranian military units were sent to the border area after Azeris attacked Soviet border installations. Soviet Azerbaijani nationalist demonstrators were fired upon by Iranian troops at the beginning of January 1990, when they attempted to do the same with Iranian border posts, indicating that they were driven by nationalist rather than religious motives.

The Soviet strategy of not antagonising Iran finally succeeded in bringing results when in 1989 Iran's pragmatic leader President Hashemi Rafsanjani went to Moscow where a major economic package was signed, in which the Soviet Union undertook to carry out a range of projects, costing up to $6 billion over a ten-year period. In return, Iranian exports of three billion cubic metres of gas per year would cover 90 per cent of the costs.[50]

The breakthrough with Iran was to be negated by the Iraqi invasion of Kuwait on 3 August 1990. Iraq's President Hussein paid no heed to a joint Shevardnadze-Baker statement demanding that Iraq withdraw from Kuwait. The most obvious victim within the Soviet Union of Iraq's invasion was to be Shevardnadze, though Gorbachev's personal prestige also was to take a severe knock. In keeping with the principles of New Thinking the Soviet Foreign Minister uncompromisingly criticised the actions of the Iraqi leader, but he found himself opposed by conservative forces who argued that Soviet standing in the international community would be seriously undermined if Moscow did not stand by its long-time ally and co-signatory of the Treaty of Friendship and Co-operation.

From the viewpoint of the opponents of New Thinking, Shevardnadze's seemingly obsequious reactions to Washington's diktats were regarded as unacceptable. To make matters worse for the Soviet conservatives, Shevardnadze suggested that Soviet troops should be sent to the Gulf as part of the coalition against Iraq. Yet Shevardnadze's opponents had actually failed to recognise the subtleties of his suggestion and took this proposal to be yet another example of Soviet kow-towing to US policies. In fact there was nothing strikingly radical about such a proposal, which he had made during the last stages of the Iran-Iraq war with the purpose of replacing the then-growing US naval presence with international forces under a UN flag. Shevardnadze was actually seeking to block the US monopoly on peace-keeping/peace-enforcing missions by including Soviet and other neutral troops.

In the light of New Thinking, Shevardnadze's reaction to the Iraqi invasion of Kuwait was completely rational. 'Now that a new world order is being built based on co-operation and inter-action, to commit an act of aggression meant to commit suicide. It was not possible, I thought' wrote Shevardnadze in his memoirs, 'for Saddam Hussein not to understand this'.[51] But the conservative forces were not impressed and regarded the crisis as an opportunity for the Soviet Union to regain some of the losses it had recently endured. Gorbachev opted for a compromise option which perhaps characterised his last two years of leadership. The Soviet leader sent Evgenii Primakov, a leading foreign policy adviser with long-standing ties with Arab leaders, particularly Saddam Hussein, on a mission to find a peaceful solution, principally by convincing the Iraqi leader to withdraw from Kuwait and save the world from impending war. It was hoped that this strategy would give credit to the Soviet Union for playing the role of international peace-maker.

Primakov was despatched to Baghdad on 4-5 October and again on 28-30 October 1990. On both occasions Primakov failed to convince Hussein to withdraw unconditionally, and in effect Gorbachev had no choice but to support whatever action was taken by the United States. On the positive side, 'Soviet verbal support for the UN resolutions earned Moscow a $1 billion credit line from Kuwait, $4 billion loan from Saudi Arabia, and a $175 million investment in a joint Soviet-Saudi bank in Alma-Ata'.[52] Unfortunately for Shevardnadze, this vocal support was to cost him his job as he was forced to resign under a barrage of communist-nationalist pressure, warning that a dictatorship in the Soviet Union was looming. Although the oil-rich monarchies provided generous compensation for the Soviet stand in the Gulf crisis, Gorbachev would have been informed that his country stood to lose an estimated $6 billion in payments for unfinished projects as well as the possibility of repayment of an estimated $5-10 billion debt for arms purchases.[53]

According to Anatolii Cherniaev (speaking at the London School of Economics on 18 October 1994), who had spent years working at the International Department and later became a Gorbachev aide, the Politburo, once the fulcrum of decision-making in Moscow, had lost virtually all its powers by the time of the crisis. The Soviet leader had set up a special operating group to monitor the conflict which included the new Foreign Minister Bessmertnykh, Defence Minister Marshal Dmitrii Iazov, KGB head Kriuchkov and MVD head Boris Pugo. It is worth noting that all the members of this group were either directly or indirectly (Bessmertnykh) implicated in the August coup against Gorbachev in 1991. The absence of New Thinking chiefs, such as Shevardnadze and Iakovlev, confirmed that Gorbachev had been forced to concede ground to the more reactionary forces of the Soviet system. But despite this Gorbachev had evidently negotiated some form of compromise with the hard-liners that prevented Moscow from pursuing a collision course with the United States. One author described the following possible scenario had Gorbachev and New Thinking not left their imprint on Soviet foreign policy:

> The Soviets would have maintained close military and political ties with the Iraqi regime right up until the invasion, would have strenuously tried to dissuade Hussein from actually crossing the border in force (if they had known about his plans), would have failed in their endeavours but would in any event have continued to support him afterward.[54]

The crushing military victory by the United States had sent a clear message to all leaders of the Middle East as well as the Soviet Union that Washington was the world's only superpower. The consequence of the Gulf War was also to have a negative effect on Gorbachev's New Thinking. 'All the parties involved in the conflict were given an object-lesson in world politics: force remains the most decisive and intelligible argument. Mikhail Gorbachev, the "prophet" of New Thinking, was weakened as a direct result of the war.'[55] To make matters even worse, there was once more a shadow cast upon the quality of Soviet-made weapons. Defence Minister Iazov was forced to admit to a parliamentary committee that Soviet defence systems had 'failed in most cases' and that the lessons of the war had forced his ministry to find 'new defence concepts'.[56]

One major beneficiary of the Gulf War was Syria, which took part in the US-led coalition and was rewarded by being reaccepted into the international community. Damascus also took the opportunity to reaffirm its friendship with the Soviet Union by sending Minister of Defence Mustafa Tlas in February 1991 to sign new bilateral military agreements. In May of 1991 Soviet Foreign Minister Aleksander Bessmertnykh toured the Middle East, stopping in Syria, Jordan, Israel and Egypt. The trip reflected the new Soviet standing in the region, with diplomatic relations open to all.

The consequences of New Thinking

Whatever the arguments about strong social, economic and political undercurrents, Gorbachev for the most part helped bring many chapters of Cold War conflicts to a peaceful close. A nuclear threat remained; but it was more likely to come from North Korea, Iran or Israel rather than Russia. The situation in the Middle East did not become more stable simply because the Soviet Union retreated from its previously more competitive role in the area. But Gorbachev's retreat was noble as he sought to make the most of what had been an irretrievable situation.

In his last months of power, Gorbachev strove to change every detail of the diplomatic service. Pankin described the system before the reforms when 'every Embassy was divided between Foreign Ministry diplomats and the KGB, "the neighbours"'. It was the

Communist Party rather than the ambassador which 'wielded enormous influence there through resident Party Secretaries appointed by the Central Committee and beyond the control of either the Foreign Ministry or the KGB'.[57] Communist Party Secretaries held meetings in which the ambassador sat as an ordinary member on a regular basis. These Party Secretaries effectively ensured that the ambassador followed the party line and they had the power to force his departure. Gorbachev ordered a complete review of this overlapping system which greatly burdened the implementation of foreign policy. The old guard was tenacious in its will to keep a hold of its power and influence. As Shevardnadze complained: 'Suddenly, I would find out that people were manipulating things behind my back, damaging our hard-won reputation as a reliable partner, and undermining our diplomatic successes.'[58]

But the elevation of the likes of Karen Brutents and Primakov because of their expertise rather than their political reliability and loyalty was surely a positive step. Alexei Vassiliev, who was consultant to the Foreign Affairs Committee and deputy director of the Institute of Oriental Studies, represented a new breed of Middle East specialists in Russia whose thinking broke with the past. He explained his country's new policy in a leading Arab journal: 'The Soviet Union's omission of ideology in foreign policy means the preservation of long-standing relations with radical regimes, but with wider co-operation and mutual interest to include all states, regardless of the path of development it had chosen.'[59] Vassiliev countered criticisms by hard-line Arab regimes critical of New Thinking by arguing that 'Soviet-US relations do not work against the Arabs. For example, the efforts of the Soviet Union and the United States helped to stop the Iran-Iraq war, and there were also shared efforts with regard to Lebanon.'[60]

Others from the Soviet old-guard criticised Gorbachev for incompetence and argued that he should have taken a leaf out of Stalin's book by covering up weaknesses with a hardened stand and by bluffing the West with carefully timed bluster into making concessions. The theorists behind New Thinking, however, pointed out that such arguments completely missed the point. Moscow genuinely wanted to create an atmosphere of trust, by building clearly definable borders to foreign policy, such as having good relations with Israel and Gulf Arab states while maintaining ties with traditional allies and encouraging them to adopt a more moderate line. Gorbachev often liked to state: 'We want political and legal methods to prevail in solving whatever problems may arise. Our ideal is a world community of states based on the rule of law subordinating their foreign policies to law.'[61]

In addition, the principle of democracy and openness had become firmly set by the last two years of Gorbachev's rule. This factor played a key part in the failure of the anti-Gorbachev *putsch* in August 1991. Immediately after Gorbachev's return to the Kremlin, efforts were quickened to establish full relations with Israel. One senior Soviet diplomat was quoted as saying that 'Israel proved through its pro-democracy stance that they want to establish sincere and business-like relations'.[62] The same attitude was adopted with moderate Arab states such as Jordan, Lebanon and Saudi Arabia.

New Thinking was intended to displace Brezhnev's ambiguous and somewhat fork-tongued policies that had led to a growing gulf of mistrust between the USSR and the Arab world. Besides, there was an economic dimension to this policy: 'The Soviet search for participation in the international economic system and for credits from and trade with the West necessitates a new, less threatening Soviet image.'[63] However, even liberals such as Andrei Kozyrev, as late as 1989, foresaw a socialist compromise with the West as a stable world system. Writing with Alexei Shumikhin, Kozyrev was in line with the view of New Thinking that the 'transference of the confrontation between West and East to the arena of developing countries, assisted by both sides, added to their unprecedented backwardness'.[64] He called on the world's economic giants to encourage an international model that was similar throughout the globe. This could be a 'realistic practicability, and not a globalist "class" plan', based on the harmonisation of capitalist and socialist models.[65]

Another influential foreign policy adviser under Gorbachev, later to become a foreign minister and prime minister for his arch-rival Boris Yeltsin, was Primakov. Perceived to be less Western-oriented than Kozyrev, Primakov's statements and views (written before Kozyrev) seemed to fall smoothly in place with New Thinking. Chiefly, Primakov argued that 'the security of some cannot be ensured at the expense of the security of others'.[66] Thus, the beginning of the rejection of the zero-sum game was taking shape. The impact of the Gorbachev leadership was highlighted by the prevalence of a new view among the country's leading foreign policy thinkers. Was it Kozyrev or Primakov who wrote the following?

It is important to note that the growing interrelationship of today's world is expressed not only in the problem of survival, which is common to all parts of the world, but also in the existence and development of a world economy and in the presence and intensification of common human interests [....]

such as those of environment and Third World poverty.[67]

One contemporary observer pointed out that 'Gorbachev explicitly acknowledges his intellectual debt to Khrushchev', but with regard to foreign policy he correctly made the crucial distinction that the last Soviet leader stressed 'the co-operative rather than the competitive dimension of US-Soviet relations'.[68] Nonetheless, Moscow drew the line at the point where compromise could have been mistaken for capitulation. In the words of Primakov, during his mediation efforts in the Gulf crisis: 'We are a superpower and we have our own line, our own policies, we are demonstrating this point.'[69]

Indeed, the Gulf War was a pointed lesson to Moscow that the idealism of New Thinking would be fruitless if it did not take into account national security and national interests. New Thinking also changed the outlook from Moscow about the inevitability of a bipolar world, and a new concept was developed which encouraged the co-ordination and co-operation of key regions; thus Europe, the Far East and eventually the Middle East began to have a growing significance of their own. It was observed at the time that 'Soviet diplomacy must no longer view world politics exclusively through the prism of US-Soviet relations'.[70] In other words, Soviet interests in Israel or Iraq for example, whether economic or geo-strategic, would not be related to the way superpower relations were going at any given period. At the same time, such interests were pursued carefully so as not to cause a rupture in relations with the United States. While Gorbachev (and Shevardnadze, Iakovlev *et al.*) put an end to many established features of Soviet foreign policy, the lessons learned from that turbulent period also helped to lay the ground-work for his successors in the new Russian Federation.

NOTES

1. Mark A. Heller, *The Dynamics of Soviet Policy in the Middle East: Between Old Thinking and New*, Tel Aviv University, 1991, p.50.
2. Joseph L. Nogee and Robert H. Donaldson, *Soviet Foreign Policy since World War II*, New York, 1988, p.336.
3. Eduard Shevardnadze, *The Future Belongs to Freedom*, London, 1991, p.54.
4. Nicolai Petro and Alvin Z. Rubinstein, *Russian Foreign Policy: From Empire to Nation State*, New York, 1997, p.9.
5. *Ibid.*, p.97.
6. Viktor Kuvaldin (Gorbachev policy adviser 1989-91), 'From Cold War to New World Order' in Gabriel Gorodetsky (ed.), *Soviet Foreign Policy 1917-1991: A Retrospective*, London, 1994, p.193.
7. Carol R. Saivetz, 'Gorbachev's Middle East Policy: the Arab dimension' in David H. Goldberg and Paul Marantz (eds), *The Decline of the Soviet Union and the Transformation of the Middle East*, San Francisco and Oxford, 1994, p.7.
8 Shevardnadze, *op. cit.*, p.61.
9. Saivetz, *op. cit.*, p.11.
10. Robert Owen Freedman, 'Soviet Foreign Policy Toward the United States and Israel in the Gorbachev Era: Jewish Emigration and Middle East Politics' in Goldberg and Marantz, *op. cit.*, p.59.
11. W. Raymond Duncan and Carolyn McGiffert Ekedahl, *Moscow and the Third World under Gorbachev*, Boulder, CO, 1990, p.119.
12. *Ibid.*
13. *World Affairs Report*, vol.20, no.2, January-March 1990, p.129.
14. Freedman, *op cit.*, p.70.
15. *Ibid.*, p.63.
16. *Ibid.*
17. *Ibid.*, p.64.
18. *Ibid.*, p.67.
19. *Ibid.*, p.69.
20. Boris Pankin, *The Last Hundred Days of the Soviet Union*, London, 1996, p.215.
21. *Ibid.*, p.216.
22. *Ibid.*, p.53.
23. Robert Boardman, 'Gorbachev, the Russian Federation, and the Rediscovery of the United Nations' in Goldberg and Marantz, *op. cit.*, p.145.
24. Galia Golan, *Soviet Policies in the Middle East from World War Two to Gorbachev*, Cambridge, 1990, p. 279.
25. Efraim Karsh, *Soviet Policy Towards Syria since 1970*, London, 1991, p.170.
26. *Ibid.*
27. Yuri Glukhov, 'Vvod siriiskikh voisk' (The Entry of Syrian Troops), *Pravda*, 22 February 1987, p.5.
28. Igor Beliaev and John Marks, *Common Ground on Terrorism*, London, 1991, p.58.
29. Heller, *op. cit.*, p.73.

30. Galia Golan, 'The Soviet Union and the Palestinian Issue' in George W. Breslauer (ed.), *Soviet Strategy in the Middle East*, Boston, MA, 1990, p.90.
31. Galia Golan, 'Gorbachev's Middle East Strategy' in Breslauer, *op. cit.*, p.158.
32. *World Affairs Report*, vol.20, no.2, Jan-March 1990, p.130.
33. Duncan and Ekedahl, *op. cit.*, p.123.
34. Heller, *op. cit.*, p.76.
35. Jiri Valenta and Frank Cobulka, *Gorbachev's New Thinking and Third World Conflicts*, London, 1990, p.71.
36. Heller, *op. cit.*, p.77.
37. *Pravda* (22 Sept. 1987, p.5), in *Current Digest of the Soviet Press*, vol.39, no.18, 1987.
38. James Brown, *Delicately Poised Allies: Greece and Turkey*, London, 1994, p.98.
39. Turkkay Ataou, 'Turkey, the CIS and Eastern Europe' in Ianon Balkir and Allan M. Williams (eds), *Turkey and Europe*, London and New York, 1993, p.196.
40. Caspar Weinberger, 'Security Arrangements in the Gulf', *Gulf Cooperation Council Reports*, no.3, 1988, p.12.
41. Alvin Z. Rubinstein, *Moscow's Third World Strategy*, Princeton, NJ, 1988, p.282.
42. 'Zaiavlenie covetskogo pravitel'stva (Soviet Government Statement), *Pravda*, 9 January 1987, p.1.
43. *Ibid.*
44. Pavel Demchenko, 'Mezhdunarodnoe obozpenie' (International Survey), *Pravda*, 25 January 1987, p.4.
45. *Tass*, 'Predsedatel' presidiuma Verkhovnogo soveta SSSR prinial ministra Irana' (Chairman of the Presidium of the Supreme Soviet of the CCCP Receives Iranian Minister), in *Pravda*, 14 February 1987, p.2.
46. *Izvestiia* 22 Sept. 1987, in *Current Digest of the Soviet Press*, vol.39, no.18, p.5.
47. *World Affairs Report*, vol.20, no.2, Jan-March, p.156. In the original report in *Literaturnaia gazeta*, 7 Feb. 1990, Beliaev pointed out that there were nine million Azeris and that better results would be achieved if both sides co-operated.
48. *Ibid.*, p.86.
49. Anthony Hyman, 'Soviet-Iranian Relations: the End of Rapprochement?', *Report on the USSR*, vol.2, no.4, 26 Jan. 1990, p.17.
50. *Ibid.*, p.18.
51. Shevardnadze, *op. cit.*, p.101.
52. Saivetz, *op cit.*, p.17.
53. Stephen Page, 'New Political Thinking and Soviet Policy Toward Regional Conflict in the Middle East' in Goldberg and Marantz, *op. cit.*, p.59.
54. Heller, *op. cit.* p.77.
55. Kuvaldin, *op. cit.*, p.196.
56. 'Soviet Weapons Fail Combat Test', *New Arabia*, no.2, 4 March 1991, p.7.
57. Pankin, p.139.
58. Shevardnadze, *op. cit.*, p.xvi.
59. Alexei Vassiliev, 'Al-siassia al-sofietia fi al-sharq al-awsat' (Soviet Policy in the Middle East), *Al-Hayat*, 26 July 1990, p.9.

60. *Ibid.*
61. Mikhail Gorbachev, *The Meaning of My Life*, Edinburgh, 1990, p.105.
62. Annika Savill, 'Moscow's New World Order', *The Independent*, 27 July 1991, p.4.
63. Carol R. Saivetz, 'Soviet Policy in the Middle East: Gorbachev's Imprint' in Roger E. Kanet *et al.* (eds), *Soviet Foreign Policy in Transition*, Cambridge, 1992, p.202.
64. Andrei Kozyrev and A. Shumikhin, 'Vostok i zapad v "tret"em mire' (East and West in the "Third" World) in *Mezhdunarodnaia zhizn'*, Moscow, Feb 1989, p.70.
65. *Ibid.*, p.74.
66. Evgenii Primakov, 'A New Philosophy of Foreign Policy', *Pravda*, 10 July 1987 in *USSR Documents – the Gorbachev Reforms*, Gulf Breeze FL, 1988, p.330.
67. *Ibid.*, p.329.
68. Heller, *op. cit.*, p.55.
69. Carol R. Saivetz, 'Moscow and the Gulf War: The Policies of a Collapsing Superpower' in Gorodetsky, *op. cit.*, p.200.
70. Alexander Rahr, 'New Thinking Takes Hold in Foreign Policy Establishment', *RFE/RL Report on the USSR*, vol.1 no.1, 6 January 1989, p.4.

4

PROBLEMS, DEBATES, IDEAS: FORMING A NATIONAL FOREIGN POLICY UNDER YELTSIN

The break-up of the Soviet Union did not ease Moscow's geo-strategic concerns, but added to them. Russia remained a huge country, spanning Asia from the Far East to Europe, and this imposing geographic factor had always been impossible for Moscow's policy makers to ignore, whether they were tsarist, communist or democratic. This was, in the words of one historian, reflected in the 'continuity and consistency of Soviet strategic thinking over the past 60 years (and Russian perceptions for 300 years before that)'.[1] The emergence of many new and often volatile neighbours led to a new range of difficulties which needed consideration. Russia's multi-continental form united different nationalities and creeds; its distinct cultural heritage was neither Eastern nor Western, yet it took something from both. Authors and poets, as epitomised by the great Dostoyevsky, lauded the spiritual purity of the Russian people, whose suffering in their history was undeniably bitter and unrelenting. This experience, Russia's artists believed, provided their country with a special message for the world. Discarding this interpretation of the Russian psyche and worldview as unscientific would miss the point that foreign policy, like any strategy, requires a motivating idea.

As was pointed out in the previous chapter, Gorbachev's reforms reoriented Soviet foreign policy firmly towards the West. Ultimately, the Soviet Union was beyond salvation and Gorbachev was replaced in Moscow by Boris Yeltsin. The democratically elected leader of the Russian Federation had markedly different practical considerations from his predecessor. Nonetheless, the age old dilemmas that plagued Russia's relationship with the outside world continued to divide its political élite. But before looking at relations between Russia and the key countries of the Middle

East (in the following chapters), this chapter will take a general look at the administrative reforms and political and ideological debates which characterised Russia's foreign policy in the first five years under Yeltsin.

The end of the USSR

Yeltsin appointed Andrei Kozyrev as Russia's foreign minister in October 1990 although there was still a Soviet foreign minister. Yeltsin's actions in undermining the Soviet Union were fruitful from a personal political perspective, but it was nonetheless a gamble which threatened stability both within the former Soviet borders, and in the international arena. Yeltsin conspired for a Russian breakaway from the USSR in order to undermine the Soviet system: 'The process, touched off by Yeltsin's Russia in June [1990], was not only disruptive of the *status quo* but also undermined the effort at political reform of relationships between the centre and the republics launched that spring with work on a new Union Treaty.'[2] The relevance of this point was that it left lingering doubts over his personality and style of leadership throughout his presidency.

When he saw his opportunity, Yeltsin moved quickly to seize power and push Gorbachev aside. On 23 August 1991 during a televised appearance at the Russian Supreme Soviet, Yeltsin openly undercut Gorbachev, one day after his return from the coup, by physically pushing him aside as he decreed the suspension of the Russian Communist Party. These developments were of much concern to Moscow's Middle East allies, and to the Central Asian republics, most notably Kazakhstan. As the largest of the so-called Muslim republics, Kazakhstan was in reality heavily populated by Russians, with close historic links to its northern neighbour. It shared with the other four republics of Central Asia a fear that a breakaway from Russia would have a devastating economic effect. Despite such fears, by the end of December 1991 the inevitable had happened and each of the fifteen republics followed its own path: the USSR was replaced by a loose political entity known as the Commonwealth of Independent States (CIS). On 24 December 1991 Russia took over the UN Security Council seat previously occupied by the USSR.

The most immediate concern for Moscow under Yeltsin was

to maintain order within the Russian Federation and sustain a level of acceptable military security for the new borders. The armed forces, with all their military resources, had to find a new strategy based on Russia's security rather than that of the Soviet Union. Russia's international military capacity was greatly compromised by the break-up of the Soviet Union and by the eruption of local conflicts in neighbouring republics, particularly in the Caucasus region. The creation of new republics had a far-reaching impact on relations between Russia and the Middle East because it meant that there were no longer any common borders between the Russian Federation and Turkey and Iran. In the past, the Soviet command post for possible Middle Eastern operations was in the Trans-Caucasus Military District, but in the post-Soviet period Moscow became ever more dependent upon the co-operation of local governments for the right to station troops in an area which was of vital strategic importance for Russia.

In internal affairs, Yeltsin faced a strong and vocal opposition composed of powerful groups from the Soviet era which, as in Gorbachev's time, were highly averse to reform. By 1993 there was a paralysis in decision making as Yeltsin's backing in the Congress of People's Deputies, the parliament established by Gorbachev, had declined to below 200 out of a body of over 1,000 members. The Russian president won a victory over parliament and his rivals in April 1993 in a tightly fought referendum, and in September he dissolved the Congress of People's Deputies and announced new parliamentary elections. His leading political rivals, Vice President Aleksandr Rutskoi and Parliamentary Speaker Ruslan Khasbulatov, claimed that this was an auto-coup by the president and made their own bid for power, leading Yeltsin to use army tanks to crush the resistance. The conclusive assault on the parliament building on 4 October 1993 was followed by new parliamentary elections in December. The use of the army and the results of the new parliamentary elections to the Russian Duma were damaging to Yeltsin and highlighted the importance of the military in the country's political battles. The political instability and the perception that there was deep hostility towards the West from senior army ranks and other important political institutions, in a view directly contrary to that of Kozyrev's, had a significant bearing on Yeltsin's original foreign policy objectives.

Yeltsin and the West

By far the most important priority for Yeltsin, in terms of foreign policy, was to maintain good relations with the West, a continuation of Gorbachev's New Thinking. Diplomatic relations with Europe and the United States warmed, and co-operation replaced conflict, though both sides continued to target their nuclear weapons at each other. Sympathisers of Gorbachev had argued that the West had hesitated to support him fully, despite the rhetoric of its leaders, because there was an unwillingness to rescue the Soviet Union after being a bitter enemy for so many years. It was therefore expected that the establishment of a democratic Russia with political, economic and social ideals similar to those of the West might convince Washington and its allies to bring the new country into the fold.

In the hopeful days immediately following the collapse of the Soviet Union, the question of what would happen if Russia's vital interests were not harmonious with the general mood of the international community did not seem to arise. In his first year in office, Kozyrev was a leading proponent of the view that Russia should pursue a totally pro-Western policy. Only the West had the means to provide economic assistance, he argued, and it also offered a shining example of a successful democratic system, which was still fragile in Russia. Until the summer of 1992, Yeltsin gave his foreign minister full backing in this radical pro-Western view. In that time, Kozyrev 'enjoyed unprecedented dominance' in the foreign policy sphere, allowing him to follow 'an uncompromising pro-Western line aimed at integrating Russia into what he called "the democratic Northern Hemisphere"'.[3]

That this pro-Western approach would inevitably sacrifice relations with traditional 'Eastern allies' hardly bothered the Kremlin élite in early 1992. Iraq, Syria and Iran, for example, were facing immense economic difficulties which made them more of a burden than a benefit. The new government was seeking to transform the state economy from its dependency on arms sales to a more diverse economic system. In effect, there seemed to be a genuine and well-defined vision which placed Russia in the Western family. Kozyrev assured the West: '[Russia] will be a normal great power. Its national interests will be a priority. But these will be interests understandable to democratic countries and Russia will be defending them through interaction with partners, not through confrontation.'[4]

However, the failure of 'shock therapy' to produce immediate economic results damaged the radical reformers, and Western refusal to provide the necessary funds to rescue their economic plans placed yet another nail in the coffin of the pro-Western radicals. Russia and its CIS partners found themselves in a similar position to countries of the less-developed world, 'negotiating from weakness with the Western powers over terms for aid, investment, and technology transfer, and for access to their raw materials, markets, and cheap labour forces'.[5] This growing realisation that the relationship between Russia and the United States was not founded on an equal basis led policy makers in Moscow to re-evaluate the nature of bilateral ties.

There were also reasons directly linked to foreign policy which greatly weakened the position of the pro-Western radicals. Kozyrev, who was a leading figure, was partly responsible for the failure to assert the position of the Foreign Ministry at a time when various other state institutions took it upon themselves to follow their own foreign policy line. One commentator observed that in Soviet times the Politburo was at the top of a pyramid which implemented foreign policy. During the early period 'each branch of power considered itself a Politburo and thought it had the right to pursue its own diplomacy'.[6] There was an atmosphere of uncertainty and chaos in the direction of the country's foreign policy, making it 'difficult to predict whether Russia would follow a path of gradual institutionalisation, consensus building, and partnership with the Western powers or slide into political decay, demagogy, and dictatorship', which would lead to aggressive international behaviour.[7] It was widely recognised that the challenges facing Kozyrev were not easy: reforming the relationship between state and government institutions; organising new mechanisms for foreign policy making; formulating a new policy which was in touch with the political élite and public opinion. But Kozyrev failed even to begin tackling these problems. Instead, despite claiming to want to establish a pragmatic foreign policy, Kozyrev pursued an ideologically driven policy in which he became closely associated with a group of thinkers who wanted the Westernisation of Russia's political, economic and cultural spheres. This label adhered to Kozyrev despite his later efforts at consensus building.

The rejection of a policy seeking to imitate and aggrandise the West had strong roots in Russian society. There were historic reasons dating back to tsarist and communist suspicions of Western moral decay and US neo-imperialism, as well as cultural reasons which rejected excessive individualism. In addition, it was not in the interest of certain political groups to encourage political reform, and they sought to win public support by criticising the government's pro-Western policies. These parties, ranging from neo-communist to extreme nationalist, were able to exploit the hurt national pride of many Russians. They were successful, to some extent, because they played a part in forcing Yeltsin to tone down his pro-Western line and adopt a more consensus-building approach. However, it is necessary here to make a crucial and central point: the rejection of the approach adopted during the first year under Yeltsin was not simply for the sake of political expediency, but because of a genuine realisation by the Kremlin leadership that the policies of the radical pro-Western liberals were essentially flawed.

Both the government and its opposition had concluded by 1993 that the promise of $24 billion in Western aid was unlikely to be fulfilled. Radical reformers in the government became discredited or were under extreme political pressure, with many being gradually replaced by moderate reformers. This internal shift of power was to have an impact on the country's international outlook. One Russian diplomat noted that the radical Atlanticists, as they were referred to in the early 1990s, viewed 'the United States as a senior partner and as the recognised leader of the Western, democratic, free world'. As a natural consequence, Moscow had tacitly accepted a subordinate role to Washington.[8] But with the discrediting of the leaders of this policy it became politically impossible to include them in a government which was increasingly under pressure to create an independent and pragmatic foreign policy.

Some interpreted the weakening position of the radical reformers as indicative of the undermining of Russian democracy and reform in general, and the re-emergence of belligerent and anti-democratic forces. The Georgian President Eduard Shevardnadze, the last Soviet foreign minister, told an audience in London's Chatham House as late as 1995 that he believed a return to the Cold War was not impossible: 'Having spent a lot of money on ending the

Cold War, the West did not invest in support of democracy and freedom.'[9] Shevardnadze had first-hand experience of Russian military involvement in his country's civil war which forced Tbilisi to compromise its national independence and recognise Moscow's dominance in the area of the former USSR. Yet Moscow's reorientation away from the West was largely forced upon it by the growing instability around it, rather than as a direct response to anti-Western forces in the country. Speaking in 1993 about possible threats to Russia, Defence Minister Pavel Grachev said that 'the most probable scenario is not a direct armed invasion of Russia but her gradual entanglement in conflicts in neighbouring nations and regions. Given the complex interrelation and interdependence of the various states and peoples, any armed conflict may evolve into a large-scale war.'[10]

Washington's actions in the early 1990s did not help the leadership in Moscow in their efforts to justify closer co-operation with the West. When Yeltsin came to power the main bone of contention with the West had been the war in the former Yugoslavia. The Russian leadership became increasingly vocal in its opposition to Washington's efforts to weaken Serbia and its Serb allies in Bosnia. The events in Bosnia had important implications with regard to Yeltsin's international policy by reflecting the Kremlin's wish to regain lost prestige in the international community and, perhaps more importantly, from the Russian people. The Kremlin began to underline Moscow's responsibility for Russians at home and abroad, claiming to act as their political and military guardian. This pledge appeared to include some responsibility for the Christian Orthodox Serbs, who were regarded by Russians as ethnically related. Ethnicity and nationalism seemed to replace communism as Russia's ideological guiding force. Russia's relations with the West were also strained as plans for NATO's eastward expansion began to unfold. Opposition to the prospect of a Western military alliance incorporating Eastern European countries, which had historically been regarded as part of a security zone, did not include only Russian extreme nationalists or neo-communists but ordinary people as well. For decades under communism 'Soviet peoples were indoctrinated with the dogma of so-called "capitalist encirclement".'[11] It was never properly explained to ordinary Russians why the West needed NATO expansion if the Cold War had supposedly ended. Plans for such expansion strengthened the hand of policy makers whose thinking was within the framework of Russian national security interests rather than close co-operation with the West. Defence Minister Igor Rodionov's words explicitly revealed the limits of co-operation with the West: 'Of course, NATO countries are free to decide what to do in their own house. But when imminent changes alarm its neighbours and threaten their security – that is inadmissible recklessness.'[12]

Despite differences over NATO expansion and Bosnia, there was a very low possibility that Yeltsin would antagonise the West to the point of re-igniting the Cold War. By 1996 Russian foreign policy was being presented to the West as pragmatic and conciliatory without ideological enemies. But it was also a policy which became more direct about asserting its national interests. Russia's efforts to become more involved in the Middle East were closely tied to the Kremlin's attitude towards the West. The early ascendancy of democratic forces prevented closer ties with traditional allies in the region because 'in its values, Russian policy [was] based on, and aimed at, the promotion of fundamental Western values'. Kozyrev's definition of this was 'individual liberty and market economy'.[13] As foreign minister, Kozyrev sought to reconcile these principles with the growing practical problems confronting his government such as domestic political opposition and international crises and situations which tested Russia's co-operation with the West in the light of pressing national interests. Kozyrev's effective dismissal as foreign minister was a consequence of his failure to do this.

Russia's redefinition of the Middle East

The construction of a policy guided by national interest ran parallel to revitalised activity in the Middle East, particularly after 1992. According to a leading Moscow academic and government adviser, what had developed in the first five-year period since 1991 with regard to the Middle East was a reappraisal of priorities and perceptions. Thus, whereas in the Soviet era certain countries in the Middle East were supported for ideological reasons, under Yeltsin there was a higher emphasis placed on the geo-strategic and economic aspect of relations. Consequently, 'while in the Soviet Cold War era Egypt was one of the most important places where the USSR was confronting the United States, it no longer constituted any strategic value for Russia. Turkey and Iran, on the other hand, have become much more important than they used to be.'[14]

As Moscow placed a greater emphasis on CIS security, the need for a more stable and productive relationship with Turkey and Iran acquired a greater urgency. Countries such as Iraq and Syria also remained important for strategic reasons as well as for their ability to consume Russian technology and weapons. Just before the collapse of the Soviet Union, one author poignantly reminded his readers that while Moscow stopped supporting 'Syrian aspirations for strategic parity with Israel, a further impoverished USSR might be tempted to sell arms for hard currency'.[15] A struggling Russian economy would likely have been similarly attracted to the prospect of quick profits through arms sales. By contrast, Palestinian-Israeli relations or Jordanian-Israeli relations had little effect on Russia's national security; thus they were of little importance for Moscow other than bringing the possibility of enhancing its prestige.

The influence of countries such as Iran, Turkey and to some extent Saudi Arabia on the Muslim republics of the CIS ensured that Russian foreign policy makers paid attention to these potential rivals. The 1980s were characterised by Gorbachev's New Thinking, the end of the Cold War, the liberation of Eastern Europe and German unification. However, the post-Soviet period was described by some as 'the time of the new independent states which are erecting their own foreign policies on the ruins of the Soviet empire'.[16] Existing within these newly independent states were aspirations which threatened seriously to curtail Russia's regional influence, as for example 'in Uzbekistan, the longing for a vast Central Asian state, a revival of the old idea of grand Turkestan', took on a new zeal.[17]

Moscow had to take into account the Muslim factor, 'that is, a policy by the Muslim republics oriented towards and possibly determined by interests in links with the Muslim countries of the Middle East and Asia'.[18] In addition, the growing friction between Russia and its neighbours, particularly over the potentially explosive issue of Russians living in the former Soviet republics, strengthened the identification of the Central Asian people with Islam.

Moscow's preoccupation with considerations that were, geographically speaking, on its doorstep masked the trend that Russia was setting its sights further. During Yeltsin's first year in office, Russia had ostensibly very little interest in the Middle East, with its influence perceived as being marginal. Israeli Foreign Minister and former Prime Minister Shimon Peres bluntly expressed this point in reference to the Middle East peace talks: 'The United States contributed more than any other country to the success of these negotiations. The Americans set the time and venue for the meetings, and guaranteed that Russia be given its rightful place as co-sponsor.'[19] Here Peres's most telling remark was the implication that it was Washington's generosity which guaranteed the Russian status; otherwise, its role might have been in doubt. Critics of the Soviet Union, such as Israel, suggested that Soviet withdrawal from the region had the positive effect of lessening the threat of war. Tel Aviv generally showed hostility to the possibility that Russia might return to the region in force because it did not want a strong counterbalance to its US benefactor. Moscow's exclusion had removed 'the potential threat to world peace caused by the superpowers being drawn into confrontation with each other through the actions of their uncontrollable Middle Eastern protégés'.[20]

There was the equally tenable argument that the superpower rivalry maintained its own checks and balances and indirectly helped preserve the *status quo* in the Middle East by preventing one side in the Arab-Israeli conflict from over-running the other. The Russian leadership was well aware that a more forceful drive to re-enter the Middle East would have led to renewed confrontation with the West under certain circumstances; for example if Russia unilaterally had declared a resumption of full relations with Iraq. While this did not take place, and was not seriously contemplated during the 1990s, it raised one interesting question: how much was Moscow prepared to risk in order to regain a strong position in the Middle East? Russia's limited capabilities, considering that it had little to offer except weapons which were recognised as being inferior to Western military equipment, made a substantial contribution towards answering that particular question. The so-called 'Atlanticists versus Eurasianists' debate was essentially a struggle to dominate Russia's foreign policy outlook, and had potentially decisive repercussions on relations with the Middle East. This polarisation of views posed for Moscow an uncompromising dilemma: Washington was highly likely to be antagonised if old alliances, such as those with Syria, Iraq and

Iran, were upgraded, yet Russia faced the prospect of losing old partners if it was to kow-tow to US demands in the Middle East. Syria was a good example of a country finely balanced between the two powers. Clinton's meeting with President Asad and Syria's participation in the US-led peace talks was largely due to Moscow's lack of assertiveness and a recognition that only Washington had the ability to influence events in the Middle East. With regard to Iraq, Russia faced strong competition from France to win important contracts.

But predictions during the first year of Russia's political scene that 'the post-communist Russian leadership will go even further than Gorbachev in its retreat from the Third World' were ultimately mistaken.[21] What happened was the reverse, with the post-Soviet leadership gradually distancing itself from various initiatives associated with the Gorbachev era. For example, Kozyrev's visit to Iraq in November 1994 added weight to Baghdad's claim that it had agreed to recognise the Kuwaiti borders, which was in effect fortifying the call for the sanctions to be lifted. This diplomatic manoeuvre was highly publicised and it restored Moscow's position as favourite over its foreign competitors with the ruling regime in Baghdad. The Russian move was a bold one because it did not meet with Washington's approval. Moreover, it could have risked relations with pro-Western Arab states such as Saudi Arabia, which was a leading player in the anti-Iraq coalition, as well as with Israel. *Al-Hayat* and *Asharq Al-Awsat*, two of the most influential Arab papers (both Saudi-funded) had front-page photographs of Kozyrev comfortably seated next to Iraqi Deputy Prime Minister Tariq Aziz at a parliamentary session with the portrait of a youthful Saddam Hussein hanging behind them. The front page headline in *Asharq Al-Awsat* read: 'Kozyrev Witnesses Saddam's Decision to Recognise Kuwaiti Borders'. The sight must have shaken the Gulf monarchies who dreaded a resurgent Saddam Hussein taking his revenge and who were haunted by the image of a split in the Security Council alliance against Iraq. The Kozyrev visit, which lasted several days, was also great political capital for Hussein who used the visit to tell his people that the days of the sanctions and the hardships were numbered. As for Russia, it signalled to the Iraqi people that the blame for their problems rested squarely on the shoulders of the United States and Britain.

Kozyrev's visit was clearly measured and thought out, signalling that Russia was not quite ready to give up its position in the Middle East. In substance though, Russia made no unilateral effort to undermine the United States and the whole event was diplomatic theatre. Nonetheless, the visit did come at a time when the United States was on the verge of taking decisive action to help the Bosnian government against the Bosnian Serbs and their Serbian allies, and there was more than a hint by Moscow that Russia could still be a disruptive force if Washington failed to show enough respect for its opinions. Nonetheless, Yeltsin and Clinton were determined to prevent any cracks from emerging at such an early stage of the relationship between the two countries. No further steps were taken, either in Bosnia or Iraq, which would have antagonised the two parties. When just forty days later, at the end of December 1994, Russian planes were flattening the city of Grozny in Chechnia at the cost of many lives, Clinton's response was that the small Muslim republic was part of the Russian Federation and that such 'teething troubles' in post-Soviet Russia were to be expected. High ranking officials from Moscow were despatched to all of Iraq's neighbouring states, including a visit by Prime Minister Viktor Chernomyrdin to the Gulf Co-operation states, around the time of the Iraqi episode, to consolidate and enhance trade links with those countries.

Writing in the leading Arab newspaper, *Al-Hayat*, Deputy Foreign Minister Viktor Posuvaliuk attempted to explain Russia's position in the area. An interesting feature of the article was its tone, which was not apologetic, but critical of the Arabs. He conceded that Russia was undergoing a difficult transition period. 'By the same token, many of those who beat the drum of Russia's weakness don't wish to discuss their difficulties and problems, and let's be honest, they exist and they are not minor.'[22] Posuvaliuk provided various examples of the way Russia's position in the Middle East differed from that of the United States. In a word, he pointed out that Moscow rejected Washington's 'all or nothing' approach regarding sanctions against Iraq. Russia, he said, supported the idea of rewarding the Iraqi regime for every positive step it took towards becoming a responsible member of the international community. Posuvaliuk also cited the fact that Moscow had played a key role in convincing Iraq to recognise Kuwaiti sovereignty and the existing borders between them. In addition, he noted that Russia's position towards Iran, Libya and Syria did not agree with that of the United States. Then he rhetorically asked the Arab reader to consider which country other than Russia took such an independent line from Washington with regard to the Middle East and had the potential to influence international affairs: 'Other than being a great power and permanent member of the Security Council and a neighbour, it is also a Eurasian country with no equal.'[23]

Posuvaliuk did accept that Russia's policy in the Middle East had changed considerably from the past. Moscow did not seek relations only with anti-Western countries but with all the states of the region. This included Israel and the Gulf Co-operation Countries. This was indicative of Russian objectives in the area to build slowly but widely by keeping relations healthy and productive with as many countries as possible.

Debates, reforms and the Middle East

In the first year of government under Yeltsin, the debate over foreign policy continued in the same vein as that which had existed under Gorbachev. There was a split between those who perceived that Russia's interests were overwhelmingly linked to the Western world, and those who were highly suspicious of the West in general and the United States in particular. The former group, generally referred to as Atlanticists, argued that Russia had nothing to gain from old Soviet ties with dictatorial regimes such as those of Syria and Iraq. The latter group was more complex in that it was a combination of neo-communists, Russian nationalists/fascists and interest groups (mainly in the arms industry) who were wary of reforms, and people who had simply been deeply indoctrinated about Western conspiracies to undermine their country. The term 'Eurasianist' was most commonly accepted to describe this amalgamation of opinions, despite certain flaws. For example, a major element of Russian nationalism did not wish to be associated with either European or Asian cultures but regarded itself as superior to both. However, broadly speaking, the term was accepted because it implied that Russia was a great power in both Europe and Asia and that its national security demanded that it gave priority to its position in both continents. Francis Fukuyama and other Western analysts suggested that there were historic examples which contradicted the view of the Eurasianist approach as inevitable. He cited the example of the founding fathers of modern Turkey following the collapse of the Ottoman Empire who cast away plans for a great Turkic empire and adopted the principle of 'a "small Turkey"...'[24] Hence for modern day Russia too, the geo-strategic factor 'can be of uncertain or ambiguous meaning and subject to rapid erosion as a result of technological advance'.[25] Sergei Stankevich questioned this argument by pointing out that Turkish aspirations remained alive but the country had been forced to bow to direct European advances which contained it in its current borders. Turkey's efforts at expanding its influence were highly visible in Central Asia, Cyprus and the Middle East where it faced hostility from the Kurds and disputed borders with Syria. Moreover, friction existed with Bulgaria and Greece.[26] The Russian comparison was on a far larger scale, and its nuclear status threatened a potentially greater impact.

Influential foreign policy makers in Moscow began openly favouring a Russian course that protected its traditional interests, particularly in the Middle East. Vladimir Lukin, the parliament's Foreign Affairs Committee chairman, pointed out that Russia had 'deep, historic interests' that needed to be 'protected not only to avoid regional imbalances, but also to prevent the disruption of the social and political balance inside Russia itself'.[27] And referring specifically to relations with Turkey and Iran, Lukin added that 'Russia's primary interest lies in preventing open conflict with third countries for influence in the developing vacuum of Central Asia and the Transcaucasus.'[28]

Kozyrev and his neglect of relations with countries outside the Western world became the target of bitter criticism from the media and senior Russian political figures. A barrage of anti-Kozyrev reporting portrayed the Foreign Minister as weak and dominated by the West. Aleksei Pushkov interpreted Kozyrev's policy in the following way:

> [Russia] should obediently follow the United States. [...] This was the source of Kozyrev's idea of a strategic partnership that assumed a subordinate role for Moscow in matters of world politics. In exchange for Russia's consent to be America's younger brother, Washington was expected to provide financial assistance, a flow of investment, and technological modernisation.[29]

This approach was seen by the radical pro-Westerners of Russia as part of the German-Japanese path to development following their defeat in the Second World War. This perspective was deemed unacceptable by Pushkov and many others in Moscow because, they pointed out, Russia had not lost a military war in the way that Germany and Japan had, when the victors dictated the terms for peace. The changes that took place in the Soviet Union were to a large extent caused by internal dynamics rather than external forces. Moreover, the lack of financial means and limp political will in Washington to save the new democratic Russia created the general impression that any possibility of 'a strategic alliance between Russia and the United States was doomed to failure from the start'. [30] Kozyrev's refusal to make sufficient compromises on his foreign policy principles and his labelling of all those who criticised his views as part of the 'Red-Brown' alliance were also criticised by the media. Kozyrev's mission, argued Pushkov, was not to promote national interest but to achieve a victory in the sphere of ideological debates. [31]

More specific subdivisions were gradually to evolve from the more general Eurasian-Atlanticist schism, with many scholars contented to establish a basic Left-Right-Centre approach as a general explanation of the political divisions in Moscow. Margot Light categorised the debate as being between liberal Westernisers, 'who favoured a market economy and held pro-Western views', and fundamentalist nationalists, 'the people who combined extreme Nationalism with antipathy towards economic reform'. [32] After 1992, she argued, there was a spread of nationalism which created a new group of pragmatic nationalists, 'who proposed a more integrationalist stance towards the other successor states' as well as 'a more independent policy *vis-à-vis* the West'. [33] The liberal Westernisers and pragmatic nationalists shared the belief that democracy should be consolidated in Russia and that a market economy was desirable. Alex Pravda and Neil Malcolm both accepted these general lines of division, with the former linking them to domestic political battle lines. Pravda saw the categories of debate in foreign policy as being a carbon copy of splits in domestic affairs between the radical reformers, conservative oppositionists and centrists. The first group was characterised by the early Kozyrev period when market reformers were dominant in the government and represented by the likes of Egor Gaidar. As

Kozyrev changed his policies, the centrists became more dominant in the government, in response to the growing electoral strength of the opposition. According to Pravda, the pragmatic nationalists 'were concerned to ensure that radical conservatives did not manage to appropriate patriotism and use it to legitimise fundamentalist nationalism'.[34]

The above interpretation, while generally useful, did not point to the more subtle, and sometimes obvious, differences which existed between the groups. From 1993 to 1996 five distinctly identifiable groups had evolved: pro-Western radicals, pragmatic pro-Westerners, centrist-nationalists, pragmatic nationalists/occidentalists and extreme nationalists. The pro-Western radicals were dominant until late-1992, with Kozyrev representing a policy of seeking to join the Western family at the expense of Russia's Eastern links. In this sense there is agreement with the interpretations of Light, Pravda *et al*. However, it was incorrect to place the broad range of opinions between the liberal Westernisers and fundamentalist nationalists under the heading of pragmatic nationalists because within this middle ground there were important divisions. The second category of my list, the pragmatic pro-Westerners, embodied Kozyrev and other former pro-Western radicals who in principle remained highly committed towards Western ideals and towards Russia becoming a part of the Western family, but who also accepted that the domestic political climate and international scene did not allow for this to take place as quickly as had been originally hoped. Therefore Kozyrev was forced into reversing his former neglect of relations with former Soviet states in Central Asia and the Caucasus as well as with key states in Asia such as China, India, Iran and Iraq.

It was also inaccurate to place the fundamentalist nationalists under the banner of the one anti-Western opposition movement because a distinction arose between the pragmatic nationalists/occidentalists and extreme nationalists. The latter group, which received wide media coverage because of the antics of its figure-head Vladimir Zhirinovskii, had in reality a non-existent effect on Russian foreign policy. Its ideas of restoring the Russian empire, by force if necessary, were widely perceived to be eccentric and clownish by most Russians. However, the proposals of the Communist opposition, headed by Gennadii Ziuganov, did partially succeed in changing the government's policy of concentrating too heavily on the West for the sake of economic rewards. This pragmatic nationalist view noted that Russia remained a great power with important historic and political links with the East, which would enable it to form strong alliances to balance Western power and ultimately serve Russian interests. This group was in its core suspicious of the West and argued that Russia needed to remain vigilant in order to protect itself from Western intentions. However, Ziuganov and his allies also noted that a strong Russia could co-exist peacefully with the Western world.

The nationalist-centrist position was epitomised by the policies of Foreign Minister Primakov in 1996. Malcolm *et al.*, and many other scholars, failed to point out that his policies were not simply formed as a consequence of merging domestic political debates by taking the most acceptable arguments and ideas from the pragmatic pro-Westerners and pragmatic nationalists. Instead, it was a policy in its own right which was totally non-ideological, and in principle neither opposed to nor in favour of East or West. It simply sought to follow what was best for Russian geo-strategic and economic interests, taking into account the diminished strength of the country *vis-à-vis* the West. Contrary to Pravda's linkage of domestic divisions with the foreign policy debate, Primakov sought to extract the Ministry of Foreign Affairs from the domestic political scene altogether. In this sense at least, Primakov sought to emulate the British Foreign Office's reputation for strong loyalty to the state rather than to any particular political party.

According to some scholars, the differences of view and tone in Russian political circles were so great that it was better not to attempt to seek labels for them at all. One such commentry argued that seven groupings were not enough to cover the full spectrum of opinions:

> Westerniser, Liberal Moderate Reformer, Moderate Reformer, Conservative Moderate Reformer, Democratic Socialist, Communist, and Nationalist. Beyond these differences of perspective, however, the politics of foreign policy is also complicated by antagonisms, not necessarily related to policy, between cliques and factions in different governmental agencies.[35]

But it would be useless to take into account too many varying nuances; therefore the five groupings already mentioned best describe the emergence of the main groups by 1998. On the whole, the policy making élite, and public opinion, made a gradual but clear shift from the position of the pro-Western radicals to that of the centrist-nationalists between 1991 and 1998.

The evolving policy under Yeltsin was accompanied by major structural reforms and underwent three key phases. The first lasted until late 1992, when the pro-Western radicals were strongest; the second phase was a period of uncertainty between late 1992 and the end of 1995; finally, a stable and recognisable policy was established in 1996 which coincided with the appointment of Evgenii Primakov as Foreign Minister. Yeltsin's election victory in the middle of 1996 added to the sense of consistency in Russia's policies, including those directed towards the Middle East. The president, particularly after the adoption of the 1993 Constitution, took personal charge in the field of foreign policy. The directors of the Federal Security Service (FSB) and of the Foreign Intelligence Service (SVR), and the commander-in-chief of the Border Troops, were all appointed members of the presidential staff. Moreover, the ministers of defence and of foreign affairs, who were answerable to Yeltsin as members of the government, also reported directly to him as 'members of the President's Security Council'.[36]

The reversal of the early enthusiasm under Kozyrev did not go unnoticed in the West. An article by James Meek in the *Guardian*, written at the time of Iraq's recognition of Kuwaiti borders, asserted that 'Russia's determination to be the acknowledged godmother, if not midwife, to Iraqi recognition of Kuwait signals Moscow's growing belief that, while it can no longer sway world politics single-handed, it can be a serious counterweight to the United States when acting in concert with a second country'.[37] In becoming more ambitious in his foreign policy, Yeltsin was 'not simply trying to pander to the country's current nationalist-patriotic mood', but 'taking a realistic view of Russia's best prospective trading partners'. These were not so much the United States and the European Union but the major Asian and Middle Eastern powers.[38] Iraq for example was among the few Third World nations capable of repaying its £4.5 billion debt, once sanctions were lifted.

The earliest signal of change under Kozyrev was the formulation of a foreign policy doctrine, despite his earlier reluctance to do so because he had argued that the ideologisation of foreign policy in the Soviet era had had a negative result on the country. Kozyrev's acquiescence was in part due to the force of old habits, and partly because it informed (and assured) other governments about where Russia stood on various issues. But according to one analyst, the practical and beneficial purpose of a foreign policy was 'probably internal to the Foreign Ministry itself'.[39] Many Foreign Ministry officials in Smolensk Square and in embassies around the world simply did not know what Russia's official position was on a long list of international disputes and general matters. Considering the tumultuous changes that had taken place in 1991, it was hardly surprising that there was a need for a consistent set of guidelines and policies.

The low morale of the Ministry of Foreign Affairs was not helped by many practical problems which were threatening the institution's whole operation. Poor pay and the lure of working for the private sector for the highly sought-after ministry officials led to a staff drain. Some figures showed that by the middle of 1993, the number of employees in Moscow was cut by almost a quarter, 'to around 3,000, of whom 60 per cent were described as diplomats'. It was also estimated that resignations numbered 'around 500 a year (twenty times the rate in the 1960s and 1970s)', leading to a serious failure to fill empty posts with qualified personnel.[40]

Overall, the initial phase of Moscow's foreign policy until the summer of 1992 had been highly reactive: with the immediate aims of defining Russia's strong position within the CIS, inheriting the Soviet role in international organisations such as the United Nations, and complete co-operation with the United States. This approach faced strong criticisms, which were to a large extent fair, that Russia was a great power without a long-term vision of itself in the world. Consequently, in August 1992 the Council on Foreign and Defence Policy, a non-governmental organisation which included leading figures from the foreign affairs and defence-security establishments, published 'A Strategy for Russia'. This document was simultaneously released with a 'Concept on Foreign Policy' (MFA) which underwent fiery debate and many revisions until it was finally presented to parliament in February 1993. The most striking aspect of both documents was the growing emphasis on the Near Abroad, in reference to the other CIS countries and the Baltic states, and the implication that relations with the United States had cooled down from the earlier euphoria. The 'Concept' was finally approved by Yeltsin in April 1993, taking many ideas from the 'Strategy for Russia'.

A second 'Strategy for Russia' was published in May 1994 which was even more hard-line than the earlier draft, though it was critical of senior government officials who were prone to 'great power rhetoric'. It vehemently opposed NATO expansion into Eastern Europe, and encouraged Russia to be more active in the Near Abroad. The overall tone of the updated proposal was that in Moscow's relations with the United States, 'unnecessary deterioration of relations should be avoided, but at the same time Russia's own interests should not be undermined'.[41] By 1994 the voice of the pro-Western radicals was almost completely silenced. Their vision, which dominated in early 1992, was seen as 'an aberration, or at least naïve and utopian'.[42] The lack of trust from Russia's defence and security élites towards the Foreign Ministry over relations with other CIS countries led to major inter-departmental differences. It was often observed that the Ministry of Defence 'appeared to usurp diplomatic functions', to the dismay of the Foreign Ministry, which was sometimes not even consulted about decisions.[43]

The Russian media, backed by influential political figures, began to point to an arc of instability which stretched from Central Asia (particularly Tajikistan), through northern parts of the Middle East and the Caucasus, up to the Balkans. This volatile area, Kozyrev's critics argued, could not be neglected for the sake of bridge-building with the West. Leading figures in Moscow began to point to the Muslim factor, which had been much less prominent in Soviet times. It was being regularly remarked in the press that in the territory of the former Soviet Union there were eighty million Muslims, as well as the tens of millions in countries neighbouring the CIS. 'The geo-political significance of the Muslim East demands not only the consideration of people as a resource, and of the extensive territory, but in the strategic location of the region, with trade-economic opportunities powered in the spiritual-historic potential of the Islamic Community.'[44]

It was not coincidental that the multi-ethnic aspect of Russian nationalism, as it became more widespread, carried implications of unifying the civilisations of the East, and in particular the historic interaction between Orthodoxy and Islam. It was also recognised that such manifestations would inevitably lead to a distancing from the Western world. The close interaction between Russia and the Muslim world, one report suggested, 'could predetermine the attraction of our country too soon, towards traditional eastern civilisation, than is allowed for her to show in certain countries of the "rich north"'.[45]

In certain respects it was ironic that the democratic climate in Russia undermined the most democratically-minded political leaders in Moscow. With regard to the domestic scene, Russia had a genuinely pluralistic political system where differences and disagreements were aired and shared and secrets became more difficult to keep. Unlike former foreign ministers Gromyko and Molotov for example, Kozyrev's foreign policy had to be justifiable to the Russian Duma and ultimately to the people. In one instance, Kozyrev's trip to Iraq was criticised by Vladimir Lukin, as likely to 'antagonise the United States'.[46]

A few academic figures interpreted this pluralism to be a sign of chaos and disorder. In the words of one such observer:

Far from being unified, the contemporary Russian State consists of an agglomeration of semi-autonomous bureaucracies organised in a loose hierarchy, on top of which sits the President. He wields considerable formal powers but has much less practical and operational control over his nominal subordinates. [...] The very term 'Russian foreign policy' is in many cases inherently misleading, since it implies that the Russian state is a unitary 'rational actor'.[47]

Yeltsin's decision to create the posts of his own foreign-policy aide, Dmitrii Riurikov, and a national-security aide, Iurii Baturin, who both undertook diplomatic missions, seemed to add to the confusion by adding separate tracks to foreign policy making. Yet it could similarly be argued that in the Western world, particularly the United States, plurality in foreign policy making was a reality. In Washington political, ethnic, military, industrial and countless other lobbies operate to influence policy. The president of the United States also has to balance the policies of the State Department, Congress, the Defense Department, intelligence bureaux, his own national security advisers and sometimes public opinion and the media. In all, despite dangers of miscommunication and a clash of interests (and even in the United States mistakes sometimes do occur in foreign policy making), such diversity is an acceptable part of a pluralistic democratic society. Therefore, in defence of the Russian example, efforts to broaden the base of opinions and ideas should not be negatively perceived as a sign of chaos but rather as a positive shift away from the Soviet model when the fate of hundreds of millions of people was decided by two or three ageing men, immersed in the propaganda of inevitable class conflict.

It was acknowledged by the Kremlin that while different ideas were welcome, there was a distinct failure by Kozyrev to adopt a far-reaching set of policies which would somehow bring together the mainstream collection of arguments about the best course for the country and deal with the most immediate problems facing Russia, such as inter-CIS relations and other important Asiatic neighbours. There was also an urgent demand to break the institutional gridlock which had made decision-making impossible by 1993. To counter accusations of disorder, Yeltsin acted decisively to ensure a more coherent foreign policy. The new Constitution of 1993 served to change the relationship between government and parliament to the detriment of the latter. The Russian Constitution until then had given the parliament the right to lay the framework of foreign policy making for the president to implement. Until October 1993, the Russian parliament had shown itself to be increasingly defiant and acting independently from the Kremlin and the Foreign Ministry. This, and rivalry between various government bodies, led President Yeltsin to issue a decree on 3 November, in order to reassert the position of the Foreign Ministry. It stated that the 'Russian Foreign Ministry will be entrusted with the function of co-ordinating and monitoring work by other Russian ministries, committees and departments to ensure a unified political line by the Russian Federation in relations with foreign states...'[48]

The task of finding a new and more prominent role for the Foreign Ministry seemed to overwhelm Kozyrev. Yeltsin's State Secretary Gennadii Burbulis, an ally of Kozyrev, sought to resolve the disarray in Russia's foreign policy making by encouraging a more direct presidential involvement. However, the Kremlin was heavily weighed down by domestic crises and challenges and could not afford to use up limited resources over the details of international affairs. Kozyrev's inabilities were becoming increasingly apparent, both in international affairs and in making his ministry more effective in dealing with internal political debates. Yeltsin's patience with his foreign minister was being increasingly tested, until he openly complained that 'everyone who feels like interfering does so, and all the Foreign Ministry does is to shut itself up in its own diplomatic debates and visits'.[49]

The 1993 Constitution, in attempting to unify the whole decision-making process, stated that 'the President "directs the foreign policy of the Russian Federation" (within the framework set by the constitution and laws of the country) (Arts.80, 86)... He forms and presides over the Security Council and conducts international negotiations (Art.83).'[50] Yeltsin accompanied this with a change of emphasis in the country's national policy in order to fit a broader consensus. While Russia's retreat from Latin America and most of Africa was seen by most political factions as logical, the pro-Western radicals' neglect of important regions such as the Middle East was heavily criticised. But Moscow's re-emerging interest in the area was not encouraged by the United States. By 1993 it was already being noted that 'serious security co-operation may not materialise in the future between the two nations...with abundant signs that deep-rooted suspicions will be hard to eradicate'.[51] Powerful lobbies in the United States argued that for Washington to protect its international interests, such as those in the Middle East, it should halt cuts in the defence sector, which also employed a large workforce.

Military leaders in Moscow argued that Russia would 'have to be armed against ever more sophisticated weaponry among (unnamed) nations to the south, and perhaps even against independent armies being established by some of the former Soviet republics'.[52] While border issues were tangible aspects of geostrategic politics, there were less visible conditions which were difficult to ignore. The arms trade, world energy prices, Islamic fundamentalism and of course the threat of nuclear attack, whether it was intercontinental or local, all undermined Moscow's outlook on the world. Consequently, the middle ground of Russian foreign policy making became more pragmatic in its thinking by the start of 1993, and Kozyrev was at the forefront of this shift from a radical to a pragmatic pro-Western position. This meant that the main priority of seeking close co-operation with the West would remain unchanged, but a new and special emphasis was given to relations with other CIS countries and regions which were of particular interest to Russia. In addition, the zealous and ideologically -driven association with the Western world was substantially toned down.

As the pro-Western thinkers were to split into ideological and pragmatic factions, the so-called Eurasianists were to do the same. Most importantly, the ideas of extreme Russian nationalists, or neo-imperialists, were rejected by parties and groups who sought to appear electable. The Russian Communist Party was the main threat to Yeltsin's government and was a genuine contender for election victory after 1993. Its political agenda was based on the failure of the pro-Western leadership to succeed in its Western-backed market reforms, which included the ending of subsidies for services and goods which had been taken for granted in the Soviet era. Their counterview was that Russia possessed all the material and human resources it needed to follow its own unique course. It had also inherited from the Soviet Union a network of friends and allies in key regions which would enable it to trade and re-establish its role as a great power. The West, they believed, would then acknowledge Russia's great power position and the two powers would learn to co-exist peacefully, each dominating its own geo-political space.

This should be contrasted with the extreme nationalist view, mainly represented by Vladimir Zhirinovskii's Liberal Democratic Party, which held some bizarre perceptions of world affairs. Zhirinovskii argued for a restoration of the Russian empire and its expansion so that Russians could have direct access to the Mediterranean and the Indian Ocean. It took the Eurasianist idea to the extreme, with visions of massive spheres of influence based on 'East-West frontiers. Rabidly suspicious of US intentions and their idea of a new world order, 'they saw a plot by America to construct a world government'.[53] They did not rule out the use of military force to achieve national objectives and xenophobia was a dominant strand in the thinking of its leading members.

Needless to say the neo-imperialist view remained on the fringes, but the pragmatic occidentalists/Russian nationalists gained a great deal of public and media sympathy and some of their suggestions were actually adopted by the ruling élite. According to one author, this was an unsurprising 'reassertion of Russian nationalism', considering the country was facing a major 'identity crisis'.[54] But the increasingly nationalist tone of Moscow's policy was not praised by all. Pro-Western thinkers were concerned that Russia was falling back into the trap of thinking it was much stronger than it really was. They argued that placing too much emphasis on great-power status demanded 'a strong economic base, capable of sustaining massive military power over extended periods', and warned that Russia was 'in danger of becoming a supernova state, expanding slowly outwards on its periphery while collapsing internally'.[55]

But despite such risks, Russian foreign policy evolved into a national, pragmatic policy, as epitomised by Primakov, whom some in the West mistook for being a hard-liner, or anti-Westerner. In fact, he was neither, but simply a realist centrist whose style was less idealistic than that of Kozyrev or Shevardnadze. The Yeltsin leadership had to take into account the general disillusionment with the West, which provided political ammunition for the Russian nationalist armoury. Under Stalin, Moscow's chief concern was to create a buffer zone in Eastern Europe and to concentrate on major southern neighbours such as Turkey, Iran and China. Khrushchev revolutionised Moscow's thinking by urging his bureaucrats to adopt a more globalist world view. Gorbachev too attempted to impose a more globally-aware outlook from Moscow but the two men shared the unfortunate position of being the only leaders to be deposed from power since 1917. Moscow's political establishment and Russian public opinion in general regarded the two former leaders as being failures, both domestically and in foreign policy.

Washington's energetic drive to expand NATO and to openly reject plans for Russian involvement in key regions, including the Middle East, nullified many of the arguments of the radical pro-Westerners. Moscow's chief concern was that NATO expansion would leave Russia too vulnerable because it would become completely surrounded by powerful and potentially dangerous international regional threats. This would include NATO to the West, the Muslim countries to the south and China to the East. Moscow's leadership almost unintentionally found itself confronted with potential threats that were close to its borders, and this included the Middle East, where Iran and Iraq were regarded as being 'perennial sources of trouble in the Southern Theatre of Operation'.[56] The efforts by Iran and Turkey to achieve closer ties with the Muslim republics in the CIS were also being closely monitored in Moscow, and the deployment of US forces in the Persian Gulf region since 1991 was an added source of concern for Russia's foreign policy chiefs.

The perception that the move towards a less Western-oriented policy was brought on by the October 1993 clash with parliament and the electoral successes of Zhirinovskii failed to acknowledge the changes taking place within the establishment. As already noted, the central apparatus itself began to change its position and this dated back to May 1992 with the publication of a draft of Russia's Military Doctrine, which was adopted in November 1993. Under the heading 'Possible Causes of War', it listed the 'violation of the rights of...persons who identify themselves ethnically and culturally with [Russia]'.[57] The Foreign Ministry's own doctrine of April 1993 echoed the Military Doctrine when it stated that Russians in the Near Abroad would have their rights secured by Moscow 'through persuasion, and in extreme cases also through the use of force'.[58]

These forceful statements were misinterpreted to mean that Russia was actively seeking confrontation in the quest for reasserting its domination over the former Soviet territories. But the doctrine was only a part of the wider recognition that the country needed to create basic guidelines for its military forces. In the words of one defence analyst in the United Kingdom:

> There are excellent reasons why a military doctrine should be published. It is somewhat analogous to a defence White Paper. Democratic accountability demands it. Russia's potential and actual security partners, not to mention neighbouring states in the 'near abroad', need to know about Russia's attitudes if they are to trust the country and co-operate confidently with it. The armed forces themselves need the direction given by an open security policy, for every officer and soldier needs to know what he is training for and why. [...][59]

One consequence of Kozyrev's failure was that many of the agreements he signed with the West were viewed with suspicion by various ministries, particularly by the Defence Ministry and President Yeltsin himself, who sharply rebuked his foreign minister several times, leading to his forced resignation. For many of Kozyrev's rivals, the natural replacement for the existing policy would be 'the creation, in response to NATO's planned expansion, of a military-political bloc of CIS countries; an emphasis in foreign policy and foreign trade on such countries as Iraq, Iran and other radical Arab regimes', and the return to the special relationship with Cuba.[60] Pushkov represented the general trend of opinion which rejected Kozyrev's world view. In its place, it was argued that Russia should isolate regions of top priority – Europe, the Balkans, the Middle East, South Asia and the Far East – by virtue of its geo-strategic position as an Eurasian power.

Moscow used whatever levers of influence it had to become directly involved in the affairs of its former Soviet neighbours, whether it was the civil war in Tajikistan or Georgia's fight with Abkhazian separatists. This led the Georgian ambassador in Moscow to say that his country's 'independence depended to a great extent on the position of Russia'.[61] Russia's involvement was not only via military means, for it had other methods at its disposal. This was made abundantly clear in Kozyrev's warning to the government in Alma Ata in 1993: 'Russia is prepared to defend its citizens living in Kazakhstan...and in this purpose will use all its power, including economic sanctions and credit and financial policy.'[62]

The radical pro-Westerners were highly concerned that the increasing entanglement in the affairs of Russia's Asian neighbours would serve to undermine the reforms intended to create a society based on Western democratic and economic ideals. 'Historically, Russia's tremendous space seemed to demand an authoritarian form of government', and historians noted that the imperialist policy of 'co-optation by Russia of other nations at different stages of economic, cultural, and political development played a very significant role in obstructing the process of democratisation and the path of economic development'.[63]

According to one observer, by 1994 Russian foreign policy had become 'hardnosed and aggressive, taking on precisely the character that President Boris Yeltsin and Foreign Minister Andrei Kozyrev had vocally resisted in 1991 and 1992'.[64] An article in a Russian newspaper by Kozyrev, entitled 'Peace with a Sword', highlighted this shifting rhetoric. He stressed that only Russia was responsible for the stability of the region of the former Soviet Union and criticised those in the West who attacked Russia's actions as a continuation of past ambitions by suggesting that 'perhaps their suspicion of Moscow's "neo-imperial plans" conceals their own similar ambitions'.[65]

In September 1993, Kozyrev was quite direct in his assessment of what Russia needed to do in the Near Abroad: 'If we do not master the political will and practical means – that is to be blunt, troops and equipment – to conduct peacekeeping missions in the zones of the former Soviet Union, this vacuum will be filled by other forces, first of all, by the forces of political extremism, which, ultimately, threaten Russia herself.'[66]

An article in the *Daily Telegraph* in early 1996 which quoted the views of a Russian ultra-nationalist sought to imply that his views were becoming more prevalent in Moscow. Anton Surikov, a leading voice of the old Soviet military-industrial complex, had called for the restoration of nuclear weapons in Belarus 'to deter the eastward expansion of Nato, and the Russian army should prepare to invade the Baltic states, which were allowed to escape the Kremlin yoke in 1991, unless they treat their Russian minorities better'.[67] The article pointed out that 'his ideas might have seemed ludicrous a year ago. But such is the swing in Russian politics to the old, Soviet way of thinking that his views have become fashionable in the military establishment.'[68] Yet the article actually reflected the failure of the Western media to understand the real motives of Russia's foreign policy and to distinguish between the views of loose-cannon individuals and the influential core of Moscow's policy-making élite.

Although Primakov took over as Foreign Minister at the beginning of 1996, Kozyrev's end had been forecast since the autumn of 1995. From then on, a clearer definition of Russia's foreign policy was in place. In the words of Sergei Karaganov, 'the formation of a rather broad consensus on foreign policy is quite likely now. But it was unrealistic to expect such a consensus to form around Kozyrev.'[69] In his last years in office, Kozyrev changed his position too often, until he was no longer trusted by either democrats or by the so-called hard-liners on the West. Kozyrev was too closely 'associated with the early years of his tenure at the Foreign Ministry, when his policy of "what can I do for you?" evoked strong feelings of humiliation among Russia's élite, whether they supported the policy of *rapprochement* with the West or not'.[70] In fact Kozyrev's weak position at the end of his tenure in office reached the point that one commentator noted that the defence minister, and 'not the head of the diplomatic office (as would normally be the case)… is achieving foreign policy results'.[71]

There were a few who were prepared to spring to Kozyrev's defence. One observer wrote that claims that Kozyrev had changed his position in his last years were not accurate. Instead, it was argued that he had stayed 'true to what was practically his first declaration [as Foreign Minister] that the foreign policy he intended to conduct was the "president's policy". Faithful to that declaration, he is evolving along with the "general line".'[72] However, with 1996 being election year, Yeltsin correctly assessed that Kozyrev had become a political liability and replaced him with the widely respected head of the SVR, Primakov. Once Primakov had assumed the position of Foreign Minister, Moscow's policy was dominated by his centrist position. It was essentially a compromise between the views of the pragmatic nationalists and the pragmatic pro-Westernisers. The basic tenet of this position was that 'since the international system is a self-help world, states must treat security as their highest priority to survive, assuming that even a benign political environment in which no obvious threats exist can change rapidly'.[73] While the centrists believed that Russia had a unique role in the world, they did not in principle reject good relations with the West as long as they did not conflict with Russia's interests.

Conclusion: Primakov hones a national policy

In his first year, Yeltsin went a step further than New Thinking by completely abandoning the socialist model, 'eliminating ideological ambiguity, and expanding the basis for common US-Russian values and objectives'.[74] But this was not enough, as a more thorough basis for international affairs was required for post-Soviet Russia. The transformation within the Russian system did not alter the basic geographic and diplomatic concerns of that country. By 1998, Moscow had been modestly successful in founding a recognisable, steady and broadly acceptable foreign policy.

In an interview with *Izvestiia* in March 1996, Primakov told the interviewer that there was widespread consensus between the Foreign Ministry and the ultra-nationalist/neo-communist-dominated parliament. When asked about the proposed expansion of NATO, Primakov's answer was no less direct: 'The expansion of NATO is not in the interest of Russian society, and it seems to me that it has also manifested the unity of Russian society, and the unity of the Ministry of Foreign Affairs with all factions in Parliament. The expansion of NATO is created for the weakening of our geo-political situation.'[75]

Primakov also criticised Russian foreign policy in the first two years since 1991, thus indirectly making his point against Kozyrev. The new foreign minister said that in this 'defining stage we followed everything in order to balance relations [with Washington]. Here I quote Mao Tse Tung who said: "when you want to straighten it is necessary to bend". We had bent excessively.'[76] He rejected the concept of a strategic alliance with the United States in favour of a more pragmatic relationship based upon a 'civilised partnership'.

Primakov was highly popular among Russia's political élite and the media. He represented a professionalism and sense of purpose which were missing under Kozyrev. One article reflected the widespread praise being heaped on Primakov following his visit to the UN in New York, where he 'dined with counterparts from thirty different countries'. Among the countries they represented from the Middle East were Iran, Israel, Iraq and Kuwait. He then met UN Secretary-General Boutros Boutros-Ghali 'and then, as an after-dinner cigar, he gave an interview to CNN'.[77] It was therefore unsurprising that there was widespread backing for Primakov to replace the beleaguered Chernomyrdin as Prime Minister in the autumn of 1998.

In the new spirit of pragmatism which was a dominant characteristic in 1996, there was no longer a rejection of everything related to the Soviet era. There was a new *rationale* which stated that some aspects of Soviet foreign policy were useful, therefore it would be folly to discard them simply because they were linked to that time. Newspapers portrayed former Soviet Foreign Minister Andrei Gromyko in a positive light. In an interview with his son, Anatoli Gromyko, the long-serving Cold War warrior was described as a thorough professional and referred to as a first class diplomat.[78] In another article, Gromyko was praised for his ability to 'show that compensating for internal weakness by means of a successful foreign policy is, to a certain extent, a possibility and thus essential'.[79] The author of the article was Karaganov, chairman of the Council on Foreign and Defence Policy and member of the Presidential Council, who had an influential voice in foreign policy making circles.

The presidential elections in the spring of 1996 appeared to settle many of the uncertainties of the national foreign policy. Yeltsin cleverly neutralised his opponents on this issue by stealing their thunder. 'The appointment of Evgenii Primakov led to almost a complete absence of debate in the country about foreign policy', wrote Karaganov in another article.[80] One article suggested that 'Yeltsin and Ziuganov, the main contenders in the presidential elections, tried to outbid one another in Russian patriotism'.[81] The incumbent president had skilfully linked foreign policy and domestic affairs by including the centrists to broaden his base. But the facts showed that the changes were also being spurred by national considerations. For example, in 1995 'Russian arms exports reached $3 billion, an increase of 80 per cent over 1994'.[82]

The first major test of Primakov's policy in the Middle East was in April 1996, when Israeli jets bombed Lebanon in an operation called Grapes of Wrath. Primakov announced that Russia intended to raise its profile in the region. But the new foreign minister found himself embroiled in the complexities of the Middle East, and was undermined by the determination of the United States to prevent third parties from getting involved, leading the *Izvestiia* correspondent to say it was 'Primakov's first defeat'.[83] The United States and Israel worked together to ensure Russia's exclusion from a peace-making role. But the real blow was that President Asad of Syria, Russia's ostensible long-time ally, did not demand the participation of his 'friends' in Moscow in the Monitoring Committee set up to oversee the cease-fire on the Israeli-Lebanese border. Indeed, considering that Primakov was supposed to be a specialist on the region, his failure to achieve anything during his trip to the capitals involved in the fighting must have been a deep source of frustration, if not embarrassment for him.

But overall, Moscow's political élite highly valued Primakov's expertise and experience. Aleksandr Iakovlev, who helped Primakov's career rise under Gorbachev, defended the foreign minister by saying that the 'democrats are wrong for taking a hostile line against him, calling him a conservative. He is not a conservative, but simply doesn't rush to conclusions.'[84] Russian foreign policy had, perhaps for the first time since the demise of the Soviet Union, become more predictable and consistent. It laid a special emphasis on regional security, particularly within the CIS; not upon 'the principle "let's restore the USSR," but according to the principle "let's restore what's good for Russia and its citizens"'.[85] Moscow's direct military intervention (some would call it invasion) in Chechnia underlined the Russian government's determination to defend national interests even at the risk of losing support from the international community as well as the domestic electorate. Many liberals in Moscow, including former acting Prime Minister Egor Gaidar, criticised Yeltsin's actions as contrary to his democratic agenda.

The most important backing that Primakov received was from the president himself. Yeltsin, who was preoccupied with the elections and pressing domestic issues, needed a foreign minister who could be trusted to act on his own initiative. Presidential support strengthened the position of the Foreign Ministry and unified policy making. Following changes in law affecting foreign policy, it was established that 'no document pertaining to this sphere may be submitted to the President's staff unless it has been cleared by the Foreign Ministry, [and] no representative of the executive branch (except diplomats, of course) may express an official view of foreign policy matters'.[86]

Primakov also proved dextrous in disassociating himself from domestic political rivalries. When asked in an interview if he could work with the country's main power brokers, Chubais, Lebed and Rodionov, the foreign minister's answer was neutral yet to the point. 'I am interested above all in their understanding that the MFA is the inter-coordinator of the foreign policy course of Russia. All three understand this. Moreover, Chubais, Lebed and Rodionov want to strengthen the position of the MFA as the central policy-making organ of the state.'[87]

In 1994 one Russian observer had protested that Moscow should be clear about its intentions: 'This would put an end to false rumours, speculation and hints that, unlike its democratic path in domestic policy, its foreign policy course may be reversible and that, if need be, it may resort to power methods of restoring its superimperial grandeur.'[88] Moscow was largely successful in redressing this situation by 1998. Russia's policies were reinvented to create new priorities for itself. This included the Middle East as much as any region. A senior Foreign Ministry official explained to me in October of that year how Russia had come to see the world. 'There are established rules and interests in bilateral relations which govern them and govern alliances in different areas of the world. Therefore, I see the status of the Middle East as having, and going to have, a very high place on the list of priorities.' He added that Russian interests could be damaged 'if we are not properly prepared at key moments with regard to developments in the Middle East'.[89]

However, towards the end of 1996, it was the head of the Foreign Ministry who provided the most telling description of Russia's international outlook.

When I say that Russia does not have permanent enemies but that it has permanent interests, I am not presenting anything new. [...] But during the Soviet period we swerved from this. National interests were often sacrificed for the sake of the struggle against a permanent enemy or the support of permanent allies.[90]

Primakov rejected the strategic alliance with the West, espoused by Kozyrev, and promoted the idea of equal partnership. According to him, the former 'is when the parties join their interests to fight a common enemy or when they even sacrifice some of their interests to the struggle against that enemy. On the other hand, partnership is when the two sides each have their own interests, but when there are, in addition, fields of coinciding interests.'[91]

Domestically, he argued that foreign policy should be based on a broad consensus of what is good for Russia – effectively, a national policy based on solid foundations which prevents it from being blown off course by the prevailing political wind. 'Foreign policy differs from domestic policy in that it should be based on national consensus. Take the example of other countries: Is US policy partisan? If Labour come to power in Britain, would it change the strategic course of Great Britain?'[92] Primakov's success in creating a coherent and steady policy laid the framework for less confused relations with the West and the Middle East.

NOTES

1. John Hemsley, 'Introduction' in John Hemsley (ed.), *The Lost Empire: Perceptions of Soviet Policy Shifts in the 1990s*, London, 1991, p.xxii.
2. Raymond Garthoff, *The Great Transition: American-Soviet Relations and the End of the Cold War*, Washington, DC, 1994, p.430.
3. Neil Malcolm, 'Foreign Policy Making' in Neil Malcolm, Alex Pravda, Margot Light and Roy Allison (eds), *Internal Factors in Russian Foreign Policy*, Oxford, 1996, p.132.
4. David Mackenzie, *From Messianism to Collapse*, New York, 1994, p.264.
5. Neil Malcolm and Alex Pravda, 'Introduction' in Malcolm *et al.*, *op. cit.*, p.5.

6. Evgenii Bazhanov, 'Top Priorities of Russia's Foreign Policy', *New Times*, October 1995, p.32.
7. Neil Malcolm, 'Russian Foreign Policy Decision-Making' in Peter Shearman (ed.), *Russian Foreign Policy Since 1990*, Oxford, 1995, p.23.
8. Vladimir O. Pechatnov, 'Russia's Current Perception of America' in Allen G. Lynch and Kenneth W. Thomson (eds), *Soviet and Post-Soviet Russia in a World in Change*, London, 1994, p.211.
9. E. Shevardnadze, speech given by Georgia's president at the Royal Institute of International Affairs, London, on 16 February 1995.
10. Leon Aron, 'The Emergent Priorities of Russian Foreign Policy' in Leon Aron and Kenneth M. Jensen (eds), *The Emergence of Russian Foreign Policy*, Washington, DC, 1995, p.24.
11. Viktor Posuvaliuk, 'Mara ukhra...' an mowqa' Russiya' (Once again on Russia's position), *Al-Hayat*, 12 June 1995, p.17.
12. Defence Minister of Russian Federation Col.-General Igor Rodionov, 'Russia and NATO: Life after Bergen', *Moscow News*, 9-15 October 1996, p.1.
13. Rosemary Hollis, 'Russia's New Priorities and the Middle East' in Rosemary Hollis (ed.), *The Soviets, their Successors and the Middle East*, London, 1993, p.120.
14. Interview with Vitaly Naumkin, deputy director of the Institute of Oriental Studies, Russian Academy of Sciences, conducted in Moscow, October 1996.
15. Amnon Sella, 'Soviet Collective Security Perception' in Hemsley, *op. cit.*, p.61.
16. Peter Gladkov, 'Superpowers No More' in Manus Midlarsky, John Vasquez and Peter Gladkov (eds), *From Rivalry to Co-operation, Russian and American Perspectives on the Post-Cold War Era*, New York, 1994, p.195.
17. Hafeez Malik, *Soviet-Pakistan Relations and Post-Soviet Dynamics, 1947-92*, London, 1994, p.338.
18. Galia Golan, *Moscow and the Middle East: New Thinking on Regional Conflict*, London, 1992, pp.79-80.
19. Shimon Peres, *The New Middle East*, Dorchester, 1993, p.9.
20. Anthony Parsons, *Prospects for Peace and Stability in the Middle East*, London, 1993, p.3.
21. Hollis, *op. cit.*, p.121.
22. Posuvaliuk, *op. cit.*, p.17.
23. *Ibid.*
24. Francis Fukuyama, 'The Ambiguity of "National Interest"' in Stephen Sestanovich (ed.), *Rethinking Russia's National Interests*, Washington, DC, 1994, p.13.
25. *Ibid.*, p.16.
26. Sergei Stankevich, 'Toward a New National Idea' in Sestanovich (ed.), *Rethinking Russia's National Interest*, p.18.
27. Vladimir Lukin, 'Russia and its Interests' in Sestanovich (ed.), *op. cit.*, p.109.
28. *Ibid.*
29. Aleksei Pushkov, 'Kozyrev's Foreign Policy: What Should Replace it?', *Moscow News (The Current Digest of Post-Soviet Press)*, 20 December 1995, p.6.

30. *Ibid.*
31. *Ibid.*
32. Margot Light, 'Foreign Policy Thinking' in Malcolm *et al.*, *op. cit.*, p.34.
33. *Ibid.*
34. Alex Pravda, 'The Public Politics of Foreign Policy', in Malcolm *et al.*, *op. cit.*, p.179.
35. Amin Saikal and William Maley, 'From Soviet to Russian Foreign Policy' in Amin Saikal and William Maley (eds), *Russia in Search of its Future*, Cambridge, 1995, p.107.
36. Neil Malcolm, 'Foreign Policy Making' in Malcolm *et al.*, *op. cit.*, p.109.
37. James Meek, 'Russia Courts World Stage', *Guardian*, 11 November 1994, p.16.
38. *Ibid.*
39. *Ibid.*
40. Malcolm, 'Foreign Policy Making', *op. cit.*, p.118.
41. Light, *op. cit.* p.74.
42. *Ibid.*, p.87.
43. Malcolm, 'Foreign Policy Making', *op. cit.*, p.125.
44. Evgenii Nikitenko and Nikolai Pikov, 'Duga Nestabil'nosti' (The arc of instability), *Nezavisimaia gazeta*, 4 December 1996, p.5.
45. *Ibid.*
46. Meek, *op. cit.*, p.16.
47. Scott Parrish, 'Russia: Chaos in Foreign Policy Decision-making', *Transition*, vol.2 no.10, 17 May 1996.
48. Malcolm, 'Russian Foreign Policy Decision-Making', *op. cit.*, p.28.
49. *Ibid.*
50. *Ibid.*, p.27.
51. James Goodby, 'Introduction' in James E. Goodby and Benoit Morel (eds), *The Limited Partnership: Building a Russian-US Security Commiunity*, Oxford, 1993, p.4.
52. Fred Charles Ikle, 'The Case for a Russian-U.S. Security Community' in Goodby and Morel, *op. cit.*, p.10.
53. Light, *op. cit.*, p.49.
54. Renée de Nevers, *Russia's Strategic Renovation*, International Institute for Strategic Studies, Adelphi Paper 289, 1994, p.5.
55. *Ibid.*, pp.6-7.
56. Edward B. Atkeson, 'Theatre Forces in the Commonwealth of Independent States' in Goodby and Morel, *op. cit.*, p.118.
57. Uri Ra'anan, 'Imperial Elements in Russia's Doctrines and Operations' in Uri Ra'anan and Kate Martin (eds), *Russia: A Return to Imperialism?*, London, 1996, p.20.
58. *Ibid.*, p.21.
59. Charles Dick, 'The Military Doctrine of the Russian Federation', *Jane's Intelligence Review*, Special Report no.1, January 1994, p.1.
60. Pushkov, *op. cit.*, p.8.
61. Sergei Grigoriev, 'Neo-Imperialism: The Underlying Factors' in Ra'anan and Martin (eds), *op. cit.*, p.5.
62. *Ibid.*, p.6.

63. *Ibid.*, p.14.
64. Suzanne Crow, 'Why has Russian Foreign Policy Changed', *RFE/Radio Liberty Research Report*, vol.3, no.18, 6 May 1994, p.1.
65. Andrei Kozyrev, 'Peace with a Sword', *Moscow News*, 9–15 September 1994, p.4.
66. Aron, *op. cit.*, p.28.
67. Alan Philps, '"Dr. Strangelove" puts peace in doubts', *Daily Telegraph*, 13 February 1996, p.18.
68. *Ibid.*
69. Ivan Rodin, 'Gadat', chto budet s Andreem Kozyrevym, bessmyslenno' (It is Useless to Guess What Will Happen to Andrei Kozyrev), *Nezavisimaia gazeta* (interviewing Sergei Karaganov), 21 October 1995, p.2.
70. *Ibid.*
71. Svetlana Petrova, 'Eshche raz o sud'be glavy rossiiskogo MIDa' (Again on the fate of Russia's foreign minister chief), *Nezavisimaia gazeta*, 2 December 1995, p.2.
72. Vladimir Simonov, 'Compromises are Inevitable, if Not Now then Later', *Komersant-Daily* 6 May 1995, p.4, *The Current Digest...*, vol.XLVII, no.18, 31 May 1995, p.27.
73. De Nevers, *op. cit.*, p.30.
74. Sharyl Cross and Marina Obortova (eds), *The New Chapter in United States-Russian Relations*, London, 1994, p.4.
75. Stanislav Kondrashov, 'Rossiia ishchet novoe mesto v mire' (Russia searches for a new place in the world), Interview with Primakov, *Izvestiia*, 6 March 1996, p.3.
76. *Ibid.*
77. Dmitrii Radyshevsky, 'Table Cloth Diplomacy by Primakov in New York', *Moscow News*, no.39, 9–16 October 1996, p.5.
78. Nikolai Samokhin, 'Chelovyek 'net' ili diplomat No.1?' (Mr No or diplomat number one?), *Nezavisimaia gazeta*, 31 December 1996, p.5.
79. Sergei Karaganov, 'Problemy stoiashchie pered Primakovym' (Problems facing Primakov), *Nezavisimaia gazeta*, 18 January 1996, p.2.
80. Sergei Karaganov, 'Kommunisty ukhodiat bez boia' (Communists back down without a fight), *Moskovskie novosti*, no.25, 23–30 June 1996, p.5.
81. Neil Malcolm and Alex Pravda, 'Democratisation and Russian Foreign Policy', *International Affairs* (RIIA), vol.72, no.3, July 1996, p.538.
82. *Ibid.*, p.550.
83. Maksim Youssin, 'Vashington bol'she ne khochet delit' s Moskvoi lavri mirotvortsa' (Washington no longer wants to share laurels of peacemaker with Moscow), *Izvestiia*, 30 April 1996, p.3.
84. Leonid Mlechin, 'Temnye ochki meshaiut uvidyet' istinnoe litso ministra' (The dark glasses hide the true face of the minister), *Izvestiia*, 15 May 1996, p.6.
85. Karaganov, 'Communists back down', *op. cit.*, p.5.
86. Leonid Gankin, 'Zalpi rezervnogo Fronta' (Volleys of the reserve front), *Moskovskie Novosti*, 23–30 June 1996, p.5.
87. Stanislav Kondrashov, 'Diplomaticheskoe Evangelie ot Evgeniia v kanune

vtorogo votsareniia Borisa' (Evgenii's diplomatic gospel on the eve of Boris's second accession to the throne), *Izvestiia*, 9 August 1996.

88. Andrei Grachev, 'Russia's Foreign Policy is a Tale of Sound and Fury', *Moscow News*, 23-9 December 1994, p.7.

89. Interview conducted in Moscow with Sergei Kepechenko, deputy director of the Middle East Department of the Russian Ministry of Foreign Affairs in October 1996.

90. Andrei Lipski, 'Ministr, Kotorogo ne rugaet oppositsiia' (The minister not cursed by the opposition), *Obshchaia gazeta*, 19-25 September 1996, p.4.

91. *Ibid.*

92. *Ibid.*

5

RUSSIAN-ISRAELI RELATIONS: FACING THE INEVITABLE

One of the most startling transformations in Russian policy in the Middle East in the early 1990s was the nature of relations between Moscow and Tel Aviv, considering that in the Soviet era, until Mikhail Gorbachev took power, Israel was regarded as an enemy of the USSR and a prime threat to its interests in the region. But because Gorbachev had already initiated so many drastic yet unexpected turnabouts in foreign policy (in Europe, Afghanistan and so on), by the time the two countries had established diplomatic relations in 1991 the world hardly noticed.

A few days after the Soviet ambassador took up residence in Tel Aviv, the USSR had disappeared as a national entity. Yeltsin persisted on the course of improving relations inherited from Gorbachev but certain practical difficulties, such as those relating to the Arab-Israeli dispute, seemed to re-impose themselves with the passing of time. The US-Israeli alliance, Israel's aggressive policies towards its Arab neighbours and Russia's co-operative relations with Syria, Iraq and Iran all created tension in bilateral relations, which by 1996 was no longer concealed by Moscow. But there were new aspects to the relationship between the two countries which helped to solidify the links between Russia and Israel and give Moscow a more balanced role in the region as a whole. One such important development was the flourishing trade between the two countries.

Problems of the past in Soviet-Israeli diplomatic relations

Ironically, Stalin was the first world leader to recognise the Jewish state in 1948 but then suddenly cooled relations because of his concerns regarding 'Western imperialism' and the influence an Israeli state might have on his own Jewish population. These concerns were in one way or another present throughout the Soviet era up till its very last days.

Soviet antipathy towards Israel continued with Brezhnev, who took decisive action in June 1967 by breaking off all forms of ties with Tel Aviv to compensate for the embarrassing defeat of its Arab allies. Moscow then played an active role at the United Nations Security Council where it adopted a series of measures calling on Israel to return land that had been taken from Arabs during the Six Day War. The animosity between Moscow and Tel Aviv continued throughout the 1970s, despite *détente*, as tension in the Middle East remained high. The Soviet Union provided the Arabs with an ever increasing quantity of modern weapons and technical assistance through manpower, and some Israelis suspected without concrete evidence that a number of Soviet troops were front-line participants in the 1973 war.

According to UN Resolutions 242 and 338, Arab-Israeli negotiations were to be based on the principle that Israel would return Arab land occupied since 1967 in exchange for recognition of Israel's right to exist. However, it was felt by some in Moscow that the 1967 decision to sever relations was a blunder because it seriously limited Soviet diplomatic efforts in the Middle East. The restrictions imposed on Moscow by its decision to break relations were made more evident when the United States brokered a peace agreement between Israel and Egypt, which was concluded in 1979. Both the United States and the Soviet Union wanted to avoid any situation which would lead to a direct confrontation between the superpowers. This possibility worried the United States to the extent that President Richard Nixon warned in a televised interview on 1 July 1970 that 'the Middle East is terribly dangerous', and the situation threatened to push the superpowers 'into a confrontation that neither of them wants'.[1]

During the 1970s, attempts by Moscow to restore relations with Israel in order to devise a peace plan for the area were met with various obstacles. First, there was the October War of 1973 in which Moscow could not appear to betray the Arab countries it had supported for so many years. And when in the late 1970s Egypt signed the peace treaty with Israel, Moscow's chief allies Syria, Libya and the PLO formed the Front of Steadfastness and Confrontation aimed at countering Washington's efforts to break the Arab coalition against Israel. The USSR believed it was vital to back this coalition as it was perceived to be a solid platform to check US influence in the area. For Washington's foreign policy makers, Arab countries which could be prized away from the confrontationist bloc to make peace with Israel would mean a loss for the Soviet-led world and a gain for the United States. Washington's most successful envoy in those important years of the early 1970s was Henry Kissinger, who was known for his shuttle diplomacy between Hafez Asad of Syria, Egypt's Anwar Sadat and Israel's Golda Meir. The Soviet Union, in comparison, refused to deal directly with Israel, which seriously undermined its own efforts at mediation.

The first comprehensive US peace plan had been devised under Secretary of State William Rogers and while Israel's response was critical of both procedural and substantive aspects of the plan, it was a first step in opening the way for Kissinger to work for a mediation. Israeli misgivings about the Rogers Plan actually served to enhance the image of the United States as an honest broker. Meanwhile, the Soviet Union had since 1967 found itself enmeshed in Arab politics and was unable to extract itself from the Arab-Israeli conflict without risk of losing strategic gains it held in the area. Between 1967 and 1973 there was increasing Soviet participation in Egypt's air defence, 'posing danger of a direct clash with Israel'.[2] The loss of Egypt, however, allowed Moscow to concentrate its attention on Syria, which became Israel's most outspoken enemy and the USSR's most important ally in the Middle East. In other words, from Israel's point of view the Soviet Union had shown continuity in its support for the most violent anti-Israeli regimes, whatever the composition of its leadership or the country they ruled.

Soviet policy presented the Jewish state as nothing more than a 'tool' of the West. In reality, the relationship between Israel and the United States was far more complicated and differences often arose. Israel was by far the largest recipient of US aid, $3 billion annually, which included the most up-to-date military hardware. Nonetheless, there were many points of friction in the relationship, among them the decision by Washington to strengthen ties with Saudi Arabia, which was to some extent elevated to equal status with Israel in the fight against Soviet and pro-Soviet expansion in the 1980s. The first instance of this was in 1978 when Washington sold F-15s and other advanced weapons to

Saudi Arabia despite a visit to Washington by Israeli Prime Minister Menachem Begin aimed at preventing such action. On realising that the Carter administration would not be swayed the Israeli leader openly criticised the United States.

The bombing and destruction of the French-built Iraqi nuclear research facility (Osirak) near Baghdad on 7 June 1981 by Israeli jets (US-supplied F-16s, escorted by F-15s), a mission undertaken without prior consultation with the United States, led to direct criticism from the State Department the following day:

> The United States government condemns the reported Israeli air strike on the Iraqi nuclear facility, the unprecedented character of which cannot but seriously add to the already tense situation in the area. Available evidence suggests US-provided equipment was employed in possible violation of the applicable agreement under which it was sold to Israel. [...][3]

Despite the Israeli misdemeanour, no action was taken because of the special relationship between the two countries and the strength of the Jewish lobby in the United States.

Attitudes and perceptions

Soviet criticisms of Israel were often laced with doses of anti-Semitism. What worried many Israelis was that many of the Soviet propaganda scriptwriters and foreign policy makers continued to hold influential positions in post-Soviet Russia. Soviet insinuations about a world Jewish conspiracy to dominate the political institutions of Washington and the banking centres in New York as well as the media were evident in the Soviet press through political commentaries and cartoons. The situation worsened when the United States under Jimmy Carter and later Ronald Reagan pressed Moscow to permit Jews to leave the Soviet Union. Western insistence regarding this matter, which it termed a human rights issue, made Soviet leaders even more suspicious of their Jewish population and more critical of Israel and its policies. From the Soviet perspective, Israel was a tool that Washington was using to chisel away at Soviet interests abroad, and at the internal social stability of the USSR itself.

One study (by Yeshayahu Nir in 1976) looked at the Arab-Israeli conflict through Soviet caricatures. One cartoon, drawn in 1979, depicted an Israeli soldier (with an eye-patch resembling that of Moshe Dayan, the former Israeli defence minister), drawing with his bayonet a Star of David made from human bones. The painter (soldier) in the cartoon wrote above the star 'Greater Israel' (in Russian) and the caption under the cartoon read: 'The Expres-SIONIST from Tel Aviv'.[4] Some Soviet anti-Israeli propaganda likened Jewish settlers to Nazis, something that Moscow would have known to be a sensitive issue to Jews. One cartoon, for example, depicted a Jewish worker carrying a bloodied axe marked with the Star of David; the worker's shadow bore a deliberate resemblance to Adolf Hitler except that the shadow axe was marked with a Swastika. The cartoon was entitled 'In His Own Shadow'.[5] Since Gorbachev's New Thinking such attacks became much less common and blatant anti-Semitism rarely emanated from the ruling élite.

During the run-up to the 1996 presidential elections there was concern, particularly from the pro-Israeli Jewish lobby in the United States, that there was a revival of anti-Semitism in Russia. Vladimir Zhirinovskii's Liberal Democratic Party was clearly anti-Israeli and not sympathetic to Jews. However, it was Gennadii Ziuganov, the principal challenger to Boris Yeltsin, who was the target of accusations by Jews in Israel and their counterparts in the United States. According to reports in the Israeli-friendly press in the United States, 'top officials of the National Conference on Soviet Jewry' met with Strobe Talbot (US ambassador-at-large for the former Soviet Union) as part of a campaign to lobby President Clinton 'over a new wave of Russian anti-Semitism'.[6]

One report listed a series of events which were intended to support this view:

> The April 3 decision by the Yeltsin government to withdraw accreditation of the Israel-based Jewish Agency, which has been supporting the revival of communal Jewish life in Russia; the April 19 bombing of a Jewish communal centre in Yaroslavl, 130 miles north of Moscow; the interruption of Jewish history classes and instruction on emigration to Israel by Interior Ministry agents in the town of Piatigorsk on April 30; the mailing of notices to large numbers of Jewish youths warning them that they may be drafted into the Russian army; the release of a new security edict that, if endorsed, could make emigration from Russia more difficult.[7]

Ziuganov's comments in his book, *Beyond the Horizon*, that the Jewish diaspora held a controlling interest in the West's economic life was taken to mean that he endorsed the world Jewish conspiracy theory.[8]

However, such allegations were largely due to hypersensitivity on the part of the Jewish-backed media and were usually prevalent in less credible journals, particularly as there was negligible evidence to suggest that the Kremlin or the Ministry of Foreign Affairs encouraged anti-Jewish activity. The real differences between the two countries were largely political, concerning Russia's role in the regional conflict. There was also friction over Israel's reluctance to transfer to Russia from the Soviet Union legal rights of valuable land holdings in Jerusalem. It would have been an impossible task for Israeli foreign policy makers to prove that there was an inherent anti-Semitism among Russians and particularly among its ruling élite. Foreign policy makers from both countries made a special effort to banish such suspicions for the sake of national interests.

Russian national interests and Israel

With regard to Israel, the first year under Yeltsin saw little activity because Moscow needed time to find its feet as a new state, had to face more pressing external problems such as relations with the other independent republics of the former Soviet Union and had to maintain co-operation with the West. But Moscow's aspiration to re-establish itself more broadly in international affairs re-emerged. As Hannes Adomeit observed in one article, 'There is hardly an opportunity let slip these days [January 1995] by Russian officials to proclaim Russia once again to be "a great power".'[9] Russia's retreat was described as a temporary measure and a 'return to a more assertive and unilateralist policy was therefore to be considered quite normal and indeed predictable'.[10]

To a varying degree, pragmatic and extreme nationalists called for a return to the old Soviet policy of supporting traditional allies in the region such as Syria and Iraq against pro-US states such as Israel. These groups argued that the policies of Moscow in the late 1980s and early 1990s were naïve to expect close partnership with the West.[11] Demands from these anti-government forces to move away from such a policy were not necessarily built on the basis of conflict as much as out of a belief that Russia's 'great power' status gave it the right to have its own spheres of influence in the same way that Washington did.

Radical pro-Westerners countered that Russia's policy of diversifying relations applied to the Middle East and so having relations with Israel was seen as a normal state of affairs. Moreover, efforts to have good relations with Israel were encouraged because of the possible benefits, mainly economic and technical, that could be gained from such ties. Relations with Israel would also enable Moscow to play a more meaningful diplomatic role as an arbitrator in the Middle East peace process, and Brezhnev's earlier error of neglecting this point served as a reminder to those opposing this view. Those favouring good relations with Israel, which included all pro-Westerners and centrist-nationalists, pointed out that the Arabs had already made large strides in terms of recognition and peace agreements with the Jewish state. Therefore, Moscow's policy would have appeared to be reactive and short-sighted if it stood by one or two hard-line regimes while the rest of the Arab countries raised the level of diplomatic and economic relations with Israel.

Israeli Prime Minister Yitzhak Rabin's belief that policy planning had to be free from past ideas and constructed within the framework of a completely changed world order did not dampen Israeli pleasure at Moscow's subdued role in the Middle East. Rabin belonged to a generation of leaders in Israel who viewed the Soviet Union in a certain light, as his comments, made in 1993, showed:

> I would say that today no Arab leader, be he Saddam Hussein – and he learnt the hard way – President Asad or Qadhafi, can rely anymore on the Soviet umbrella under which he has sheltered for 31 years...the Syrians cannot rely anymore on the prospect that, in time of war, when events turn against them, the red phone from Moscow to Washington will ring and the request will be sent: 'stop the Israelis'.[12]

The Soviet Union's standing as a major military supplier, which was of concern to the Israelis, had become substantially diminished in the first years of Yeltsin's rule. According to one source, global sales fell from 'a fairly stable $12 billion a year in the 1980s to $7.8 billion in 1991, $3 billion in 1992 and $2.5 billion in 1993', and in ranking it dropped from first, or second behind the United

States, to sixth (as Russia) in 1993.[13] Such statistics infuriated Russian nationalists and centrists because they believed that acquiescence to Washington was costing their country billions in lost revenue, and they argued that 'participation in the sanctions against Iraq, Libya and the former Yugoslavia alone had cost the country up to $30 billion in lost contracts'.[14]

Israel, however, continued to be unhappy with the amount and type of weapons being sold by Russia to its regional foes especially since countries such as Iran and Syria were not participants in the peace process and had not compromised on their aim to retrieve lost Arab lands by any means, including force. Rabin noted that 'the arms procurement policies of these countries has as much bearing on regional peace as those of the parties to the negotiations, if not more so'.[15] Israel possessed sophisticated missiles and a nuclear capability, which was justified by its leaders as being necessary to maintain a balance with its much larger neighbours. Rabin pointed out that 'the name of the game of the arms race today in the region, and particularly in the Arab and Muslim countries, is weapons of mass destruction, and long range delivery systems, which, in the Middle East context, means essentially ground-to-ground missiles'.[16] Israeli political and military leaders were greatly concerned that economic collapse in Russia would lead to a decision from Moscow to supply their enemies with large quantities of such missiles. Since 1991 Russia had shown restraint in sales of weapons of mass destruction, and long-range delivery systems procured by Syria and Iran originated from the Far East, namely China and North Korea.

Rabin had made it clear that he was unhappy with Russia's role in arming Iran, which he believed to be the biggest threat to the Middle East. However, while Tehran supported militant Islamic organisations, it was highly unlikely that Iran would launch a full-scale conventional military attack on Israel, considering that its armies would have to cross several countries to reach Israel. Iraq and Jordan were certain to refuse Iranian troops on their soil even if it was for the cause of 'liberating' Palestine. Secondly, Israel's fear of a missile attack through biological or chemical weapons was also not too strongly founded because Tel Aviv possessed a far more destructive nuclear deterrent. Iran's huge expenditure on military hardware was actually aimed at sending a message to its most immediate neighbours – particularly the

Arab world. Iran was also worried about instability in Central Asia, the Taliban threat in Afghanistan and a new member to the nuclear club, Pakistan. Hence the war of words between Iran and Israel was mainly seen as an exercise in propaganda aimed at satisfying domestic political needs rather than a genuine fear of a full-scale war.

In long-term thinking, Israeli concerns about the nuclearisation of the region were based on solid arguments. Iran's missile technology was relatively basic in the early 1990s, but its modernisation threatened to alter the strategic balance of the region because of Israel's disadvantage in terms of size. Moreover, Israeli leaders[17] felt that the relatively pragmatic influence of President Rafsanjani, replaced by Khatami, was under pressure from radical Islamic fundamentalists, particularly as the economic situation of the country was rapidly deteriorating.

Israeli fears about Russian military supplies to the region indirectly served to make bilateral relations more valuable. Because Iran had an agreement with Russia worth billions of dollars for the supply of conventional weapons – MiG-29s and Su-24s – and with countries of the Far East for ground-to-ground missiles and the development of nuclear capabilities, Rabin made it his policy to work with, rather than against, both Russia and China in an effort to entice them away from closer relations with the regime in Tehran. The Jewish state instigated relations with China in January 1992. Israel promised greater assistance in technological development and other sectors in return for a pledge from Moscow (and Beijing) not to provide certain types of weapons to Iran and other 'dangerous' states such as Syria. This example highlighted the point that Russia was still regarded as being important by the Middle East states and, in turn, Moscow gradually found that it had much to gain from keeping a noticeable profile in the region.

The Middle East peace process

Under the Labour government of Yitzhak Rabin, and then Shimon Peres, Israel made the strategic decision to counter the threat of war by making peace with its neighbours. Israel's strategy went beyond making peace with individual countries, but instead endeavoured to create a regional peace in the Middle East 'where there will be a common infrastructure of energy, of water, of roads, open skies...' according to Israeli Deputy Foreign Minister Yossi Beilin.[18] Throughout the history of the Arab-Israeli dispute, forces dedicated to conflict had the upper hand, but Beilin remarked in 1994 that 'today there is something new for the first time in many years – there is a coalition of the moderate forces, of the pragmatic forces in the Middle East...'.[19] From this perspective the role of Russia was important: Israel wanted Russia to use the remaining influence it had with the opponents of the peace process in order to convince them that there was no other option but negotiations. Syrian consent to enter into negotiations with Israel was largely given because Gorbachev had made it clear to President Asad that the Soviet Union refused to provide further support for his objective to reach strategic parity with the Jewish state.

The problem faced by Moscow was that the two major political parties in Israel were generally dismissive of direct Russian involvement in the peace process. Rabin's successful election campaign placed a strong emphasis on promoting relations with the United States. One of the very first episodes which reflected Israel's lack of concern for Russian sensibilities was during the third round of peace talks held in Moscow when members from Moledet and Tehiya (two right-wing parties in the Likud coalition) withdrew from the government to disrupt the talks in Russia. 'Delegates had begun to address the granting of transitional autonomy to the Palestinians in the West Bank and Gaza Strip.'[20] Such behaviour by the Israeli delegates would have been unlikely in Washington.

Rabin came to power as leader of a left-wing-based coalition on 23 June 1992 at a time when relations between Israel and the United States had been severely tested by the behaviour of Rabin's predecessor Yitzhak Shamir, leader of the ruling Likud, who had been deliberately attempting to block Washington's efforts to initiate the peace process. One interesting suggestion was that Likud had, in August 1991, claimed that one of a number of conditions to which Washington 'had agreed in return for Israel's participation in the regional peace conference scheduled for October was the re-establishment of full diplomatic relations with the USSR'.[21] The explanation for this was straightforward: Shamir wanted to speed up the rate of Jewish emigration from the USSR to Israel, though the full extent of his plans upset world opinion because he wanted these immigrants to expand settlements on occupied lands which would in effect have concluded the outcome of negotiations over territories (in Israel's favour) before they had even begun.

Shamir's decision in January 1992 to deport twelve Palestinians added to the tension between Washington and Tel Aviv. Officials from the Israeli government protested to the United States over the wording of the UN Security Council Resolution condemning Israel's planned deportation, objecting to the reference to 'occupied Palestinian territories', which Israel did not accept. But the lowest point in the history of relations between Washington and Tel Aviv, also in 1992, was when the Bush administration withheld $10 billion of loan guarantees until Israel made a commitment to halt settlements on occupied Arab land. The pugnacious Shamir responded through Israeli army radio: 'I think almost all the political factions in Israel would not accept a situation in which the American administration would dictate our policy, whether about settlements today or about other territorial issues tomorrow.'[22]

Russian leaders found it increasingly difficult not to criticise Israel for actions which were in obvious breach of international law, despite efforts to create a more positive working environment between the two countries. When Shamir met Russian officials in January of 1992 the two sides discussed possibilities of improving bilateral ties, especially ways in which Israel could help in updating telecommunications networks and in the storage of agricultural produce. The purpose of the visit by the Israelis was to attend the Moscow round of the peace conference but in his speech Foreign Minister David Levy reflected his country's attitude towards the Russians compared with the United States:

> My deep appreciation to the host, the government of an independent Russia [but]...special thanks goes to the US nation and President for the exemplary, brave leadership which the entire world has witnessed and to US Secretary of State Baker for his contribution and determination in moving this historic wheel: the peace process.[23]

In March of that year Levy indirectly criticised Russia soon after he announced that he would be again travelling to Moscow. His criticisms were actually aimed at Syria but the Russian government could not have failed to miss the point: 'Syria is following its Iraqi sister, and the missiles it is purchasing are noted for their even more precise technology. Syria is also making an effort to develop chemical weapons, and deals for the procurement of advanced Russian and East European tanks are being struck.'[24] The comparison of Syria with Iraq was not unintentional, nor was the implication of Russian involvement. Levy was a moderate in the Likud camp and he found it difficult to agree with his more belligerent leader, Shamir. In fact Levy resigned in March in protest at Shamir's neglect of the special relationship between his country and the US. 'Although the US did not identify with Israel's policy and the two countries differ on matters of substance', Levy argued that the relationship should be 'cherished because there is no substitute'.[25] Rabin's election victory in June was in large part due to his promise to restore good relations with Washington, and to pursue the peace option.

At a Labour Party conference Rabin told his audience that 'in terms of Israel's relations with the world, we have always known, and we learned...just how important friends are. Most important to us is the friendship of the only large superpower.'[26] While Rabin's coming to power led to more harmonious relations between Israel and the United States, it did not change Israel's continued occupation of Palestinian territories and its poor human rights record towards the Arab population, which often led to strained relations between Tel Aviv and Moscow. For example when the Speaker of the Russian parliament Ruslan Khasbulatov arrived in Israel in January 1993, the Jewish state was being internationally criticised for the deportation of 415 Palestinians to the mountains of southern Lebanon. On 6th January Khasbulatov was forced to comment despite his efforts to avoid direct criticisms of the Israeli government. 'We in the Russian parliament have a profound appreciation of the Rabin government's policy of negotiation and substantive concessions, but we do not think the expulsions promoted that policy.'[27]

When the United Nations threatened to impose sanctions for the expulsions and the peace talks were in danger of collapsing, Russia was unable to play a constructive role and had to resign itself to being overshadowed by the United States. This point was acknowledged by Rabin: 'The USA, for its part, undertook to prevent decisions in international forums – I do not want to say where, you can understand that for yourselves – to prevent any decisions which have operational significance for Israel.'[28]

Throughout 1993, Russia generally played a very small role in the Middle East peace talks and bilateral relations between the two countries were not substantial. In July Yossi Beilin, deputy foreign minister, went to Moscow but only to meet with the Palestinian representative Faisal Husseini. In September Rabin met Russia's Deputy Foreign Minister Anatoli Adamishin and asked him to use his country's influence with its Middle Eastern 'friends', primarily Syria, to win their support for the Declaration of Principles signed between the PLO and Israel. Russia was represented at the signing ceremony, in September 1993, though many commentators pointed out that they were hardly noticed. An Israeli reporter summed up the feeling in his country about Russia when he wrote that Moscow was not 'an active participant in the process, nor is it briefed on developments on a regular basis. The Russians are merely invited to the White House to sign documents already agreed upon, perhaps out of nostalgia for the Madrid Conference where Russia was co-sponsor.'[29]

In turn, some quarters in the Russian press had shown similar scepticism about Israel's commitment to the peace process, but they did agree with their Israeli counterparts that Washington and not Moscow would instigate the real changes. An article written just before the Madrid Conference argued that the peace process would be detrimental to the Palestinians and the author rightly predicted that Israel would continue to expand and build settlements. Beliakov argued, with fair accuracy, that the United States and Israel would bring Yasser Arafat into their camp to control Palestinian militants, and to further undermine Moscow's influence in the Middle East by taking away one of its last remaining allies. The peace process would in effect 'become an instrument to twist the Palestinian arm'.[30]

Yeltsin's government did display a shift to a more balanced tone in statements regarding Israel. For example, when Israeli jets bombed southern Lebanon in July 1993 Moscow's response echoed that of most European countries except Britain, which generally followed Washington's lead. A Russian Foreign Ministry statement on the attacks said that 'Moscow considers Israel's reaction to the actions of extremist groups to be disproportionate'.[31] By the standard of Soviet statements regarding Israel, the fact that the attacks were described as a 'reaction' was a considerable difference to the old rhetoric of militant Zionist expansionism. And a report from (the non-governmental) *Izvestiia* was even more understanding of the Israeli position:

> Continuing shelling of Israel by Hezbollah militia men using rocket launchers is forcing the Israeli Army command to continue the operations. [...] For two hours before each attack, Israel warns Lebanese village residents by radio of planned strikes against Hezbollah command centres and bases located in their areas, thereby giving the population a chance to clear out.[32]

Similar language emanated from Moscow when Israel bombed Lebanon in early June 1994, again as a response to Hezbollah Katiusha shelling. 'Only at the negotiating table can agreements be reached guaranteeing both the restoration of the territorial integrity of Lebanon and the mutual security of this state and Israel',[33] a government statement suggested. Thus, it was not the Israeli presence in Lebanon which was regarded as the problem, as was explained as being the case before the Gorbachev era, but the military actions of both sides to resolve the dispute in their favour. This position was established to a large extent because of the lingering influence of New Thinking and the early influence of the pro-Western radicals around Yeltsin since 1992. The pro-Western radical influence in government in the early years under Yeltsin led to the contention that support for militant groups such as Hezbollah could no longer be justifiably supported. It was believed to be necessary for Moscow to distance itself from the Brezhnev era, when support for terrorist organisations and non-state militant groups was deemed an acceptable part of the struggle against Western imperialism, for the credibility of post-Soviet Russia as a new democratic state to have any value.

The pro-Western pragmatists and centrist-nationalists rejected the ideological and political hostility displayed towards Israel by the pragmatic and extreme nationalists, arguing instead that while Russia had a right as a democratic state to criticise Israeli violations of international laws, efforts to promote the positive aspects of relations were both desirable and beneficial to national interests. The new Russian position was described by Adamishin as part of a new policy that was guided by a different perspective. 'Now, with more pragmatism, we try to have good relations with a greater number of countries, certainly not considering one country against another, but having a conception of all for peace and stability.'[34]

Obstacles in Russian-Israeli relations

Russian foreign policy in the region since mid-1993 began to attribute greater importance to its role in the peace process as a consequence of the growing criticism of Kozyrev's policies. During the Israeli bombing of Lebanon in July 1993 a Russian Foreign Ministry spokesman said that 'this dangerous relapse into military confrontation in the Middle East is especially alarming in light of the fact that the Russian and American co-chairmen of the Middle East peace process are currently trying to narrow the differences between the positions of the talks participants'.[35]

The Russian Foreign Ministry's aim to play up its role in the peace talks was not helped by Rabin's constant and deliberate remarks about Washington being the only real power-broker. Moreover, the fact that Moscow was often left uninformed about latest developments in negotiations placed its leaders in an awkward position when trying to justify the importance of their position. Under Kozyrev, the Russian opposition media was merciless in its mockery of the Foreign Ministry's pretensions. One writer remarked that 'formally speaking, Russia is also a sponsor of the Washington meetings, but it has been relegated to a supernumerary role, playing the part of a character who appears onstage when it's time to utter the historic phrase "dinner is served"'.[36] The views of the author, Iuri Glukhov, reflected those of Russia's pragmatic and extreme nationalists, bitter at what they saw as their country's decline in the international order. With regard to Israel's continued attacks on southern Lebanon, the author lamented that the Russian Foreign Ministry had 'spoken out after a long silence, calling the Israeli actions "inappropriate to the situation". That's all. Without any condemnation or indignation over the international banditry.'[37]

The motivating factor behind such arguments was the belief that Russian interests were more closely linked to its traditional Arab allies than indicated by the conclusions of the pro-Western democrats' assessment of the world order. A Russian foreign policy study, sponsored by the Foreign Ministry, pointed out that Moscow's aims for the Middle East would be:

[....] ensuring the country's national security; preventing the spread of politico-military fires in the Middle East, which would cause even greater instability in the Caucasus and Central Asia; and making effective use of the Arab countries' considerable potential to help solve Russia's economic problems during its renewal process.[38]

In light of this, one Russian commentator asked the question: 'Just how do we intend to build relations with the enormous Arab world when we fail to say clearly that part of it is occupied, that we see this and that we will help liberate these lands?'[39]

In a meeting between Peres and Deputy Foreign Minister Viktor Posuvaliuk in August 1994, the latter attempted to involve Moscow in an Arab-Israeli settlement over Jerusalem, partly because of Russia's substantial church holdings. The Russian envoy's expectation that he would be given a more sympathetic hearing was firmly suppressed by Peres, who stated that 'the issue of Jerusalem is politically closed...'.[40] While Moscow had a non-existent role in the Israeli-Jordanian peace agreement, signed on 26 July 1994 in Washington, Moscow's policy makers expected the Syrian-Israeli track to give them a more prominent role. However this ambition became a major source of tension between Russia and Israel, as reports that the Foreign Ministry was 'drafting its own proposals for a solution to the Golan Heights problem'[41] were met with cynicism by both Washington and Tel Aviv. Israel's Labour leadership maintained a clear aim to work on the Syrian track in tight co-ordination with Washington without any outside interference, and Moscow was often left uninformed about various proposals and developments in negotiations. For example, when on 22 June 1994 Foreign Minister Peres announced that new proposals to the Syrians had been made, the Deputy Director of the Near East and Africa Department Alexander Sheim admitted that 'the Russian Foreign Ministry knows nothing about [such] proposals to Syria' which were aimed at finding a way out of the then suspended peace talks.[42]

After the Hebron massacre on 25 February 1994, when a Jewish settler machine-gunned dozens of Palestinians praying in a mosque, Russia's efforts to step up its involvement in the region became more overt. The event had threatened to bring about what many commentators had begun to warn against: that extremists on all sides of the dispute were regaining the upper hand so that the region would once again become embroiled in conflict. Kozyrev arrived in Tunis on 11 March to try to breathe new life into the peace process, and in particular into the Gaza and Jericho First agreement which provided the Palestinians with limited autonomy in return for a PLO pledge to end its armed struggle.

Posuvaliuk, Yeltsin's special representative to the Middle East who accompanied Kozyrev on his trip, spoke in rather abstract terms about the best way of furthering the peace process in which, 'as a phenomenon that involves combining two viewpoints, no compromise is ideal if you look at it from only one of the sides'.[43] This seemed to contradict calls from Russian nationalists to take a moral and political stand with the Arabs because the policy supported neither the Israeli nor Arab position but the agreements which both sides were concluding as a consequence of the negotiation process. This effectively made Russian policy more favourable to the Israelis who were in a stronger position and who already had powerful support from Washington. Critics of this policy in Russia and the Arab world argued that Moscow's support for the peace process at any cost was in fact peace at the expense of Palestinian rights, which complemented the US-Israeli position. When Posuvaliuk was asked to answer criticisms that the PLO-Israeli peace agreement had failed to deal with key issues such as the fate of Israeli settlements on occupied territories, the status of Jerusalem and of possible Palestinian statehood, the Russian envoy said that it was correct not to do so because 'the boat could not be overloaded'.[44] The Foreign Ministry had sent an envoy to the Middle East in March of that year, Igor Ivanov, who did adopt a position less favourable to Israel. He backed PLO calls for an international force to be present in the occupied territories, a position strongly rejected by Israel because it preferred the Palestinian cause to be forgotten as a world issue and wanted to deal with it as a local problem.

On 24 April 1994, Rabin headed a delegation on an official visit to Moscow. This was the first such visit in the history of the two countries. The result of the visit was the signing of six agreements between the two governments covering the fields of scientific-technical, cultural-educational and medical-touristic co-operation. Prime Minister Chernomyrdin, who represented the Russian side, said that 'Russia and Israel have favourable prospects for expanding co-operation in various spheres including the economy and military spheres'.[45] Chernomyrdin also assured Rabin that Russian Jews were safe from anti-Semitism. Commenting on the visit, Posuvaliuk said that Russia's praise for Arafat in the past should be extended to include Rabin: 'In our view these are courageous political leaders...For Rabin it is an enormous psychological strain to drive around the city and see everywhere "Rabin, Rabin the traitor".'[46]

Posuvaliuk's praise concealed some deep-seated differences between the two countries and the political reality revealed that Russian interests with Israel's enemies made it difficult for Moscow to take relations with Israel much further beyond the point they had reached. Russian arms sales to Israel's enemies began to increase after 1993, leading to renewed concern about Moscow's role in the region. The United Nations arms register – published 14 October 1994 – listed that 'Russia exported 100 tanks, 80 armoured combat vehicles (ACVs), and one warship to Iran in 1993, making the latter Russia's largest arms customer'.[47]

Moscow's stepping up of its activities in the Middle East led to a warning from Rabin 'against the involvement of Russia in the peace process without co-ordination with the Americans'.[48] Igor Ivanov responded to the statement by saying that since Russia was also a co-sponsor in the peace process it had as much right as the United States to attempt to 'adopt separate initiatives'.[49] This remark upset the Israelis and the United States, forcing Kozyrev to reassert that Moscow sought co-operation with Washington: 'We are in daily contact, we are acting in unison, in complete accord', the Foreign Minister claimed.[50] Nonetheless, the Israelis (and many Russians) felt that Russian interests were ultimately tied to the Arabs and that Moscow's leadership spoke in a language that contradicted their country's actions. For example, Yeltsin had promised Rabin in May 1994 that Russia would not deliver military equipment to Syria. Yet shortly before this, Vice-Premier Oleg Soskovets had visited Damascus and 'signed an agreement on the sale of the latest arms to Syria'. It was also widely reported that Moscow 'proposed strategic co-operation to Damascus'.[51]

In October 1995 Deputy Foreign Minister Eli Dayan travelled to Moscow with the purpose of expressing Israel's expectations of Russia. In an interview with the newspaper *Moskovskie novosti* he openly requested from Russia's leaders a role that would enable a breakthrough in the peace talks between Israel and Syria. Dayan diplomatically announced that his country had 'complete trust in Russia'.[52] He added that Washington's role on this particular track of the peace talks faced certain obstacles: 'We understand that their capabilities are not limitless. Now the ball is in Russia's court, and, drawing on its traditional connections in the Arab world, it can achieve a real breakthrough in the peace process.'[53] The Israeli government had chosen to take this step because of a marked increase of activities by Hezbollah in southern Lebanon which was costing Israeli lives on a regular basis. But it would have been politically suicidal for the Labour government to withdraw from southern Lebanon without proving to the Israeli electorate that a watertight security arrangement was assured. Iran and Syria were exploiting this entrapment to put more pressure on Israel for their own political advantage: Tehran's proxy-militia Hezbollah gained support and strength in Lebanon, giving it a more weighty voice in Middle East affairs, while Damascus used its alliance with Iran and support for Hezbollah as a strong card on the bargaining table. In this context, Dayan explained that the purpose of his visit was 'to convince President Asad to agree to an Israeli-Syrian summit. [...] We would also like Russia to convince Syria and Iran to renounce attempts to destabilise the situation in southern Lebanon and to back terrorists from Hezbollah.'[54]

Evidence suggested that in early 1995 Israel had held some hope that Russia could play a beneficial role, indicating that Moscow's policy in the region was bearing some fruit. Tel Aviv understated differences over increased armed sales to Iran and Syria, with Israel's ambassador to Moscow, Professor Aliza Shenhar, saying she was 'fully satisfied' with Moscow's general arms sales and policy in the Middle East.[55] She added that the Chechnia conflict was an internal matter for Russia and Israel 'cannot bring more pressure as far as human rights are concerned because Israel faces similar problems'.[56] This was a reference to terrorist attacks by Palestinian groups (allegedly backed by Iran and Syria) which opposed the peace agreement between the PLO and Israel. Russia's condemnation of Hamas and Islamic Jihad was equal to those of the United States and Israel in its clarity. Kozyrev was personally committed to the peace process because it promised a new democratic and more secular order in the Middle East that was close to his beliefs. He also knew very well, as was the case in his own country, that there were groups prepared to use any means to resist the establishment of this new order. Following a bomb attack in late-spring 1995 on an Israeli bus in Tel Aviv, Kozyrev warned that 'opponents of the peace process still exist...[and that we] must not lull ourselves into believing that resistance to the process is on the wane'.[57]

Bilateral relations increased and on 6 June 1995 Moscow hosted Russian-Israeli consultations under the chairmanship of Deputy Foreign Ministers Posuvaliuk and Beilin. The Israeli delegation was met by Kozyrev and both countries seemed to have high expectations of the meetings. Both parties agreed that 'a working committee will operate on a regular basis, overseeing its workings twice a year taking it in turns between Russia and Israel'.[58] In September 1995 Rabin made yet another visit to Moscow but the Russian side was unhappy at his insistence on discussing the sale of nuclear equipment to Iran because it wanted to shift the focus on issues concerning Russian-Israeli relations and the Russian role in the Middle East peace process. Nonetheless both sides were able to agree that they should enhance military co-operation. This was to be the last visit to Russia by Rabin, as he was assassinated by a Jewish extremist on 4 November 1995.

Despite the loss of Rabin, who alongside Arafat played a central role in the making of war and peace in the region, Russian-Israeli relations maintained their earlier momentum. In December 1995, Defence Minister Pavel Grachev went to Israel, the first visit of its kind, with the purpose of establishing military and technical relations between the two countries. The visit was hailed in Russia as a breakthrough for Russian influence in the Middle East. As one commentator noted: 'Russia is establishing relations in a very important and delicate sphere with a state that plays a key role in the region.'[59] Grachev's success was at the expense of Kozyrev, who had lost all credibility in Moscow, making the work of the Foreign Ministry largely superfluous. Towards the end of 1995, constant rumours in the Russian press that Kozyrev would be released from his position by Yeltsin added to the paralysis that existed in the Ministry of Foreign Affairs. Kozyrev was finally replaced in early 1996 by Evgenii Primakov, who was regarded as well-connected in the Arab world and more suspicious of the West and Israel.

Primakov and Israel

Israel's Ambassador Shenhar immediately played down the new Foreign Minister's connections with the Soviet system: 'Even though Primakov was part of the Soviet foreign policy, he now sees Middle Eastern problems in a different light.'[60] This diplomatic politeness however was soon submerged by the difficult realities of bilateral relations. In early February, for example, Russia expelled an Israeli diplomat who was accused of espionage. Meanwhile, Israel accused Russia of stepping up its covert activities in the Jewish state, a claim that was denied by Moscow in a rather unconvincing manner: 'Russian intelligence officers do not do anything in Israel that their Israeli counterparts would not do in Russia.'[61]

With regard to Palestinian-Israeli relations, Primakov was consistent with Kozyrev's line of strongly condemning terrorism and he continued to support the negotiations between the two parties. When an Iranian-backed group executed a suicide bomb plan in early March 1996, Primakov sent a telegram to his counterpart Ehud Barak condemning the attack and others that had preceded it. Russia's response to such violence differed from that of the United States in that Washington's statements were highly interactive with Jewish emotions and sentiments at the expense of more rational responses. Russia's position, as represented by Primakov, was similar in tone and substance to most West European reactions. For example, following the suicide bomb attack in early March, Foreign Ministry spokesman Mikhail Demurin stated that Russia 'decidedly condemns the criminal, irrational acts of extremists who are fighting against the real wishes of both the Palestinian and Israeli people for peace...'.[62]

The spate of violence in the Middle East resulted in the convening of an international conference against terrorism at the Egyptian sea-side resort of Sharm al-Shaykh on 13 March. Yeltsin spoke in a language that gave much stronger support to Israel than was usual for his Foreign Ministry. He stressed the urgency of saving the peace process which for most of 1996 seemed to be close to collapse:

> How can this goal be achieved? First, all of Israel's healthy forces, the authorities led by Prime Minister Peres, should know that they enjoy not only moral but also practical support of the world

community. This should give Israel confidence that continuing the process of peaceful settlement to the conflict with the Arabs is the only path.[63]

Yeltsin's support for the government of Peres, which was facing elections at the end of May, was identical to Bill Clinton's strategy since the opposition Likud party took a far more belligerent line. However, Yeltsin was not blindly following Washington's line, though it was possible that the presence of his US counterpart could have had an influence on the tone of the speech. Moscow had supported the idea of a Middle East peace process since the Brezhnev era, but the break from the Soviet past was that the Russian president could be relied upon to play a leading and constructive role in such a conference as Sharm al-Shaykh.

In Russia, support for Israel was not as naturally forthcoming as Yeltsin's official policy. The Liberal Democratic Party leader Vladimir Zhirinovskii never had enough support to be a legitimate threat to the leadership by democratic means, but his extreme nationalist views were a manifestation of populist, if not slightly twisted, views that many Russians held. In a message to Pat Buchanan, during his bid for the leadership of the Republican party in the United States in late February, Zhirinovskii wrote: 'You describe the US Congress as an "Israeli-occupied territory". It is the same case with us in Russia. That is why in order to survive, the United States and Russia could use part of their territories to allot places for the settlement of this small but importunate tribe.'[64]

The views of Zhirinovskii never had any real bearing on Yeltsin's foreign policy towards the Middle East. Nonetheless, events in April 1996 led to some of the strongest criticisms from Moscow of the Jewish state since the collapse of the Soviet Union. The launch of Israel's military attacks on Lebanon, called Operation Grapes of Wrath, met with an immediate response from the Foreign Ministry in Moscow: 'We cannot fail now to be concerned by the fact that once again Lebanon's sovereignty has been violated and it is difficult to call the Israeli army's action an appropriate response to the actions of the extremists.'[65] In addition, Moscow demanded Israeli compliance with UN Security Council Resolution 425, which stipulated that only the withdrawal of Israeli troops from southern Lebanon would lead to the security of both countries.

A few days later, when Israeli war jets targeted civilian targets and the capital city Beirut, Russia's diplomatic language became more critical: 'It is inadmissible to resort to air strikes against an independent and sovereign state, including the residential quarters of its capital – Beirut.'[66] Anti-Israeli groups, including the communist faction of the State Duma and some sections of the Russian press, called the Jewish state the only real terrorist in the Middle East, rather than the Islamic group Hezbollah. But the Israeli attack on the United Nations base in south Lebanon, which was sheltering Shi'ite refugees, resulted in the strongest criticisms from the most senior sources of the Russian government. President Yeltsin's statement on the tragedy was without ambiguity: 'I must say with absolute certainty that what is happening in Lebanon is totally unacceptable. [...] The Israeli military operation in Lebanon must be halted immediately. One must put an end to this total infringement of the sovereignty of Lebanon, which will lead to a real humanitarian catastrophe in that country.'[67]

Primakov was dispatched to the Middle East in the hope that Moscow could genuinely prove to Israel and the world that it had a useful part to play. Cynics could have argued that the presence of the French and US foreign ministers – as well as the Iranian – during the crisis would have made Russia's absence an admission of failure in the country's policy in the region, thus it was imperative at least to make a show of playing an important role. However, in this case Primakov genuinely believed that something could have been achieved. Israeli Prime Minister Peres wanted to broker a cease-fire with Hezbollah that would protect the Jewish villages of northern Israel and Primakov sought to convince Peres that he could play an important role because of Russia's 'special' relationship with Syria and Iran, who were Hezbollah's puppet masters. Unfortunately for the Russian foreign minister, the whole affair was to back-fire, leaving Russia embarrassed and totally excluded from the eventual settlement. Both the United States and Israel made it clear that Russian interference was not helpful.

Primakov tried to claim on his return to Russia that his tour of the region in April 1996 was successful in that he met with leaders of Syria, Israel and Lebanon as well as foreign ministers from France, Italy and Iran, but he could not boast of any tangible achievements in resolving the crisis. While he joined the international community in condemning Hezbollah shelling, he added that 'only with the withdrawal of Israeli forces from Lebanese territory will it be possible to transfer full responsibility [for Hezbollah's actions] to the Lebanese and Syrian governments, whose troops are also deployed in Lebanon'.[68] Primakov's statements clearly placed the blame upon the Israelis for being the cause of instability but, reading between the lines, there was not a detectable hint of support for Hezbollah as a political group. Instead, the government in Beirut was encouraged to take responsibility for Lebanon's southern border with Israel. In addition, the reminder that Syrian troops were also deployed in Lebanon implied that Israel was not the only occupying force on Lebanese territory, a reference that would hardly have been welcomed in Damascus. President Yeltsin called upon both Israel and the pro-Iranian group 'to immediately stop fighting and find an agreement'.[69]

Primakov was offended by Israeli suggestions that his efforts in the conflict added to the chaos of an already complicated situation, and the fact that Secretary of State Christopher carried on in his diplomatic efforts during the crisis without giving Russia any significance added to the Russian Foreign Minister's sense of frustration. His counter-response to the US-Israeli attitude was defiant: 'We have our own interests there [the Middle East] and our own responsibilities. [...] We are valued as a co-chairman of the Madrid Conference. This was especially noticeable in the Arab countries.'[70] This omission of Israel's lack of appreciation of the Russian role was not accidental, but sent a deliberate message that if Tel Aviv and Washington continued to neglect Moscow's efforts in the region, then Russia had ample friends in the Arab world to make its presence felt despite them. Primakov also added a direct criticism of Washington's insensitivity to Moscow's work, saying that he found it easier to co-operate 'with France and the European Union, regrettably, more than with the USA'.[71]

The Russian media did not fail to notice the failings of their foreign minister in his mission. The Russian daily *Segodnia* pointed out that it was the United States which held all the important cards in the Middle East. Even with regard to Syria, it was reported that Peres had requested from Christopher 'his help in finding progress with Syrian President Hafez Asad regarding the peace process'.[72] The main irony of this situation was that Primakov was appointed, in part, because he supposedly had many contacts in the Arab world. He studied and spoke Arabic and his appointment to the post of foreign minister was welcomed by most Arab leaders. But despite the antagonisms with the United States and Israel, Moscow did not over-react or make extreme comments in favour of the Arabs. Domestically, Primakov did not pander to the views of the pragmatic and extreme nationalists by reverting to Soviet-style slogans of Zionist aggression and US imperialism in the Middle East. Primakov's message was consistent, as it was throughout his tenure as foreign minister, in that he wished Moscow to play a meaningful role in a settlement that would bring the Arabs and Israelis together in order to avoid the possibility that Russia would be excluded from the region altogether.

In general, Primakov's centrist views were in line with the mainstream of Russia's media and political élite, which had become increasingly convinced by 1996 that it was necessary for Russia to maintain some role in the Middle East because of geo-strategic and economic factors. Israel's importance was two-fold: economically, it was a dominant force in the region which could provide Russia with important technology in the fields of agriculture and medicine, amongst many others; politically, winning the goodwill of Tel Aviv would almost certainly have allowed Russia to play a more influential role in the Middle East and lessen Washington's strong-hold there. In addition, good Russian-Israeli relations would dampen suspicions in the West about Moscow's intentions in the Middle East, particularly among those circles which perceived Russia to be a supporter of hard-line regimes, and enhance its image as a serious and constructive player in the region. That Primakov found it difficult to reconcile these aims with Israeli and US demands that Moscow should lessen its co-operation with some of Israel's enemies such as Syria and Iran, was largely because of Russia's fruitful economic and political links with countries which happened to be enemies of Israel. But it was also because Russia, in line with most countries of the international community, genuinely found certain aspects of Israeli policy, such as the expansion of settlements on occupied land, the refusal to negotiate over the status of Jerusalem, and the bombing of civilian targets in Lebanon, morally difficult to justify. Washington's zealous support for Israel was interpreted in Russia (as in most of the world), as not being based on international law, or a sense of righteousness, but on the more direct assessment of the US national interest.

Russia's foreign policy in 1996 was crafted with the purpose of being non-antagonistic and digestible to popular opinion, perhaps to redress the failures of Kozyrev. Moscow did not want to appear to be in line with the United States and Israel simply for the sake of being pro-Western, at the expense of its national interest. Nonetheless, Primakov did not take Middle East policy to the level encouraged by extreme nationalists. There were many forces in Russia which were very antagonistic towards the state of Israel, a view epitomised by the *Pravda* correspondent Israel Shamir. His regular articles were very little different from those of the Soviet era, warning the reader of Israeli plots with US connivance to dominate the Middle East and completely isolate Russia.

One such article, entitled 'Five per cent Justice', highlighted the plight of Peter Boutros, a Palestinian Christian from the village of Ikrit in northern Galilee, whose land had been owned by his family for generations, 'but instead of feeding them, it belongs to a Jewish kibbutz. Boutros, like hundreds of his countrymen, was deprived of his land, his home, his village, because he is Christian, Palestinian Arab, and not Jewish.'[73] The article recounted the history of the village back to 1948 when the Jewish army gave the inhabitants twenty-four hours notice to leave their land. Shamir wrote that terrorism was part of Jewish military strategy, and when the Arabs left the village, 'Israeli troops blew up their homes with dynamite, surrounded the fields with fences and gave the land to Jewish settlers'.[74] In 1994 the Rabin government established a parliamentary commission, due to pressure from left-wing and Arab MPs, to examine the plight of the displaced Palestinians of Ikrit and it was decided that compensation was in order: 'Those who lived in Ikrit (and the neighbouring village of Biram) received a refund of 5 per cent of their land,' and a few were allowed to return to their village, though they were 'forbidden to work on their own land – they can only work as farm labourers or hired workers in neighbouring Jewish farms'.[75]

The significance of the writings of Shamir and others like him was not that they were political statements about the Israeli occupation of Arab lands, or the reasons behind the violence in the Middle East, but rather that they were a reflection of the Russian sense of morality, which was opposed to what were regarded as

Western materialistic tendencies and the Israeli-US interpretation of justice: might is right. Although the Soviet Union had disintegrated and the Cold War long been declared at an end, perceptions continued to exist in Russia that Moscow should uphold virtue and justice in its inner society as well as in international affairs.

Cynics argued that such views disguised the self-interest and hard political aims of certain cliques in Russia which were closely associated with the Soviet system and who feared Western influence. But such cliques, and their political methods and aims, did not exist only among the neo-communists or ultra-nationalists; they had also become increasingly associated with Yeltsin. In other words, the mainstream political parties of Russia resembled each other more than they differed in the general thrust of their foreign as well as their domestic outlook. Primakov, as head of the ministry in Smolensk Square, personified the new outlook which came into existence by 1996.

The victory of hard-liner Benyamin Netanyahu in the Israeli elections in June 1996 created tension and international concern that the region would become embroiled in conflict once more. The official response from the Russian Foreign Ministry was mildly optimistic: 'We proceed on the assumption that after the new Israeli government comes to power the development of mutually beneficial Russian-Israeli ties in various spheres will continue in the interests of the people of our countries.'[76] Yeltsin sent a telegram congratulating Netanyahu on his victory in Israel's first direct leadership elections. Unofficially, there was concern in Russia that Netanyahu was seeking confrontation and would damage the fragile peace in the Middle East. Judging by the reaction of the world's press, Russia's attitude towards Israel was not in any way unusual or extreme. In fact, the European media had shown sympathy towards the Palestinians whose future was bleak in view of Netanyahu's promise to encourage more Jewish settlers to move into their land.

Foreign Ministry officials in Moscow insisted that Netanyahu's victory did not necessarily entail worsening relations between the two countries. In one interview with an Arab paper soon after the Israeli elections, Deputy Foreign Minister Posuvaliuk spoke in a very non-committal way about Israel, saying that he did not want 'to cast a dramatic dye' upon the election of Netanyahu and the stalled peace process. He added: 'In the last months we felt a lack of importance from the Peres government in bilateral relations in one respect, but on the contrary we heard assurances and declarations from Netanyahu and his supporters that bilateral relations had been neglected in the past from the Israeli side, and that they will redress this situation upon attaining power.'[77]

Under President Jacques Chirac, France was to significantly raise its profile in the region and cause controversy by adopting an overtly pro-Arab stance. Chirac's visit to Israel in October 1996 caused a storm when he was filmed publicly arguing with Israeli security officials, sent a minister to the PLO office in Jerusalem, and called on Netanyahu to accept a Palestinian state. The tour was 'intended to demonstrate his contention that France, and more broadly, Europe, should assume a role in Middle Eastern politics in keeping with their aid to the region'.[78] Moscow's reaction to French behaviour was ostensibly supportive. According to Russian officials, their main concern was US hegemony in the Middle East; therefore the emergence of a counterbalance to Washington was welcomed. Moreover, Moscow suggested that close co-operation between Europe and Russia in the Middle East would provide a healthy balance in the conflict and help spur the stalled peace talks. However, France's actions were in many ways detrimental to Russia, not least because Paris had taken up the mantle of friend of the Arabs and the only country capable of standing up to the United States and Israel in the region. In other words, the impotence of Russian diplomacy in the Middle East was greatly magnified by the actions of Chirac.

Posuvaliuk backed Primakov's calls for a more active role for Moscow in the region. Recognising that the peace negotiations had reached a difficult stage, Posuvaliuk said that 'we intend to pursue an increasingly active policy of our own'.[79] The deputy foreign minister openly admitted that this policy was partly motivated by the need to sell arms in the region, and by other economic reasons. Posuvaliuk warned that Russia could not afford to lose its position in the region because:

> [....] as soon as we walk out of anywhere, someone is always ready to step into our shoes...in the next five years, various Middle East countries intend to buy a total of 60 to 80 billion dollars worth of arms, and it is our duty to find a niche of our own in those plans. But big arms supplies require a big-time policy...those who

order large batches of combat hardware want a lot of political strings too.[80]

Posuvaliuk refused to be drawn into taking sides in the Palestinian-Israeli negotiations, saying that Moscow would not play the part of advocate for either side. He said it was inevitable that Netanyahu would soften his hard-line stance because 'a speech for an election campaign differs from the action of a prime minister once in the seat of power'.[81] But he did suggest that Russia had its own interest in the negotiations, particularly with regard to Jerusalem. 'I would like to take this opportunity to confirm that Russia has the largest Christian Orthodox community in the world, as well as numerous Muslims, so we ask that our concern for the future of the Holy City is put under consideration.'[82]

In September 1996 there was major rioting in the West Bank following an Israeli decision to open one of the tunnels near the Al-Aqsa Mosque in Jerusalem for tourism purposes; this action was seen by the Palestinians as another scheme by their occupiers to control their national and religious affairs. This took place at a time when the situation was already tense due to Netanyahu's reneging on agreements signed by the former Israeli government and the PLO leadership. Commenting on the rioting, Demurin made a direct criticism of the Israelis. He explained that 'the fact that the Israeli authorities have unilaterally opened a tunnel near the Muslim shrine – the Al-Aqsa Mosque – provoked a spontaneous protest by the Palestinian population'.[83]

Moscow rejected Israeli efforts under Netanyahu to change the guiding principles of the peace process, and appeared to back Arab suggestions that Tel Aviv was deliberately using this argument to stall the peace process altogether. Primakov noted during his visit to the region in late October that the formula of land for peace should not be rejected only because 'in one of the countries a new government came to power'. The Russian foreign minister encouraged Israel to fulfil its international obligations and to tone down its aggressive policies against its Arab neighbours. He added, perhaps to the dismay of Israel, that Moscow would conduct its policy not only through words but also by means of actions. Primakov declared in late 1996 that 'Russia means to play a considerable and well-heard part in the orchestra' of the Middle East peace process.[84] These differences between Israel and Russia prevented relations between the two from developing beyond the reserved and frosty level which existed during 1996 and 1997.

The importance of trade relations

But in parallel with all this, the trade aspect of Israeli–Russian relations had a positive bearing for both countries. Both the Foreign Ministry and the press were pointing to the multiplying intensity of bilateral trade:[85]

RUSSIAN-ISRAELI TRADE

	1991	1992	1993	1994	1995
Trade volume in US$ millions	70	100	280	400	650

Contracts signed in 1996, including the construction of a power plant in the Negev desert, were worth $450 million alone, and overall trade was being targeted to reach $1 billion towards the end of the millennium. In the words of one article written that year, 'the Jewish state is today one of Moscow's leading trade partners in the region, leaving behind the traditional friends of the Soviet Union such as Syria…'.[86] In the light of the growing emphasis on economic relations, Moscow's relations with Israel were provided with an added dimension which was highly valued.

One significant turn of events was the visit of Natan (formerly Anatolii) Sharansky, the leading dissident in the Brezhnev era who eventually became Israel's trade and industry minister following his party's coalition with Likud. Sharansky, who spent nine years in Soviet camps, told the media in August 1991 that he had organised a special meeting at his Ministry where 'I announced that the development of economic relations with Russia should be for us now a leading priority.'[87] Sharansky said he would encourage leading Russian companies such as Gazprom, which had traditionally had strong links with Iraq and Iran, to work on Israeli projects. He added that trade between the two countries would naturally be boosted by Jewish emigrants who understood the Russian market. Sharansky's official visit to Russia was full of symbolism. His description of the turn of events in his life was that 'the circle is complete', though perhaps the analogy could be extended to the relations between the two countries, considering that Stalin was among the first leaders to recognise the state of Israel.

The ever-increasing trade between the two countries created a new dilemma in the region in that it appeared to contradict the complex and not altogether positive political and geo-strategic aspect of bilateral relations. This situation was exemplified when a military co-operation agreement was signed between Israel and Turkey in April 1996. In addition to joint aircraft training, the agreement allowed 'for access for naval vessels to each other's ports'.[88] The Israelis benefited particularly from this agreement because it allowed their pilots a much greater range of airspace training. The agreement was worrying to Moscow because it brought together two of Washington's most important allies in the Middle East in a military pact to the south-west of the CIS. Considering that at the time NATO expansion to the west of Russia was becoming an inevitability, that Saudi-Pakistani support for the Taliban in Afghanistan was destabilising the Central Asian arena, and that Washington was actively courting China, the Russian sense of encirclement was no longer based on unwarranted suspicions.

Israel's ambassador to Turkey described the two countries as being 'quite natural allies', and in March 1996 Suleyman Demirel became the first Turkish president to visit Israel.[89] The significance of these events was that they appeared to be a step towards dividing the region into two blocs: those states Washington backed, and those it wanted to isolate. Belonging to the latter category, Iran and Syria were vociferous in their criticisms of the Turkish-Israeli alliance, which was made with full US blessing. Such events led to the resumption of the image held during the Cold War era that Israel was the American wedge used to divide and conquer the region, despite Moscow's efforts not to over-dramatise the situation. Russian officials were attacking Israeli policy with growing regularity by 1996. Andrei Vdovnii, the director of the Middle East Department of the Foreign Ministry, told a leading Saudi newspaper that summer that the Arab countries had to remain calm in the face of Israel's efforts to disrupt the Middle East peace process. 'We see that the heart of the problem lies in the way the new Israeli government behaves towards the Palestinian issue, which is the basis of the problem in the Middle East.'[90]

Conclusion: between optimism and realism

In 1991 and 1992 there was genuine and well-founded optimism that Russian-Israeli relations were positively limitless in terms of co-operation and cordiality. The pro-Western radicals were dominant in Moscow's political arena and they were known for their determination to cast away the prejudices and hostility of all aspects of Soviet policy. The pro-Western radicals' desire for improved relations with the United States was closely associated with the way Moscow behaved towards one of its most important international allies. In addition, Russia's relations with hard-line regimes such as Syria and Iran were at that time negatively affected as a consequence of Gorbachev's New Thinking, the continued flow of Jewish immigrants into Israel (and the occupied territories), and Russia's general neglect of its relations with the East.

However, as Russia's relations with the West cooled, differences with Israel took on a new and larger significance. As this happened, the pro-Western radicals began losing their influence in Moscow to pragmatic pro-Westerners such as Chernomyrdin, who encouraged trade ties with Israel but was restrained in political support for Israeli actions and policies in the region which undermined the peace process. In 1993 Moscow's political élite, which included Kozyrev, was dominated by the pro-Western pragmatist position of acknowledging Washington's primary position in the Middle East but suggesting that Russia could still play a prominent role in finding a breakthrough in the Middle East peace process. Both Washington and Tel Aviv undermined Moscow's efforts to have a say in regional affairs and this led to growing criticisms in Russia from pragmatic and extreme nationalists who argued that Russia's interests were being wastefully neglected by Kozyrev and his colleagues. They also argued that Russia's neglect of traditional allies such as Iran and Iraq was costing the country billions of dollars in lost revenue.

After 1994 Russia raised its diplomatic profile in the region by improving relations with old Arab and Iranian allies, but it also persisted in seeking to improve relations with Israel, which indicated that there was not an overbearing influence of the pragmatic nationalists on the government's policy. Instead, a more centrist policy was taking shape in 1995, when Russian-Israeli relations were given a fresh impetus by Tel Aviv's encouragement of Moscow to convince the hard-line states such as Syria and

Iran to tone down their belligerent policies and statements and show support for the Israeli-Palestinian and Israeli-Jordanian peace agreements.

The appointment of Primakov in early 1996 as Foreign Minister coincided with a period of growing friction between the two countries, both of which faced leadership elections in that year. In Russia, the strong neo-communist opposition posed a serious challenge to Yeltsin, whose pro-Western policies had come under strong criticisms in the light of the growing debate about NATO expansion into Eastern Europe. In Israel, Prime Minister Peres was seen as being too much of a dove, particularly in the light of terrorist attacks by Hamas and Hezbollah, which led to calls for more stringent reactions against Israel's enemies. Operation Grapes of Wrath, launched in April 1996 against Lebanon, was intended to silence Peres' critics, but the mission was a complete failure because it did not suppress Hezbollah and at the same time the death of hundreds of innocent civilians and the destruction of homes, factories, roads and other buildings rebuilt after the twenty-year civil war led to widespread international criticism. Peres was replaced by Likud hard-liner Netanyahu, who opposed many of the concessions made to the Palestinians in the peace process. As his government reneged on various agreements with the Palestinians, and pushed forward plans to expand Jewish settlements in disputed territories, Moscow's criticisms of Tel Aviv became more frequent. However, these criticisms were not in the same vein as those emanating from pragmatic and extreme nationalists, but were more akin to the condemnation of most European capitals at the time, particularly Paris.

Thus it appeared that by 1996 Russia's policy towards Israel had reached an *impasse*, despite the growing trade links, not because Moscow had opted for a return to the anti-Israeli line of the Soviet era, but because of Israel's aggressive policies in the Middle East. There was also an acceptance by Moscow that the special relationship between Israel and the United States acted as a barrier to greater Russian involvement in the region. In the words of one leading Russian academic, 'Russia cannot be compared to the United States in terms of direct political influence in Israel.'[91] Added to this, Russian foreign policy had by 1996 defined a certain outlook on world affairs based on a domestic consensus of national interests and principles, typified by the centrist-nationalist position of Primakov. This new perspective stressed the need for the restoration of relations with traditional Arab allies, some of which were Israel's most dangerous enemies. These factors made it difficult for Moscow to create better working conditions with the Jewish state than was aimed for in the early 1990s.

NOTES

1. Bernard Reich, 'Israel in US Perspective', in Moshe Efrat and Jacob Bercovitch (eds), *Superpowers and Client States in the Middle East: The Imbalance of Influence,* London, 1991, p.72.
2. *Ibid.*, p.72.
3. *Ibid.*, p.76.
4. Yeshayahu Nir, *The Israeli-Arab Conflict in Soviet Caricatures, 1967-1973,* Tel Aviv, 1976, p.25.
5. *Ibid.*, p.96.
6. Martin Sieff, 'New Russian Anti-Semitism Worries US Jewish Leaders', *Washington Times,* 16 May 1996, p.12.
7. *Ibid.*
8. Lord Bethell, interviews with Gennadii Ziuganov and Vladimir Zhirinovskii, 'Face to Face with the Men who Threaten Yeltsin', *Evening Standard,* 3 June 1996, p.15.
9. Hannes Adomeit, 'Russia as a "Great Power"', *International Affairs,* vol.71, no.1, Jan 1995, p.35.
10. *Ibid.*
11. *Ibid.*, p.36.
12. Yitzhak Rabin, 'Prospects for Peace and Security in the Middle East', *RUSI Journal,* vol.138, no.1, February 1993, p.1.
13. Adomeit, *op. cit.*, .p.57.
14. *Ibid.*
15. Rabin, *op. cit.*, p.2.
16. *Ibid.*
17. *Ibid.*
18. Yossi Beilin, 'Peace as a Major Component in Middle Eastern Regional Security', *RUSI Journal,* vol.139, no.4, August 1994, p.8.
19. *Ibid.*
20. Tom Little, *The Middle East and North Africa – EUROPA* (40th edn.), London, 1994, p.496.
21. *Ibid.*, p.498.
22. Clyde Haberman, 'Israelis Bitter on U.S. Loan Aid', *International Herald Tribune,* 10 March 1992, p.3.
23. *BBC SWB,* ME/1290, 29 January 1992, A/1.
24. *BBC SWB,* ME/1329, 14 March 1992, A/15. Comments made on 12 March.
25. *BBC SWB,* ME/1343, 31 March 1992, p.i.
26. *BBC SWB,* ME/1624, 25 February 1993, A/4.

27. *Voice of Israel Radio* (6 January) in *BBC SWB*, ME/1580, 7 January 1993, p.i.

28. *BBC SWB*, ME/1603, 3 February 1993, A/5.

29. *Israeli Defence Forces Radio* in *SWB*, ME/1801, 20 September 1993, A/13.

30. V. Beliakov, *Pravda* (28.9.1991) in *The Soviet Union and the Middle East*, Jerusalem (The Soviet and East European Research Centre of the Hebrew University), vol.XVI, no.9, 1991, p.2.

31. Aleksei Portanskii, 'Moskva schitaet, chto Izrailiu izmeniaet chuvstvo mery' (Moscow considers Israel's sense of proportion has failed it.), *Izvestiia*, 29 July 1993, p.3.

32. *Ibid*.

33. *Itar-Tass*, Foreign Ministry statement quoted in *Central Eurasia*, FBIS-Sov-94-108, 6 June 1994, p.10.

34. *BBC SWB*, ME/1801, 20 September 1993, p.13.

35. Portanskii, *op. cit.*, p.23.

36. Iuri Glukhov, 'Uroki vsedozvolennosti' (Lessons in permissiveness), *Pravda*, no.147, 3 August 1993, p.1.

37. *Ibid*.

38. Sergei Filatov, 'Politics is a Subtle Business but One Would Like Clarity', *Pravda*, in *The Current Digest of the Post-Soviet Press*, vol XLIV, no.46, 1992, p.18.

39. *Ibid*.

40. Ben Lynfield, 'Moscow's Help Over Jerusalem Rejected', *The Times*, 27 August 1994, p.11.

41. Konstantin Eggert, 'Skromnost krasit Rossiiskuiu diplomatiiu' (Modesty adorns Russian diplomacy), *Izvestiia*, no.208 (24315), 28 October 1994, p.3.

42. Iuri Tissovsk, *Itar-Tass*, in *Central Eurasia*, FBIS-Sov-94-122, 24 June 1994, p.15.

43. Ivan Men'shikov, 'Moskva proiavliaet aktivnost' i zaiavliaet o svoei osoboi roli v regione' (Moscow displays its activity and announces its special role in the region), *Segodnia*, 12 March 1994, p.5.

44. *Ibid*.

45. I. Ivanov, *Itar-Tass* 25 April 1994, *BBC SWB* (part 1, former USSR), SU/1981, 26 April 1994, B/9.

46. *Ibid*.

47. *RFE/RL*, no.197, 17 October 1994, p.2.

48. Kozyrev interviewed by *Ostankino TV* on 1 March, *BBC SWB*, SU/1937, 5 March 1994, B/15.

49. *Voice of Israel* (Jerusalem), 3 March 1994, *BBC SWB*, SU/1939, 7 March 1994, B/9.

50. *Itar-Tass* (World Service, Moscow), 3 May 1994, *BBC SWB*, SU/1989, 5 May 1994, B/2.

51. Konstantin Kapitonov, 'Israel exchanges land for peace', *Moscow News*, 6-12 May 1994, p.3.

52. Dmitrii Sabov and Leonid Gankin interview with Israeli Deputy Foreign Minister Eli Dayan, 'Eli Dayan: The Ball is in Russia's Court' in *Moscow News*, no.75 (weekly), 29 October 1995, p.11.

53. *Ibid.*
54. *Ibid.*
55. *Interfax* (8.2.95) quoted by *Commonwealth of Independent States and the Middle East*, vol.XX, no.2-3, Jerusalem, February and March 1995, p.56.
56. *Ibid.*
57. *CIS and the Middle East*, vol.XX, no.6-7, June and July 1995, p.45.
58. 'Sovmestnoe rossiisko-izrael'skoie zaiavlenie' (Joint Russian-Israeli statement), *Diplomaticheskii vestnik*, no.8, August 1995, p.14.
59. *CIS and Middle East*, vol.XX, no.12, December 1995, p.33.
60. *Interfax*, 'Israeli Envoy: Russia's Primakov "can contribute" in Middle East', *Central Eurasia*, FBIS-Sov-96-015, 22 January 1996, p.20.
61. *Interfax* (22.2.96), *Central Eurasia*, FBIS-Sov-96-037, 23 February 1996, p.12.
62. *Interfax*, in *Central Eurasia*, FBIS-Sov-96-045, 6 March 1996, p.11.
63. *Russian Television Network*, in *Central Eurasia*, FBIS-Sov-96-051, 14 March 1996, p.9.
64. *Interfax*, *BBC SWB* (part 1, former USSR), SU/2546, 24 February 1996, B/14.
65. *Itar-Tass*, *BBC SWB* (part 1, former USSR), SU/2585, 13 April 1996, B/8.
66. *Itar-Tass*, *BBC SWB* (part 1, former USSR), SU/2589, 18 April 1996, B/18.
67. *Itar-Tass* (19.4.96), *SWB* (part 1, former USSR), SU/2591, 20 April 1996, B/8.
68. Vladimir Dunaev, 'Mirovaia diplomatiia ishchet puti vykhoda iz livanskogo krizisa' (Peace diplomacy seeks a way out from Lebanese crisis), *Segodnia*, 24 April 1996, p.8.
69. Vladimir Dunaev, 'V khode obstrela bazy OON v Livane pogibli bolee 100 bezhentsev' (More than 100 refugees killed as a result of bombing of UN base in Lebanon), *Segodnia*, 20 April 1996, p.4.
70. *Interfax* (22.4.96), *BBC SWB* (part 1, former USSR), SU/2594, 24 April 1996, B/18.
71. *Ibid.*
72. Vladimir Dunaev, 'Shimon Peres nuzhdaietsia v planirovannikh vyborakh' (Shimon Peres on need for scheduled elections), *Segodnia*, 9 February 1996, p.7.
73. Israel Shamir, 'Piat' protsentov pravosudiia' (Five per cent justice), *Pravda*, 20 March 1996, p.3.
74. *Ibid.*
75. *Ibid.*
76. *Itar-Tass* (1.6.96), *BBC SWB* (part 1, former USSR), SU/2628, June 1996, B/6.
77. Houda Al-Husseini interviewing Viktor Posuvaliuk, 'Roussiya mussamima 'ala mumarasat siyassiya nashita fi al-sharq al-awsat' (Russia insists on pursuing active peace role in the Middle East), *Al-Sharq Al-Awsat*, 5 July 1996, p.16.
78. Serge Schemann, 'Chirac and Israelis Irritated Over Visit', *New York Times*, *Middle East Clipboard*, vol.XIII, no.43, 17-23 October 1996, p.80.
79. Leonid Gankin, 'Russia-Israel: A New Partnership', *Moscow News*, 20-26 June 1996, p.5.
80. *Ibid.*

81. *Ibid.*
82. *Ibid.*
83. *Interfax*, 'Foreign Ministry voices concern over eruption of violence in Israeli–occupied territories' (26 Sept. 1996), *BBC SWB* (part 1, former USSR), SU/2729, 28 September 1996, B/16.
84. Vladimir Abarinov, 'Evgenii Primakov sokhraniaet svoi novye blizhnevostochnye initsiativy v sekrete' (Evgenii Primakov keeps his new Middle Eastern initiative secret), *Segodnia*, 30 October 1996, p.1.
85. Maksim Iusin, 'Izrail' – Nash glavnyi privoz na blizhnem vostoke' (Israel: our main importer in the Near East), *Izvestiia*, 15 February 1996, p.3.
86. *Ibid.*
87. Anton Nossik, 'Natan Sharanskii v Rossiiu poka ne sobiraetsia' (Natan Sharansky is still not prepared to visit Russia), *Segodnia*, 31 August 1996, p.4.
88. Kelley Courtier, 'Turkey, Israel Launch a Military Partnership', *Washington Post*, 16 April 1996, p.7.
89. *Ibid.*
90. Houda Husseini, interview with Andrei Vdovnii (director of the Middle East Department of the Russian Ministry of Foreign Affairs), 'Al dor al-russi wal fransi al-jadid fi al-sharq al-awsat az'aja amrika' (The new Russian-French role in the Middle East irritates the US), *Al-Sharq Al-Awsat*, 19 June 1996, p.16.
91. Personal interview with Vitalii Naumkin, deputy director at the Institute of Oriental Studies, conducted in Moscow, October 1995.

6

RUSSIA AND ISRAEL'S NEIGHBOURS:
A NEW BASIS OF RELATIONS

The improvement in ties with Israel and the general reorientation
of Russian foreign policy since the demise of the Soviet Union
appeared at times to be incompatible with Moscow's strategy of
rebuilding its relations with Israel's neighbours.[1] Syria continued
to be Israel's most bitter foe and the danger of a major military
confrontation between the two countries remained high between
1991 and 1998 because of the continued Israeli occupation of
neighbouring territories and the uncompromisingly hard line of
the leadership in Damascus. Until 1998, Moscow attempted to
develop relations with Israel's neighbours on the basis of pragmatic
and mutually beneficial bilateral relations. The challenge for Moscow was to balance this with the still unresolved Arab-Israeli
conflict. The Israeli army had been active in southern Lebanon
since the 1970s and it fortified its position there in 1982 by
creating a so-called security zone. The Golan Heights were occupied since 1967, as were parts of Jordan, while the Palestinians
were left stateless. Since the Madrid Conference in October 1991,
the peace process aimed at finding a settlement that would be
acceptable to all sides of the dispute. For Russia, which inherited
the role of co-sponsor from the Soviet Union, the occupation
of Arab territories fostered a volatile Middle East which did not
coincide with its national interests.

In the first year or so of the Yeltsin presidency the trend that
existed under Gorbachev in his last years continued: very little
involvement in the Middle East. Moscow's relations with most
Arab states at the time of the collapse of the Soviet Union were
negatively affected on a bilateral level, particularly with regard to
Syria, because of the Kremlin's overriding commitment to improving relations with the West. For many years, Syria and the
Soviet Union had the shared interest of curtailing the dominance

of US and Western-backed countries. However, Syria's involvement in the Lebanese civil war was one of the many areas of dispute with the Soviet Union. One of the main reasons for Moscow's displeasure was that from the start of the civil war in 1975 the Soviet leadership wanted the preservation of a united and sovereign Lebanon free from outside domination, be it Syrian or Israeli.

The Hashemite Kingdom of Jordan and its ruler King Hussein, long regarded as a solid Western ally, had had good working relations with the Soviet Union since well before New Thinking and Gorbachev. The British-educated King Hussein was also a shrewd political player with a talent for keeping his political and diplomatic options open. This contrasted with PLO leader Yasser Arafat, who was treated with suspicion by almost every leadership in the Middle East, ranging from Israel to Syria, from Jordan to most Lebanese groups, as well as Iran and the GCC countries. Arafat was not allowed into the United States until 1993 and his relationship with Moscow had often been tense and superficial yet, in retrospect, the Soviet Union had on occasions been the only friend that the PLO leader could turn to.

Russia's relations with these four of Israel's Arab neighbours were based on a dual approach determined by the peace process on the one hand and direct bilateral relations on the other, yet these two aspects often overlapped and influenced each other. For example, when Gorbachev allowed the speeding up of the rate of Jewish emigration from the Soviet Union to Israel, the relationship with Syria became soured because the move was seen as indirectly endorsing the growth of Jewish settlements on occupied territories and lessening the likelihood of Arab lands ever being returned.

The decline of Soviet influence

The US-led war against Iraq was decisive proof for the Arabs of Washington's leadership on the world stage, in contrast to Moscow's passivity and weakness. For Jordan and Lebanon the changing attitude was less visible because they already had strong relations with the West that were unaffected by the Soviet demise, unlike the more clearly defined transformation which affected relations with Syria and the PLO. On the whole, until Gorbachev's New

Thinking, Soviet policy in the region and its anti-Israeli stance were intended to prevent the formation of any 'pro-Western' bloc. Moscow sought to contrast its policies with Washington's statements on the issue, 'thereby locating their allies in the region on the "moral high ground" while forcing "pro-American" regimes into a defensive posture'.[2] This moral factor was a very important aspect of Soviet policy and was used to justify its support for Israel's foes. The de-ideologisation of foreign policy by Gorbachev was understood by the Arab states as meaning that the illegality of Israel's occupation ceased to be an issue worth fighting for. Upon this basis of finding a practical solution to the dispute with Israel by means of negotiations, as Gorbachev began suggesting, the Arab parties decided that it was in their greater interest to do so with US help. Arafat quickly detected the altered state of affairs and from 1988 began to move PLO policy substantially towards one that would be acceptable to Washington. He renounced terrorism and in an address to the UN General Assembly in Switzerland (the United States would not grant him a visa to go to New York) unilaterally recognised the right of Israel to exist.

The leaderships from Brezhnev to Yeltsin had all encouraged a settlement by negotiations under the guidelines set by UN Security Council Resolutions 242 and 338. But with New Thinking, Moscow changed its approach, placing Russia's policy towards Israel's neighbours within a new framework. Gorbachev also made clear a new attitude towards terrorism at the CPSU congress of February 1986: '...political assassinations, hostage taking, aircraft hijacking, explosions in streets, airports, or railway stations – this is the loathsome face of terrorism, which those inspiring it try to disguise with various kinds of cynical fabrications'.[3] This principle of total opposition to terrorism, which was sometimes ambiguous under Brezhnev, continued to be emphatically supported by Yeltsin.

Gorbachev's acceptance of the role of co-sponsor of the peace process was a symbolic gesture that the USSR was still a power, but it signalled that the two-camp world with superpowers fighting their battles through regional clients had ceased to exist.

Russia and the PLO: a friendship without commitments

As far as the PLO was concerned, New Thinking had pulled the proverbial carpet from under their feet because there was no legally-existing Palestinian state. What could the Palestinians have to offer the Soviet Union in non-ideologically based, business-like bilateral relations? Arafat managed to emerge from this dramatic transformation unharmed because he had never actually been fully dependent on the Soviet Union. Moscow was useful in countering US and Israeli efforts to undermine the PLO, but Arafat managed to strengthen his power base from the support he received from particular Arab states: Saudi Arabia until 1990, but mainly Iraq, Tunisia and Algeria.

In April 1977, almost a year after a PLO office was opened in Moscow, the first publicised meeting between Arafat and Brezhnev took place and relations seemed to have been further consolidated when in November 1978 the office was granted diplomatic status. Such gestures were recognition by Moscow that the PLO was a coherent political organisation – and not a rogue movement – that could provide significant political value in terms of prestige in the wider Arab context and as a bartering chip *vis-à-vis* the United States.

Arafat's points of friction with Moscow, until 1986, were over the existence of the state of Israel, and 'the locale of a Palestinian state (alongside or instead of Israel – either within the 1947 Partition Plan lines or the 1949-1967 borders)', and the PLO's relationship with Israel's neighbours.[4] But to the further distress of Arafat, when in 1988 he finally accepted the Soviet position, which was in essence the creation of a Palestinian state in the West Bank and the Gaza Strip, Moscow changed its standpoint under Gorbachev (and later under Yeltsin) to a settlement based on the principle of land for peace that was virtually identical to the US position. The consequence of this for Lebanon, Syria and Jordan was less drastic because only part of their land was then occupied and the extent of Israel's withdrawal from these territories in relation to security guarantees was the main issue of negotiations. Yet for the Palestinians there was a startling omission because there was no actual guarantee of statehood. Although under Yeltsin Moscow continued to be more open to the idea of Palestinian statehood when compared with Washington, Russian diplomats emphasised the need for the parties to find their own arrangement between each other.

During the first years of the post-Soviet era, Yeltsin's Middle

East policy faced opposition from his political opponents for excessive concessions to the West. They pointed out that if Yeltsin and Foreign Minister Kozyrev wished to fulfil their objective of repairing Russia's damaged relations with the Arabs, Russia ought to resume placing emphasis on the moral factor, and that there was a practical reason for doing so because it would counter US economic might, which Moscow could not hope to compete with. Russia, they suggested, needed to pursue its own set of principles and interests.

Regarding the Palestinians, Yeltsin and Kozyrev did not rapidly embrace this way of thinking. Russian participation in the Israeli-Palestinian side of the negotiations was minimal and they played no part whatsoever in the secret talks in Oslo which culminated in the Gaza-Jericho peace agreement. Moscow did not even know that they were actually taking place. With the official talks taking place in Washington, the Russian Foreign Ministry was probably provided with a general briefing on the official negotiations, and even then only sporadically. Russia had little to offer the Palestinians in the way it could other Arab states such as Syria and Jordan in terms of supplying military hardware, because there was no Palestinian army. An example of the insignificant role that Russia played in the peace talks was that a special letter of assurances had to be sent to the Palestinians from the United States to convince them to attend the Madrid Conference. The letter stated: 'The United States believes that there should be an end to the Israeli occupation which can occur only through genuine and meaningful negotiations.'[5] No letter of assurance was ever requested from the Russian side, perhaps because the Palestinians felt that it would not be worth the paper it was written on.

From his first encounters with the Soviet leadership Arafat had known that Moscow was not prepared to make huge sacrifices for the Palestinian cause. A top Arafat aide who travelled to Moscow in 1968 was quoted as having said after a long lecture by his Soviet counterparts: '"You are saying there is no way you are going to be drawn into a confrontation with the Americans for the sake of us Palestinians in particular and us Arabs in general". [...] They replied to the effect that I was understanding them perfectly.'[6] The Palestinians knew that this understanding was even more binding under Yeltsin.

One month after the collapse of the Soviet Union a round of talks was held in Moscow which by all accounts was a failure. The Syrians and Lebanese did not attend and the Palestinians were not allowed to take part because Israel refused to meet members who were residents of East Jerusalem. Sergei Filatov, commenting at the end of the round of discussions, reflected: 'It is hard to assess the Moscow meeting in a positive light. President B.N. Yeltsin didn't even pay any attention to it...'.[7] One year later, Russia's lack of diplomatic influence in the Israeli–Palestinian conflict was reconfirmed when Israel expelled 416 Palestinians to the freezing mountains of southern Lebanon, on the accusation of belonging to the militant Islamic Palestinian organisation, Hamas.

Moscow found it difficult to continue ignoring criticisms by political opponents regarding Russia's stance on the Palestinian issue. It was therefore unsurprising when Yeltsin met with PLO chairman Arafat on 19 April 1994, after the historic peace declaration of September 1993 between Israel and the Palestinians; the consequence of the meeting was a pledge by Yeltsin that his government would help create a Palestinian police force for the newly established Palestinian National Authority. While by great-power standards the offer by Moscow was modest, the Palestinians were expected to take into account the economic difficulties being faced by Russia. Moreover, the offer had great symbolic and political value: by offering help to the Palestinians Yeltsin answered his critics' questions regarding Russia's interest in the Middle East and claimed that his government was not driven by purely pragmatic factors but also by matters of principle even if they offended Israel and its Western allies. Following the summit meeting Yeltsin's office issued a statement underlining his government's broader interests by stating that 'establishing a lasting and fair peace was and remains a strategic priority for Russia in this region of vital importance'.[8]

The offer to help establish a Palestinian police force, by providing 45 DRDM-2 armoured personnel carriers and training a small group of policemen at no cost, had a more specific practical explanation. In fact, it was basically all that Russia could offer, since the Palestinians were not permitted to establish an army under the terms of the PLO-Israeli agreement. More significantly, the police force would help Arafat remain in power in the face of powerful opposition to the peace treaty from Hamas and other militant Palestinian groups. On several occasions in the past, Soviet leaders had intervened directly to save Arafat's PLO, and even his life, from Israel and Syria, particularly in Lebanon. Yeltsin's government, as far as possible, continued to support the actions of the PLO leader for similar reasons but with different motives. The Russian leadership took advantage of the PLO's lingering suspicions of US intentions to make inroads into this track of the peace process. Until September 1993, when the PLO-Israeli Declaration of Principles was signed, Arafat's criticisms of Washington's strong pro-Israeli line were highly charged. Speaking in 1993, Arafat complained that 'the denial of the Palestinian people's right to self-determination and grave violations of Palestinian human rights over decades provides us with the most striking example of double standards in the implementation of human rights'. The Palestinian leader added that 'the very clear support accorded to Israel by the USA and other states can only but encourage Israel to persist in its violation of human rights'.[9] The US response was unsurprisingly hostile to such criticism.

Russia's growing support for Arafat since the peace agreement of September 1993 was influenced by the perception that the Palestinian leader represented the moderate forces. Arafat presented himself as the leader of the democratic, secular and progressive path for his people and he made genuine efforts to fight Palestinian terrorist groups – a point which he confirmed at the White House agreement signed in October 1998 with Netanyahu. The only other alternative to Arafat was the violent and authoritarian Hamas, which had grown out of the miserable conditions of the Gaza refugee camps. It would have been difficult to envisage the democratic leadership in Moscow justifying support for them instead of the PLO. In May 1994 Kozyrev elucidated the Russian position and offered strong language in support of Arafat. He acknowledged that in the light of violent opposition to the peace process 'it must be said that this is his great contribution, his role as a brave, decisive leader. Therefore the fact that we received him in Moscow, on his visit on the eve of the signing [of the Gaza-Jericho agreement], was not simply a gesture of protocol, but was in fact an expression of support for him as the top leader.'[10] By the spring of 1994, Moscow made clear its willingness to increase its involvement in the peace process despite the domestic difficulties the new government was facing. 'We have our own worries, a lot of them. But nevertheless it cannot be said that Russia is standing aside', Kozyrev was to insist.[11] He claimed that 'it was generally acknowledged' that the visits by Arafat and Rabin to Moscow and their meetings with Boris Yeltsin 'gave a good boost to the work being carried out'.[12]

In reality, Kozyrev's claims were inaccurate because Russia had virtually no bearing on the development of the peace process, but he was correct in his assessment that the implementation of the agreement will be 'no less important a phase than the talks' leading up to it.[13] In fact, as soon as the agreement was signed there were many obstacles which threatened its legitimacy. First, the Israelis began to question, or reinterpret, certain aspects of the agreement, particularly with regard to Jericho. The Palestinian understanding of the area of Jericho was that it would be much larger than the Israeli interpretation. There were also other difficulties such as responsibility for border areas and the continued expansion of Jewish settlements which threatened to destroy the agreement before it had a chance to be implemented.

The United States continued to be the most important mediator on the Israeli–Palestinian track. But Kozyrev's extensive visit to the Middle East at the end of March 1995 suggested that Moscow had not given up on its efforts to match the United States and the shuttle diplomacy of its Secretary of State Warren Christopher. Before his departure to the area Kozyrev acknowledged that 'the Middle East peace process is facing great difficulties'.[14] But according to the Russian foreign minister this only made it more necessary for his country to become more involved in finding a solution. While Kozyrev stressed that it was Moscow's policy to co-operate more closely with Washington, he added that 'it is evident now that the efforts by one co-sponsor are not enough to add dynamism to the process'.[15]

In the spring of 1995, Russia's renewed vigour on the Palestinian–Israeli track was displayed when Kozyrev's most senior aide responsible for the Middle East, Viktor Posuvaliuk, attempted to meet with Faisal Husseini, a senior PLO official, in East Jerusalem. For Israel the issue of the status of Jerusalem was highly sensitive and a similar situation arose in March 1995 when Britain's Prime Minister John Major was forced to cancel a trip by his minister of state for foreign affairs, Douglas Hogg, to the PLO's offices in East Jerusalem because of Jewish and Israeli protests. The Russian official, however, went ahead with the planned meeting despite

Kozyrev's assurances to Israeli officials that his deputy would not do so.

The Palestinians generally received far more sympathy after 1993 with regard to the dispute over Jerusalem, when pro-Western liberals began to disappear from the Russian political stage. The press and Russian officials noted the significant political as well as religious value Jerusalem held for Christians, Muslims and Jews alike. Israeli obstinacy over the issue, refusing even to discuss the possibility of taking into consideration the perspective of Christians and Muslims, led Arafat to make strong demands in 1996 during celebrations marking the birth of Christ. A commentary in *Nezavisimaia gazeta* noted: 'The declaration of Arafat is clearly to be understood as a signal to Israelis and to all the world. Compromise is necessary!'[16]

The election of Arafat as the president of the Palestinian National Authority in January 1996 was strongly welcomed and praised by Moscow. Posuvaliuk, as deputy foreign minister, said the election of Arafat had caused 'a feeling of great satisfaction in Moscow' at the successful accomplishment of 'the first genuinely free and democratic elections in the history of Palestine'.[17] This support for the PLO and in particular Arafat had become a normal feature of Moscow's policy. Posuvaliuk described the Palestinian leader as 'a tested and long-standing friend of our country. He is one of the few who spoke favourably not only during the existence of the USSR, but also at the time of hardships for Russia.'[18] The suggestion that there was a certain continuity between the Soviet Union and Russia was in itself significant, highlighting the high esteem which Moscow had for the Palestinian leader. Posuvaliuk added:

> [Arafat] has never betrayed friendship with Russia and we have also been true to this friendship and have never stopped saying that Yassir Arafat's leadership is the embodiment of true democracy for the Palestinians. Yassir Arafat believed and believes in Russia, and we believed and believe in him. And this has been confirmed by the choice made by the people of Palestine.[19]

The references to the people and history of Palestine appeared to indicate Russian support for Palestinian statehood, a principle which was completely rejected by both Israel and the United States. Further praise was given to Arafat when in April 1996 the Palestinian National Council (the Palestinian parliament) voted to annul declarations in their charter calling for the destruction of the state of Israel. This took place at the time when the Israeli army was involved in a military offensive against Lebanon which led to many civilian casualties. According to a statement from the Russian Ministry of Foreign Affairs, 'despite this, a balanced, realistic line in support of the political course pursued by Arafat to advance the peace dialogue with Israel has prevailed at the National Council of Palestine'.[20]

The language of friendship and warmth was often reciprocated by the Palestinian leadership. Arafat often emphasised what he believed to be the special relationship that existed between the two leaderships. He consented to comment personally on this volume partly because he felt it important 'to highlight the friendship between the Russian people and the Palestinians', and when asked if there was a preference towards the neo-communists rather than Yeltsin and the democrats he interrupted with an emphatic 'no, we are friendly with all sides in Russia'.[21] This was not unusual because many of the personnel in Russia's government and political-economic élite remained in place and, if anything, progressed within the new system. Foreign Minister Primakov was a prime example of a senior official in Moscow who had long-standing ties with the Arab leadership. When asked if he preferred Primakov to his Western-oriented predecessor Kozyrev, Arafat did not mention the latter but dwelt on the relationship with his successor. 'I have known Primakov for twenty years, and he speaks Arabic fluently. And he doesn't only know me, but he is also familiar with all the Palestinian leadership.'[22] Clearly, this answer suggested that Primakov was preferred because the Middle East was less of a concern for Kozyrev, who regarded relations with the United States as the key priority. While Primakov undoubtedly placed relations with the United States at the top of Moscow's agenda, his special knowledge of the Middle East gave him the ability to act more decisively and independently from Washington, and to some extent from Yeltsin as well; something that Kozyrev failed to do in his early years in office.

Arafat was keen to show that the level of ties between the Palestinian and Russian leaderships went beyond individuals and parties, adding that 'our relations are not only with Primakov but with many others in Russia'. He pointed out that a committee was especially established to set a framework for relations between

Russia and a future Palestinian state. This committee had resulted from 'Russia's role as a co-chairman of the peace conference'.[23] But the problem of gaining anything tangible from this 'special relationship' was conceded by Arafat. When asked if Primakov had offered any specific help to the Palestinian authority the PLO leader answered: 'Not yet, you know this is still his first year [as foreign minister].'[24] Perhaps in this response there was a subtle expression of the limited ability of Russia to act decisively on behalf of the Palestinians.

But a senior Russian official interviewed in Moscow defended the Russian role and argued that it had actually become increasingly prominent since 1991. Sergei Kepechenko said that while he did not 'deny that US diplomacy was more active at some phases' of the negotiations between Palestinians and Israelis, he noted that neither power had the full capability of finding a lasting peace between the two parties.[25] He correctly noted that the 'Oslo agreement was a fruit of direct talks between the PLO and the Israeli government, concealed from both the United States and Russia'.[26] According to Kepechenko, with consideration to the view from Moscow that the Palestinian-Israeli conflict was no longer a foremost priority, Russia did not have to be present at every step of events but rather make itself available when its help was needed.

Overall, such comments served to add weight to the argument that the Palestinian issue had been relegated to a peripheral status in Russian foreign policy thinking. Even by 1998, when the centrist-nationalists had become dominant in Moscow and the pro-Western radicals were excluded from the foreign-policy élite, there was no apparent sense of urgency regarding the Palestinian issue. The deadlock in talks in late 1997 and early 1998 was widely blamed on the government of Netanyahu for failing to adhere to commitments already agreed upon between the Israeli and Palestinian sides. Yet again it was the United States that broke the deadlock. However, Moscow's position was in many instances less critical of the Likud government than many European capitals. Generally, there was strong support for Arafat – not upon the basis that he was an ally who could help to contain US influence in the region but rather because of Russia's strong endorsement of the peace process, which he had come to symbolise. Very few voices in Russia, other than some extreme nationalists, argued that Moscow should revitalise its support for the Palestinians at the expense of good relations with the United States.

Russia, Jordan and the triumph of realism

Even under Brezhnev there was never any deep animosity between Jordan and the Soviet Union, and King Hussein's official visit to Moscow in June 1976 resulted in an 'arms agreement which provided for the dispatch of a Soviet SAM system and even some Soviet advisers to Jordan'.[27] King Hussein's close relationship with the West, particularly Britain but also the United States, meant that Soviet leaders looked upon him with suspicion. But since Brezhnev there was recognition in Moscow that King Hussein's pragmatic policies and moderate stance with regard to the Arab-Israeli conflict created a positive climate for developing bilateral relations. At the same time, there was a perception in Jordan that too much reliance on the West was not in the kingdom's interest, and King Hussein skilfully followed the strategy of 'keeping your friends close and your enemies closer'. Jordan's biggest threat since the late 1960s was Syria and not Israel, with Damascus making several threats to invade the kingdom. The consequence of this was a close relationship between Jordan and Iraq, another foe of Syria. This alliance was particularly strong in the 1980s during the Iran-Iraq war, with Syria's support for Iran in the war leading to further antipathy between Amman and Damascus.

King Hussein's political survival differed from the Gulf monarchies because it was based on a measure of domestic popularity, on skilful diplomacy in terms of relations with the outside world, and on independence from the West. One such example of this was Jordan's stance in the Gulf War, in which it refused to cave in under US pressure to join the anti-Iraq coalition. For most of the 1980s, when Ronald Reagan had intensified his policies against the 'evil empire', Jordan preserved a constructive relationship with the Soviet Union.

Jordan had adopted a policy, which dated back to the late 1970s, of cultivating good relations with Moscow while things were not going well with the United States. Then, Washington had been pressurising Amman to join Egypt in signing a peace treaty with Israel but threats from Syria prevented King Hussein from doing so. However, the pro-Jewish Congress and administration in Washington did not sympathise with Jordan's predicament and arms sales to the kingdom decreased in value and quality. On 26 May 1981 King Hussein made an official visit to Moscow with the specific aim of purchasing an air defence system. In November 1981 an agreement was concluded with the Soviet Union for the purchase of twenty SAM-8 vehicle-mounted surface-to-air missile units and sixteen ZSU-244 AA gun units.[28] Jordan's request to Washington for advanced air defence equipment and jets had been flatly rejected by Congress while the Reagan administration upgraded its weapons sales supplies and support for Israel to new levels, with Alexander Haig, the secretary of state, announcing in May 1982 plans to revive strategic co-operation with Israel following a meeting with Israeli Defence Minister (the hawkish and anti-Arab) Ariel Sharon. 'The whole U.S. approach to Jordan, compared with the way it dealt with Israel caused consternation in the Arab world.'[29]

The Jordanian monarch made another trip to the Soviet Union in June 1982 to discuss the enhancement of the kingdom's air defence system and a deal was announced on 30 June, which included the purchase of SAM-8 missiles; this was concluded in 1984.[30] King Hussein attempted to ease US-Israeli concerns by assuring them that these security measures were aimed at Syria, which in 1980 massed troops on the Jordanian border and threatened to invade under the pretext that Amman had been supporting Islamic militants who had tried to overthrow the Alawite regime in Damascus. Jordan paid for the military equipment, substantially subsidised by Iraq, in hard currency. Amman made use of its diplomatic contacts to increase the chance of dialogue between Washington and Moscow mainly by openly supporting the Soviet Union's proposal for an international conference on the Middle East.

Amman was critical of Washington's failure to force an Israeli and Syrian withdrawal from Lebanon because Jordan wanted neither to become too dominant. Jordanian policy-makers also criticised Washington's increasing military support for Israel because it led to a spiralling arms race in which Moscow countered with supplies to Syria. Moreover, King Hussein criticised Washington's total support for the Israeli aim of defining the status of Jerusalem as the undisputed capital of Israel and its refusal to acknowledge the illegality of Jewish settlements on occupied territories. This, the monarch believed, made it more difficult for Arabs to make peace with Israel and jeopardised the potential role of the United States as peace-maker. King Hussein stated on 15 March 1984 that 'the US has no right to object to the presence of the Soviet Union at any new peace negotiations, but because the USSR is allied with Syria and the US with Israel, neither superpower is in a position to act as an honest broker in peace talks'.[31]

Although the differences between Jordan and Israel were not as wide-ranging or complicated as between Israel and other Arab states, and peace could have been attained much earlier, King Hussein waited until the right political moment to take this step. The fact that after 1991 the Yeltsin government continued to encourage the peace process eased Amman's international position.

In October 1992, the first visit by a high-level Russian delegation to Jordan was led by Petr Aven, the foreign economic relations minister. Aven told Jordan that the main purpose of the visit was 'to pay special attention to your question of debt, which Jordan had to the former USSR and, now to Russia as the legal successor of the USSR'.[32] Jordan had failed to keep up with all the payments for increasing Soviet arms supplies, although Moscow recognised that Jordan's record was better than other Middle Eastern countries. In fact, the Russian delegation gave high praise to the Jordanian position while openly criticising the Syrian leadership, which Aven and his colleagues had found difficult to deal with. 'The government of Jordan preferred not to complicate the talks with a protracted dispute over legal succession', one reporter noted, and 'it took little more than a day for Jordan to sign an agreement with Russia to buy back the debt accumulated in relations with the former USSR'.[33] And as if to amplify the contrast with Syria, a delegation member noted the 'exceptionally friendly tone of the talks, in which Jordan's King Hussein also took part'.[34] This did not detract from the fact that the United States remained the most valuable economic patron for Amman. Washington's ability to provide large-scale aid and reschedule debts was recognised by Moscow as a vital lever in directing the course of Middle East negotiations and strengthening bilateral ties. When in 1992 the United States 'rescheduled about $128 million of debts under an agreement' between Washington and Amman, made possible by the Agency for International Development and the Defense Department of the United States, it was viewed as but one of the many carrots that could be dangled to encourage Jordan to make peace with Israel.[35]

In late October 1992 a Russian parliamentary delegation headed by Ramazan Abdulatipov, chairman of the Council of Nationalities of the Supreme Soviet, held talks with Jordanian Prime Minister Zayed Bin Shaker. This was followed by a visit to Jordan by Chairman of the Supreme Soviet Ruslan Khasbulatov on 5 January 1993, and Lt.-Gen. Andrei Nikolaiev, first deputy chief-of-staff, who arrived in early February. Visits by Russian officials became regular and at the most senior level of government, which included Foreign Minister Kozyrev, characterising the active and positive nature of bilateral relations. Deputy Foreign Minister Viktor Posuvaliuk's visit at the end of 1994 revealed a point of friction over the Russian intervention in Chechnia. Jordan had adopted a firm position against the war and in sympathy with the Chechens, whose links with Jordan were historic. Following a meeting with Posuvaliuk, Prime Minister Abdul Salam al-Majali said he had 'clarified the Jordanian government's stance on the issue, which stresses the principle of resorting to dialogue and reason to settle controversial issues to avoid further bloodshed of innocent victims'.[36]

The Chechen community in Jordan had always been loyal to the Hashemite monarch, who in most of the Muslim world is regarded as the true protector of the holy sites of Mecca and Medina as well as Jerusalem. A chain of complicated political events led to the limitation of the influence of the Hashemite family in the Arab world after the First World War but Chechen fighters continued to be the most loyal military guards of the king. Nonetheless, in 1996 Moscow acknowledged that Jordan had toned down its support for the Chechen rebels. Sections of the Russian press, which claimed that 'Chechen fighters had been quietly receiving support from various Jordanian aid and support organisations...', acknowledged that mutual diplomatic efforts had led to reduced pro-Dudaev activity and a 'strict ban on pro-Dudaev propaganda in Jordan'.[37] The diplomatic tone of the message was indicative of the nature of Jordanian-Russian relations. The Chechen war did not lead to a deterioration in bilateral relations which were practical, business-like and non-ideological. They represented in many ways what both countries wanted from each other.

King Hussein, like Arafat, was also praised by Moscow for his active pursuit of the peace process. Following the anti-terrorism conference in Egypt in March 1996, which Yeltsin attended, offering strong support for its aims, the Russian media contrasted the positions of the different Arab countries. Syria did not attend and its Foreign Minister Faroukh Shara said that his government did not believe the conference served the interest of the Arabs. His Jordanian counterpart, Abdel Karim Kabiriti, was praised for his constructive role and support for the gathering at the Egyptian sea-side resort of Sharm al-Shaykh. Kabiriti was quoted in one report, in a comparison with the Syrian position, as saying that the 'final communiqué is extremely balanced and focused more on the problems of peace than on the fight against terrorism'.[38] This moderation by Amman was highly valued by Moscow.

Russian relations with Syria and Lebanon: the old and the new

Syria was ostensibly the most consistently pro-Soviet state in the Middle East until the mid-1980s. During that time the Soviet leadership was forced to take special account of events in Lebanon, particularly the civil war, because of the heavy involvement of Syria. Throughout the course of the conflict, Moscow had generally been critical of Syria's actions in Lebanon, but this difference of opinion did not alter the strategic alliance between the two countries. Yeltsin inherited icy relations between Damascus and Moscow from the Gorbachev era, but it did not take long for members of his government to try to revive the close relationship that existed under Brezhnev. The reasons for this had great significance because on the surface such aims contradicted the general thrust of Yeltsin's policies in the Middle East and his country's relations with the West.

Unlike the cases of Jordan and the Palestinians, Russia under Yeltsin believed that it could play a decisive role in resolving the conflict between Syria and Israel, not only regarding the Israeli occupation of the Golan Heights, but also taking into account that troops from both countries occupied Lebanon. Historically, they were the bitterest of enemies and Israelis viewed Syrians with greater suspicion than any other Arabs because the Ba'athist regime in Syria had shown itself to be brutal in the suppression of its opponents. Simultaneously, the Syrian government claimed that Israel was an expansionist Zionist state; not content with the land it already occupied, it sought to subjugate all Arabs from the Nile to the Euphrates.

The clash between Israel and Syria in Lebanon on 9 June 1982 highlighted the danger of a direct superpower involvement in the region. The battle resulted in the destruction of the Syrian SAM network in Lebanon in what was described as the largest single air battle since the Second World War, in which 'Israel downed twenty-three Syrian MiGs (by the end of the war the Israelis destroyed eighty-five Syrian planes without the loss of a single Israeli aircraft)'.[39] This clearly underlined the inferiority of Soviet weapons even if one took into account the skill factor where the Israelis also held an advantage.

From the late 1970s onwards, the Brezhnev leadership began to feel that it had little control over events in Lebanon and had decided that Syria's policy 'had entered a stage of diminishing returns'.[40] Brezhnev had taken offence, according to many observers, because Asad had falsely convinced Moscow that Syrian intervention would be short-lived, with its only objective to stabilise the situation in Lebanon. When Syrian troops intensified their assault on the leftist coalition in Lebanon and their PLO allies in mid-1976, Brezhnev sent a strongly worded letter to the Syrian leader: 'We understand neither your line of conduct nor the aims which you are pursuing in Lebanon...we are still prepared to consolidate the links of friendship between our two countries...unless Syria behaves in such a way as to cause rifts in the relations between us.'[41] Moscow's dilemma was that it wanted to support Syria in order to limit Israeli domination, but at the same time the Soviet leadership feared that Syria would interpret such support as giving a green light to military action in pursuit of its ambition of recapturing the Golan Heights and exerting full control over Lebanon.

Gorbachev's refusal to support Syria's objective of achieving strategic parity with Israel did not mean that Moscow was prepared to abandon its interests in the Middle East altogether. Arab press sources reported just before Asad's visit of spring 1990 to Moscow that the two countries were 'negotiating a secret contract to refurbish Syrian air defense systems', and that the USSR 'continued to supply SS-21s and Sukhoi 24s to Syria'.[42] Gorbachev, as Yeltsin did later, justified the sale of weapons to Syria by arguing that

Moscow had a right to sell weapons to its partners for defence purposes in the same way that the United States continued to arm Israel.

Nonetheless, since the mid-1970s Moscow had felt uneasy at the surreptitious co-operation between Damascus and Washington, with tacit US approval for some of Syria's policies in Lebanon. Washington's indirect support for Asad 'signalled not only that he was not a Soviet client but that he could be an asset to US interests in the Middle East if he were to be properly acknowledged'.[43] Syria's role in the release of Western hostages held captive in Lebanon and the fact that Syrian troops helped crush PLO forces in Lebanon in the late 1980s were not unwelcome to Washington nor Tel Aviv. Growing co-operation in relations between Syria and the United States – President Clinton, during his first term in office, met President Asad twice – was a source of concern for the Yeltsin government. Russia feared that Syrian participation in a peace deal would completely exclude Moscow from the Middle East. This scenario was not discounted since Syria had already played the role of ally to the United States in the anti-Iraqi coalition, and these factors partly explained the reason for the Russian Foreign Ministry's energetic efforts since 1993 to establish an important role in the Israeli-Syrian negotiations over the Golan Heights.

Russia's relations with Syria began badly when in October 1992 Aven travelled to Damascus as head of a delegation to discuss the question of debts that were owing to the Soviet Union. The Russian delegation described the Syrian position as 'disheartening. The very legality of holding talks on indebtedness with Russia as the USSR's legal successor was called into question.' The Syrian officials wanted to create a joint commission that would examine the legal issues relating to the Russian succession and whether Damascus owed Moscow anything at all.[44] The Russian delegation, which also included high-ranking officials from the Ministry of Finance, the Ministry of Foreign Affairs and the Ministry of Defence, met with Prime Minister Mahmoud al-Zoubi, Economic Minister Muhammad al-Imadi and Defence Minister Mustafa Tlas. The Syrians told their Russian counterparts that other former Union republics had demanded repayment of Syrian debts; 'however, the Syrian officials declined to present a single document proving that such demands have been made', the Russians claimed.[45]

The Russian delegation was clearly annoyed by the complete stubbornness of the Syrian position and took up a similarly firm position: 'Not only will the Russian government not write off any more debts or be satisfied with a lack of dependable guarantees that deliveries will henceforth be paid for promptly and in full; the Russian Federation Parliament will also reject any hint of charity in the matter.'[46]

Aven himself admitted after the meeting that 'political dialogue with Syria has been broken off for a rather lengthy period of time. As a result, negotiations on financial subjects have run into purely political problems.'[47] The Syrian leadership wanted to stifle Russian hopes of exiting from the Middle East arena after taking what it was owed. Damascus sought reassurances that Russia would continue the Soviet responsibility for refurbishing and upgrading Syria's defences. Russia refused to make such a commitment until it had received guarantees from Syria that it would be able to pay for what it had purchased in the past and what it wanted to purchase in the future.

On 2 November 1994 Kozyrev's meeting with Asad in Damascus took place in a completely different political setting. In the two years that had passed, Moscow had gradually shifted its position to the extent that it appeared as if the years between 1988-1992 had been some form of aberration. Kozyrev had on his trip commented on the necessity of 'Russia's presence in the Middle East ... to provide a balance and a counterweight' to the US-supported peace process.[48] The Syrians in turn wanted to see Russia 'reactivating' its role in the Middle East, which from their point of view would strengthen Syria's hand *vis-à-vis* the United States and Israel. Damascus had been facing mounting pressure from the United States to join the PLO and Jordan in signing a peace treaty with Israel. The agreements signed by the PLO and Jordan left Syria more isolated than ever, prompting the leadership in Damascus, which did not want to sign a treaty from a position of weakness, to see the value in reaffirming its links with Moscow.

The realisation by Moscow since 1992 that concessions to the West in the international arena would not necessarily guarantee financial aid to rescue Russia's shrinking economy served to realign Moscow's priorities. Russia's growing assertion that it should be responsible for the security of the whole of the CIS meant in effect that the Middle East would once more be across the border from Russia's most urgent security concerns. Such considerations influenced the thinking of Russia's foreign policy makers and played a part in enabling Russia and Syria to move nearer a settlement over debt repayment. In April 1994 First Deputy Prime Minister Oleg Soskovets proposed in Damascus that repayments of debts, estimated at $10 billion, could be met in part through the import of Syrian goods such as food, medicine and cotton. Damascus in turn softened its position and announced that it was determined to repay any legally outstanding debts, so opening the way for the signing of a military-technical agreement on 27 April. Syrian Defence Minister Tlas said the agreement was a 'first step' towards reviving close relations between Damascus and Moscow. He added that the agreement reflected Syria's 'privileged relations' with Russia and that Damascus had 'powerful friends' in Moscow.[49]

Moscow had become wary of US efforts to bring Syria into the fold, following two trips to Damascus in February and August 1993 by Secretary of State Warren Christopher. During the August trip Asad had vocally highlighted the value of the US role in the peace process, setting the wheels in motion for US-Russian competition with regard to resolving the Syrian-Israeli track. By the spring of 1994 these differences were barely concealed, with Moscow insisting on a more prominent role. On 14 March Kozyrev met Christopher in Vladivostok airport: 'The location represented an attempt by each side to rebuff the other: Kozyrev refused to travel to Washington to meet Christopher and Christopher refused to hold talks outside the tentative setting of the airport.'[50] Kozyrev candidly stated that 'how and in which issues should there be a close partnership, and in which should the partnership be a loose one' were matters that needed clarification and agreement from both sides.[51] In effect, Kozyrev implied that while Russia was prepared to accept a secondary role with regard to Jordan and to some extent the Palestinians, the Syrian-Israeli track was given a higher level of importance by Moscow.

On 4 May 1994 Kozyrev reaffirmed Russia's 'long-standing vital interest' in the Middle East, but he attempted to stifle Western and Israeli fears that his earlier remarks were a threat that Russia was about to act independently by saying that Moscow and Washington were 'in daily contact, we are acting in unison, in complete accord'.[52] Yet by then it had become obvious that this was not true, with US officials complaining to reporters 'about Russia's failure to consult on some issues connected with the Middle East peace process',[53] in particular, with regard to the Golan Heights negotiations.

Kozyrev was under pressure to remain vigilant with regard to Washington's aims. A group of State Duma deputies warned their government in June 1994 about US ambitions to place troops on the Golan Heights. The warning, which was reported in *Segodnia* under the headline 'Duma Deputies Rise to the Defence of the Golan Heights', reflected Russian pragmatic and extreme nationalist attitudes and perceptions.[54] According to the report, the Duma deputies had reached the conclusion that Washington's 'strategic goal of a peaceful settlement' was to 'turn the Golan Heights into a military base for the deployment of rapid reaction forces'.[55]

The deputies were in agreement with the general opinion of Middle East observers that it was Israel and not Syria which most opposed the idea because in the military sense it would limit its ability to act independently in the region, and would leave it more dependent on the United States. The deputies, who directed their message at Kozyrev and State Duma Speaker Ivan Rybkin, called for both US and Russian armed forces to be excluded from any Syrian-Israeli deal. 'In order to avert the treacherous US plans, the deputies asked the Russian Foreign Ministry to step up its influence on the process of peace settlement.'[56] In fact, the Russian Foreign Ministry had already stepped up its role on that track, but it was not as a consequence of pressure from political opponents as much as it was due to geo-strategic factors. The Syrian example reflected the Moscow leadership's predicament in balancing support for peaceful settlements to regional conflicts through co-operation with the United States on the one hand, while being more assertive in protecting its own interests on the other.

On 22 July, on the fiftieth anniversary of the establishment of diplomatic relations between Moscow and Damascus, the Russian ambassador in the Syrian capital keenly promoted the need for closer relations between the two countries. Aleksandr Zotov, in an interview in *Literaturnaia gazeta*, admitted that when he arrived in Damascus in 1989, at the height of *perestroika*, 'it was not an easy time'.[57] The ambassador also did not deny that there were differences between the two countries. He pointed out that in the past, 'if there had been no crises, there had been disagreements in the ideological sphere during that time, notably over Syrian involvement in the Lebanese civil war'.[58] However, he suggested in the interview that, under Yeltsin, the aberration of these differences was being corrected and that the two countries were working towards reactivating the traditionally close relationship between Moscow and Damascus. Zotov also defended the continuation of Russian arms sales to Syria, saying that 'thought may be given to the creation of a modern air defence system, which would be rather a stabilising factor'.[59] These comments were made at a time when radical pro-Westerners, and leaders in Israel and the United States, were arguing that increased arms sales to Syria would make the regime in Damascus less willing to compromise with Israel with regard to finding a peace settlement.

The question of debts continued to loom. Despite efforts in April 1994 by both governments to smooth over differences, the quarrel erupted into the open once more in May when *Izvestiia* reported that a high-ranking official from the Ministry of Foreign Economic Relations, Iurii Mikhailov, had refuted media claims that Russia had agreed to write off 90 per cent of Syria's debts. The report noted that Damascus wanted to write off the greater part of the $11 billion debt and defer repayment of the rest for twenty years. Mikhailov bluntly rejected the possibility and declared that 'Moscow insists on fulfilling contractual obligations under each loan with payment of the debt by 2005, at least of hard currency credits. The rest is to be paid out with goods deliveries and reinvestments in the local economy.'[60] The Russian government believed that with Syria's growing rate of oil production, economic benefits from its presence in Lebanon and financial aid from the Gulf countries, Damascus easily had the capability to repay a substantial section of the debts. Kozyrev's visit to Damascus at the end of March 1995 was yet another endeavour to resolve differences regarding the question of debts. Kozyrev asserted that 'the time has come to untie that knot and release the potential of bilateral relations'.[61] According to estimates in Moscow, this knot was worth between $7–11 billion for arms shipments alone.[62] Despite this point of contention, Kozyrev argued that co-operation between the two countries was necessary 'to prevent utter stagnation or even reversal in the process of settlement in the Middle East'.[63]

The drive to revitalise the relationship with Syria was intensified under Primakov, who received broad support for this strategy from both official and media circles. Kozyrev's neglect of bilateral relations with traditional allies such as Syria, particularly in his first years in office, meant he came under pressure not only from pragmatic and extreme nationalists but also from many moderate forces. Syria was presented as a potentially useful ally in the region and in relation to Russian national interests in general. The media revived memories of Soviet participation in construction projects which formed the infrastructure of the Syrian economy and military. In addition, during that period, 'sympathy to Damascus was underlined by the similarity of positions in fundamental political problems of the Middle East region'.[64] There was an apparent resumption of a broader realignment of interests between Syria and Russia over various issues which included the aim of preventing US domination in the region and restraining Turkish influence. However, Moscow also began to lay greater emphasis on the need to pursue economic relations with traditional partners. 'To neglect the potential of Russian-Syrian trade-economic ties and to let them go would be a serious mistake, in as much as Syria is able to play the role of "economic gateway" to Russia in the Middle East.'[65]

In 1996 there were clearer indications of Moscow's willingness to provide political support for the regime in Damascus. When asked in an Arab paper if Syria had missed its opportunity to make peace with Israel as a result of the election of Netanyahu in Israel, Deputy Foreign Minister Posuvaliuk's answer was unambiguous: 'No, I don't think Syria lost any opportunity, but President Asad worked in a clear way for the cause of peace, and he was prepared to move in this direction on the basis of land for peace. I believe that Syrian society has developed its mentality and character towards peace, and for this reason I don't believe Syria has lost any opportunity.'[66] In effect, the Russian deputy minister was saying that accusations that the Syrian leadership was stalling the peace process were incorrect and that Damascus had, on the contrary, set out to reach an agreement. The possible implication thus being that the blame for the failure of the peace process to progress lay in Israeli obstinacy.

When Primakov made his trip to Syria in 1996, there was a distinct effort to give the impression that Russia could utilise its influence in Damascus for a positive regional goal. The Russian foreign minister told reporters that 'In Damascus, I did not get the impression that the Syrians were preparing to strike Israel'.[67] This was hardly a startling revelation, but Primakov used the opportunity to announce that Moscow would not be supportive of any Syrian attack. Clearly, these were assurances intended for Israel, where he went after Syria, in an effort to raise the Russian profile on that track of the peace process. On his return to Russia, Primakov told reporters that Israeli officials 'put a very high value' on his consultations 'and for their part put forward similar assurances to Damascus'.[68]

Primakov maintained the habit of being vague on the Russian view of the Syrian role in Lebanon by calling for the withdrawal of all foreign troops from that country. The issue was a sensitive one for Damascus, which wanted to portray the military presence as a stabilising force in response to the request of the Lebanese leadership. Israel, which perceived the Syrian presence as a threat to its own security, had regularly suggested that both countries withdraw troops from Lebanon as a prerequisite to a peace deal. It was also implicitly recognised by Moscow and the West that the majority of Lebanese and the exiled opposition viewed Syria as an occupying force that used Lebanon as a bargaining chip in its negotiations with Israel.

The Syrian government responded to its sense of growing isolation after 1991 by giving more priority to Russia but it did not delude itself into thinking that it was as important as the United States in terms of finding a lasting solution in the region. In the words of a leading Russian insider on foreign policy, speaking in October 1996, 'Damascus still sees Russia as a friendly country but at the same time Asad understands that the key to the problem lies in the hands of the United States. Without the United States he cannot do anything. At the same time he is trying to use Russia as a counterbalance and source of support, especially in recent months.'[69]

In 1995 Kozyrev went to Lebanon on a widely publicised trip, where he met President Elias Hrawi and Foreign Minister Fares Bouez. Kozyrev was accompanied by a delegation of forty diplomats and businessmen, indicating that Russia was already hoping to play a part in the reconstruction of the war-ravaged economy and infrastructure.[70] Kozyrev reiterated that Moscow supported the continuation of the peace process on the basis of Resolution

425, a position very much in keeping with the policy of the Lebanese government and not wholly agreeable to Israel. Lebanon praised the visit, with Bouez noting that it was accorded 'great importance, especially as it occurs at a time when we welcome a Russian role in the peace process'.[71] Moreover, bilateral trade was encouraged, which the Lebanese foreign minister said would 'no doubt have a deep and well-founded future'.[72]

The two countries signed economic, financial and cultural agreements but Kozyrev also highlighted the political significance of the visit. He said that his aim was to 'strengthen the relations which are tied between Russia and Lebanon, which are traditional and whose roots are very old. From another perspective, we want to participate in ensuring progress on the Lebanese-Israeli track in the peace process', which he called a necessary component of a fair and comprehensive peace in the Middle East.[73] The statement fully endorsed the Syrian position that there should be a unified front in negotiations with Israel, whereas Tel Aviv would have much preferred to deal with each country separately. Kozyrev also reaffirmed the Russian position that Moscow endorsed the withdrawal of all foreign troops from Lebanese territories, which was also a reference to the 40,000-strong Syrian forces. But in 1996 a leading Russian expert with good contacts in the Foreign Ministry confirmed that 'the general view is that Lebanon is not a country which can conduct its policy independently, regardless of the Syrian factor. Unless the Syrian track is successful and the problems between Syria and Israel are solved, there would be no success on the Lebanese front.'[74]

Moscow's perception that Syria played a key role in Lebanese-Israeli negotiations was further underlined by a senior Russian Foreign Ministry official in October 1996. His comments were a substantial divergence from the Kozyrev period when Moscow endorsed any path towards a regional settlement. The Russian Foreign Ministry had by 1996 become more dismissive of Israeli suggestions that its troops would withdraw from Lebanon on condition that Syria did the same. Israeli Prime Minister Netanyahu had suggested this on the basis that Lebanon and Israel could then reach an agreement separately from Syria. Sergei Kepechenko claimed that this Israeli tactic did not have much sympathy in Moscow: 'We see such proposals as a political manoeuvre, so that the new government of Israel can escape from talks with the Syrian government and agreements with the Palestinians.'[75] Such a strikingly cynical view of the Israeli government was perhaps a reflection of the different climate that characterised the Russian Foreign Ministry in 1996 compared with the early 1990s. However, it was also necessary to place this position within the context of the harder line adopted by Israeli Prime Minister Netanyahu.

By 1995 there was a broader consensus on the need for better utilisation of Russia's traditional contacts with Israel's neighbours. The opening lines of one article entitled 'Russia, Syria and Lebanon: Half a Century of Friendship and of Fruitful Collaboration' advised: 'Don't be startled, dear reader, by this headline, which at first glance seems to promise a struggle through the pages of a journal of lectures from stale times.'[76] It enthusiastically endorsed a more active Russian policy in its relations with the two countries and reminded its readership that the history of interaction between them had been highly positive and was based on many joint interests. 'The faith on which the renewal of Russia's relations with Syria and Lebanon is founded serves as a guarantee of their effective co-operation on the path to providing a just and hopeful Middle East settlement.'[77]

With Russia moving towards a free market, Lebanon seemed a better prospect for trade and business for post-Soviet private enterprises. In the case of Syria, where the leadership in Damascus tightly controlled all imports and exports, trade agreements were almost always fixed on an inter-governmental level. But the limits of Russian economic capacity were often highlighted by the prominence Beirut attributed to the European role and the general lack of recognition afforded to Moscow's role. For example, in one interview President Hrawi, who was widely regarded as a Syrian-placed figure, commented that 'if US policy is to continue supporting Israel, contributing more than £2 billion annually to its budget, then the EU should play a more active role in assisting Lebanon'.[78] Unsurprisingly, no mention was made of Russia because its economic difficulties were known to the international community.

Kozyrev's last trip to Lebanon, in spring 1996, coincided with a period of growing violence between Hezbollah forces in the south of the country and Israeli troops. Kozyrev clearly felt that Syria held some responsibility with regard to this when he said: 'I hope the Syrians will exercise their influence in Lebanon to bring an end to the exchange of violence.'[79] By recognising Syria's key role in the Middle East, Russia could not abandon such an important regional player. In April 1996 an Israeli offensive against Lebanon caught the world's attention by the severity of its actions and its morally dubious aim of crippling the country's infrastructure, which was being rebuilt following twenty years of civil war. Israel called the offensive Operation Grapes of Wrath because it was in response to the persistent shelling of Israeli villages by Iranian-backed Hezbollah guerrillas. As the situation worsened, with the threat of Syrian involvement looming, the United States, France and Russia all sought to utilise their influence to stabilise the situation. On 16 April, after contacting Syrian Foreign Minister Faroukh Shara, Primakov said that he accepted the interpretation of events provided by Damascus: that what had taken place 'in Lebanon is unacceptable inasmuch as Israel's actions are undermining the sovereignty of the Lebanese state and are harming the civilian population and civil installations'. Primakov also contacted Israel's ambassador in Russia and informed her that the actions of the Jewish state were 'counterproductive'.[80]

On 20 April Primakov followed Christopher and the French Foreign Minister Hervé de Charette to the region. Primakov met with de Charette at the Russian Embassy in Damascus and also held a meeting with Iran's Foreign Minister Ali Akbar Velayati. The following day Primakov went to Lebanon to meet government officials while Yeltsin and Clinton were discussing the problems of the Middle East in the Kremlin. These talks, according to reports, took over thirty minutes longer than scheduled and were carried out 'in an open but sometimes rather sharp fashion', according to officials close to Clinton.[81] These events taken together could have suggested that Russia was acting from a position of strength, considering its close relations with Iran and Syria, which both had an important bearing on affairs in Lebanon. There was a brief temptation to believe that Moscow could emerge with a surprise peace deal that would upstage Washington.

In fact, the opposite happened: Russia's reputation was to some extent more damaged as a result of Operation Grapes of Wrath. The main reason for this was that the United States and Israel undertook direct measures to squeeze Russia out of any possible settlement. Christopher's behaviour during his shuttle diplomacy in the region was described as 'incomprehensible' by Yeltsin because his strategy appeared more concerned with asserting Washington's role and with finding a face-saving exit from the fighting for Israel than actually stopping the fighting itself.[82] Moscow let its dismay be known, which in itself was a reflection of the frustration that the Russian leadership felt. As Deputy Foreign Minister Igor Ivanov, elevated to the position of Foreign Minister in 1998, complained: 'Unfortunately, US representatives were not felt to be striving in a reciprocal fashion towards co-ordinated actions. It seems at present that the USA would like to some extent to monopolise its role as far as the settlement in the Near East is concerned.'[83]

The attitude of the Russian media towards the sixteen days of fighting during Operation Grapes of Wrath provided a good understanding of the political climate that existed in Moscow at the time. One of the better written features was by Mikhail Gorelik in *Novoe vremia*, entitled '16 Days of Wrath'.[84] The article provided a factual and non-emotional description of events ending on 27 April:

> Here are several figures characterising the total 16 days of military conflict, begun by the persistent shelling on Kiryat Shimona by Hezbollah's Katyushas: 127 inhabitants of northern Israel were injured, three of them seriously; around 200 peaceful Lebanese civilians perished; 50 Hezbollah guerrillas and 10 Syrian and Lebanese soldiers were killed; 1,400 homes in northern Israel were targeted.[85]

The clinical and detached approach was, at the time the article was written, becoming ever more acceptable in the Russian media. The policies of the Russian Foreign Ministry were expected to be presented in a similar vein. Yet it was also regarded as the duty of the journalist to provide an accurate explanation for human losses. So when Israeli shells hit a refugee camp in southern Lebanon, it was reported in the following way:

> The tragedy in Qana...where over 100 refugees in southern Lebanon were killed as a result of artillery shelling...[was caused by] the stationing of Hezbollah fighters in the immediate proximity of the refugee camp; the guerrillas were under intensive shelling from Tzahal divisions [Israeli forces].[86]

The controversial suggestion that Israel's actions were justified on the basis that its forces knew that Hezbollah forces were using the refugees as human shields was accompanied by the contention that Hezbollah was as ruthless as the Israelis in its attempt to achieve its military and political ends:

> It is possible to assume that Hezbollah were not too depressed upon hearing this [the death of refugees by Israeli shelling]. [...] First, the guerrillas place no value on human life (not their own, nor others) – it is better for them to use it for a greater goal; secondly, it is tactically acceptable to them to extol their victims among the international community as a principle. Thirdly, the bitterness and anger of people are directed against Israel and world opinion censures Israel. From this perspective, when there are more injuries, more crippled children, more blood, the better it is![87]

The involvement of the United States and France in the region seemed to be much more highly valued than that of Russia by all sides in the dispute, including Moscow's ostensible ally, Syria. When an international committee was established that comprised France, the United States, Syria, Lebanon and Israel to oversee a cease-fire, the most obvious absentee was Russia. During his Middle East trip, Primakov was told by Israel's Prime Minister Peres that the involvement of Moscow was complicating rather than helping the situation in the region. Russia's exclusion from the Lebanese crisis in April 1996 led Foreign Ministry officials to be more vocal in their affirmation of Moscow's continued interest in Lebanon. The set-back of being publicly snubbed by the United States and Israel, according to leading officials, did not affect Russia's policy and aims. Foreign Ministry officials explained that 'the Russian co-sponsor intends to vigorously assist the Arab-Israeli talks, which should lead to the restoration of the territorial integrity of Lebanon in accordance with Resolution 425 of the UN Security Council.' [88]

In his condemnation of Operation Grapes of Wrath, Primakov adopted the strongest anti-Israeli position since 1991, calling on the Israeli forces to withdraw from southern Lebanon. He effectively blamed the Israeli government for the instability on the Israeli-Lebanese border by suggesting that by occupying parts of their territories, Damascus and Beirut could not justify keeping so-called resistance groups such as Hezbollah under control. Primakov said that in order to achieve a breakthrough, Israel had to withdraw from Lebanese territory, 'and only after this will it be possible to place full responsibility on the Lebanese government or Syrian government which has forces in Lebanon'.[89] There was a noticeable change of emphasis in this point in that during Kozyrev's last visit he had called on Syria to use its influence in Lebanon to restrain Hezbollah. Primakov did not support the pro-Iranian group, but he was equally dismissive of Israel's justification for keeping its soldiers on Lebanese territory.

Russia's media echoed the policy of the Foreign Ministry in its emphasis on democratic ideals, the upholding of international law, and placing greater value on international institutions such as the United Nations. The United States, by contrast, clearly tilted towards the needs and concerns of Israel. More important, Washington's policy was to leave all areas of dispute fluid and open to negotiations. Thus, even UN resolutions were not accepted as binding law, but there was instead encouragement towards negotiations and allowing events to take their own course. Behind the difference in the stances between Moscow and Washington lay subtle motives. Israel, backed by the United States, had the strongest bargaining position among the negotiators and by de-emphasising the importance of international laws and institutions, it was able to use more options to achieve its objectives. Russia recognised that with the Arabs being in a militarily inferior position, international laws and UN resolutions were the best means of putting pressure on Israel.

This aspect of policy, intended to be fair and non-partisan, only succeeded in irritating all sides of the conflict. The Syrian government's interpretation of terrorism differed from that of Russia and most certainly from the view in Israel and the United States. Thus while groups such as Hezbollah were described by the Syrian regime as freedom fighters, Israel viewed them as terrorists. The leadership in Moscow generally agreed with the international consensus that such groups were terrorist because of their attacks on civilian targets. This view was often reflected in the Russian press in its criticism of Hamas and Hezbollah bombings. An interview in a Russian newspaper with Major-General Yossi Ginossar, head of the Israeli Shabak (intelligence services), on the threat of terrorist attacks was particularly sympathetic to Israel and neglected to remind readers of the Arab side of the dispute. Instead, Ginossar was quoted as saying that 'it is necessary to fight terrorism with total force'.[90] The implication of the interview was that Israel's actions were simply a reaction to Arab provocation.

Likewise, the Russian press changed its perspective in its handling of the internal affairs of Lebanon. An article in early 1996 in *Novoe vremia* provided a thorough explanation of the Lebanese civil war, with a far more even-handed perspective than was the norm in the past. The report revolved around the debate over the prolongation of the presidential term because of the still unstable situation in the country. Article 49 of the Lebanese Constitution prevented the president from remaining in his post for more than one term, but as the Russian feature pointed out, this was disregarded through a constitutional amendment under Syrian pressure because the president of Lebanon, Elias Hrawi, was generally recognised as being a puppet of Damascus. 'In October 1995 Parliament submissively prolonged the presidential term for Elias Hrawi for three years. [...] The people of Lebanon silently witnessed this...'.[91] There were none of the Soviet era clichés or propaganda blaming all of Lebanon's problems on Israel. In fact, there was equal condemnation of the roles of Syria and Iran for the country's instability, especially for their backing of Hezbollah. Damascus and Tehran were accused of undermining Lebanon's traditionally democratic culture. While 'ex-president Amin Gemayel reflects upon the "perishing of Lebanese democracy" from a long way away in America, and Michel Aoun [Lebanese army general and anti-Syrian nationalist], based in France, is appealing to his people not to lose spirit and to hope for the future', President Hrawi kow-tows to 'Syrian power'.[92] The article disputed Syrian claims that its presence in Lebanon was intended purely to maintain peace and stability in a 'friendly' neighbouring state. Despite calls from the Lebanese and the international community for Damascus to withdraw, 'the Syrian army is not abandoning Lebanon with haste... Syrians feel themselves to be at home in Lebanon. Their security service [based on the Romanian and East German models] often carried out arrests of Lebanese civilians' who appeared to question the presence of Syrian troops in their country.[93]

The article in many ways typified the transformed perspectives in Moscow with regard to Israel's neighbours; being anti-Israeli did not automatically make that country a friend of Russia. Syria could no longer act as it pleased, confident of support from Russia, because other countries in the region were equally valued. While Syria continued to be an important country in the region, the authoritarian nature of the regime made it more difficult for Russia to appear too closely associated with it. Nonetheless, Moscow could not ignore the usefulness of relations with Syria which had been developed over a period spanning decades.

Conclusion: a balanced policy

By 1998 Russian foreign policy was clearly more vocal in its desire to play a larger role in the Middle East process and in improving its relations with Israel's neighbours. During his trip to the Middle East in October 1996, Primakov continued to insist that the solution to the problems of the Middle East would not be reached by the efforts of any one power but as a result of multinational participation, working in harmony akin to an orchestra. 'We want our efforts to supplement this orchestra', so that the melody of peace can best be heard, Primakov said after his visit.[94]

Relations between Israel's neighbours and the United States had worsened by 1998 and this coincided with a more involved Russian approach to regional matters. Primakov toured the Middle East in October 1997 when he announced a twelve-point code of conduct for regional security which was interpreted as containing the most pro-Arab statements since the collapse of the Soviet Union. In December 1997 Posuvaliuk made an extensive visit to the region, meeting all the leaders of Israel's neighbours. Other than raising the profile of Russia's role, Posuvaliuk offered to mediate in negotiations to swap the remains of Israeli soldiers killed in south Lebanon for Lebanese prisoners in Israeli jails. Perhaps as an indication of the new achievements of Moscow's diplomatic leadership – somewhat at the expense of their US counterpart – Posuvaliuk was readily able to meet with the Israeli leadership, then continue on his mission for a meeting with the leader of Hezbollah Hassan Nasrallah.[95]

Washington's standing in the Arab world did not improve with Clinton's 1996 appointment of Madeleine Albright as Secretary of State. From her work as US ambassador to the United Nations, she was believed to hold anti-Arab views and was staunchly pro-Israeli, and the 'revelations' that she was of Jewish origin did not ease the concerns in Arab capitals. Albright was not the first Jewish secretary of state; Arthur Goldberg held that title in 1965 under President Lyndon Johnson, and he proved a strong supporter of the Israeli cause and was in fact active in providing vital diplomatic back-up to the Jewish state during and after the 1967 war. One leading and well-connected Arab writer, Saleem Nassar, observed that 'Arab diplomats at the UN have said that the extreme passion which Ambassador Albright showed in her defence of the Israeli position following the Qana Massacre, led to her nomination by Jewish organisations for her to be Christopher's heir in Clinton's second term'.[96] From a Western outlook, the point could be dismissed as a sign of excessive Arab paranoia, but the writer was simply expressing the perceptions that were prevalent among the political élite. Washington's actions strengthened the calls in Arab capitals for the return of Russia and Europe into the Middle East as a counterbalance to US involvement.

A bigger role for the European Union was officially encouraged by Moscow, in line with Primakov's encouragement for a multipolar world. Following the election of President Jacques Chirac in May 1995, France had taken a much more active position in the Middle East which was often not compatible with the policies of the United States and Israel. The European Union committed itself to major investments in the Arab world, including a pledge of $630 million to the Palestinian self-governing territories by the end of 1998. Such donations would invariably have led to political influence, leading some Russian commentators to note that Moscow was slightly concerned that it had a serious rival to its position in the Middle East. 'Brussels is aspiring to the niche of major friend of the Arabs. [...] It is noteworthy that the ministers of foreign affairs in Luxembourg talked about the EU's striving to be a co-sponsor of the peace process "along with the US". The other co-sponsor, Russia, wasn't even mentioned.'[97]

When Chirac paid a successful visit to the region in October 1996, Moscow must have taken note of the warm welcome he received, not only in Lebanon but also in Syria. Asad referred to him as 'my great friend, my dear friend, friend of all Syria',[98] language that was not characteristic of the astute dictator. In order to preserve its reputation as 'friend of the Arabs', Moscow was thus compelled to adopt a more critical approach to Israeli policy. Primakov skilfully played a balancing act by intensifying the tone of criticism of Israeli actions such as the building of Jewish settlements on occupied land while clearly stating Russian support for a peace deal that would fulfil all of Israel's security requirements. During his trip to the Middle East in November 1996, within days of Chirac's visit, the Russian foreign minister criticised the Israeli government for undermining agreements that had already been made and called on them to respect 'approaches that have already been agreed upon, already signed or already found'.[99] Primakov also reminded Israel and the West that Russia's role could become more prominent on the basis of its traditional ties and 'other dimensions of a great power, including the military dimension'.[100]

Syria's overwhelming reliance on Russian-built weapons for its military forces was a dominant consideration for both Damascus and Moscow. Ambassador Zotov's justification for Russia's reactivated role in building up Syrian military forces was highly worrying to Israel as well as Syria's other neighbours. In particular, both Turkey and Jordan viewed Syria with suspicion, with the former's military threats against the Ba'athist state in late 1998 highlighting this point. Therefore Moscow's actions could have appeared to raise the tension in the area. Resuming large-scale military support to Syria could also have been interpreted as tacit support for the presence of Syrian troops in Lebanon. Zotov, however, was keen to point out that Russia was not reviving the policies of the Soviet past. Consistent with the arguments of the centrist-nationalists typified by his foreign ministry chief, Primakov, Zotov contended that Russia was not taking sides in the Middle East, nor had it any interest in doing so. He reassured 'the Israelis [not] to worry about the scale of military supplies. [...] Russia understands that it is co-sponsor to the peace process in the Middle East, and peace is more important than anything else.'[101]

Russia's support for the peace process did not falter throughout the 1990s. This unambiguous strategy of promoting peace served Russian interests for various reasons. First and foremost, a large-scale eruption of violence and war would have threatened to extinguish any remaining influence Moscow had in the region and would provide the opportunity for the United States to increase its already dominant position there. Secondly, most policy makers in Moscow did not rule out the possibility that instability and the rise of extremism as a consequence of a new Arab-Israeli war could negatively affect the relationship between Russia and its new Muslim neighbours (as well as Muslims within the Federation), forcing the leadership in Moscow to direct its concerns towards increasing military expenditure, thus allowing the military establishments to become more powerful and diverting attention away from economic and democratic reforms. The leadership in Russia strongly supported King Hussein of Jordan and Arafat as leaders of the new Palestinian authority because they symbolised a new Middle East where moderation prevailed over extremism and belligerence. Moreover, King Hussein and Arafat were seen by Moscow as a bridge to co-operation with the West and integration into the world community.

The Lebanese ambassador to Moscow under Gorbachev, Mahmoud Hamoud, noted in 1996 that the Soviet Union had been consistent in its support for Lebanon by insisting on Israeli compliance with UN Resolution 425, and the same stance was adopted by the Russian leadership. Asked if Moscow could play a more meaningful role in the peace process, the ambassador responded that Lebanon

> [....] expected a bigger role from Russia, considering it is an important country on the world stage and it has a noteworthy role in the politics of the Middle East. We have noted the increasing activity of Russian officials in their visits to the region and their wish to co-operate with all sides in reaching a solution in the region.[102]

Moscow gradually succumbed to the attractions of rebuilding the damaged relationship with Damascus which centred around the possibility of arms sales, recouping the estimated $11 billion debt and forging a strategic alliance that would prevent outside powers, particularly the United States, from monopolising the region as their sphere of influence. More specifically, Syria was seen as a wedge that could split the increasing military co-operation between Turkey and Israel and prevent NATO from extending its 'security' umbrella over the Middle East.

However, the new pragmatism of Russian foreign policy did not create a dividing line of enemies and friends. Moscow cultivated its ties with all of Syria's neighbours and ensured that its support for Damascus did not cross the point whereby it would antagonise any of them too much. Primakov often reiterated the point that Russia had many options ahead of it, including the utilisation of its traditional ties as well as the cultivation of new ones, to further its national aims in the Middle East.

NOTES

1. This chapter's focus is on Arab territories occupied by Israel. Hence while Egypt is geographically a neighbour of the Jewish state, it is not included since a peace treaty had been signed between the two states in 1979.
2. Mark A. Heller, *The Dynamics of Soviet Foreign Policy in the Middle East*, Tel Aviv, 1991, p.42.
3. Galia Golan, *Gorbachev's New Thinking on Terrorism*, New York, 1990 pp.33-4.
4. Galia Golan, *Soviet Policies in the Middle East from WWII to Gorbachev*, Cambridge, 1990, p.114.
5. Madiha Rashid Al-Madfai, *Jordan, the United States and the Middle East Peace Process, 1974-1991*, Cambridge, 1993, p.241.
6. Alan Hart, *Arafat*, London, 1994, p.244.
7. Sergei Filatov, 'Zero Option', *Pravda*, 30 January 1992, p.4, in *The Current Digest of the Post-Soviet Press*, vol.XLIV, no.4, 1992, p.18.
8. *RFE/RL Daily Report*, no.75, 20 April 1994, p.1.
9. Talal Nizameddin, 'U.S. Rejects Arafat Charges of Double Standards', *UPI*, 16 June 1993.
10. *NTV* Moscow (8 May 1994), *SWB*, SU/1993, 10 May 1994, B/4.
11. *Ibid.*
12. *Interfax* (3 May 1995), *SWB*, SU/1989, 5 May 1995, B/2.
13. *Ibid.*
14. *Interfax* (28 March 1995), *SWB*, SU/2265, 30 March 1995, B/5.
15. *Ibid.*
16. Alexander Shumilin, 'Priezd v Ierusalim mozhet stat' grekhom' (Arrival in Jerusalem can become a sin), *Nezavisimaia gazeta*, 16 February 1996, p.5.
17. *Interfax* (22 January 1996), *SWB* (part 1), SU/2517, 24 January 1996, B/14.
18. *Ibid.*
19. *Ibid.*
20. *Interfax* (26 April 1996), *SWB* (part 1), SU/2598, 29 April 1996, B/14.
21. Personal interview with Palestinian President Yasser Arafat during his visit to London in early June 1996. It is worth noting that part of the reason why he agreed to give the interview was because he valued Palestinian-Russian relations so highly. His visit was only a few days after the victory of the right-wing Likud in the Israeli elections and a few weeks before the presidential elections in Russia.
22. *Ibid.*
23. *Ibid.*
24. *Ibid.*
25. Interview with Sergei Kepechenko, deputy director of Middle East Department at the Ministry of Foreign Affairs, conducted in Moscow, October 1996.
26. *Ibid.*

27. Golan, *Soviet Policies...*, *op. cit.*, p.114.
28. Al-Madfai, *op. cit.*, p.81.
29. *Ibid.*, p.81.
30. *Ibid.*, p.82.
31. *Ibid.*, p.115.
32. *SWB*, ME/1511, 14 October 1992, B/4-5. Reported from Jordan TV.
33. Sergei Parkhomenko, 'Poteria Tempa' (Losing a tempo), *Nezavisimaia gazeta*, 22 October 1992, p.4.
34. *Ibid.*
35. 'Jordan reschedules debt with U.S.', *Reuter*, Washington, 24 May 1992.
36. *Hashemite Kingdom of Jordan Radio* (25 December 1994), *SWB*, SU/2191, 3 January 1995, B/14.
37. Viktor Sokirko, 'Iordantsy bol'she ne prinimaiut ranenykh Chechentsev' (Jordan no longer taking part in Chechen crisis), *Komsomol'skaia pravda*, 16 March 1996, p.1. General Dzhokhar Dudadev led a strong Chechen Rebellion against Russian control.
38. Aleksandr Shumilin, 'Diskussii v Arabskom dome' (Debate in the Arab home), *Nezavisimaia gazeta*, 22 March 1996, p.4.
39. Golan, *Soviet Policies...*, *op. cit.*, p.127.
40. Efraim Karsh, *The Soviet Union and Syria*, London, 1988, p.34.
41. *Ibid.*, p.36.
42. Carol R. Saivetz, 'Soviet Policy in the Middle East: Gorbachev's Imprint' in Roger E Kanet, Deborah Nutter Miner, Tamara J. Resler (eds), *Soviet Foreign Policy in Transition*, Cambridge, 1992, p.205.
43. Moshe Ma'oz, *Asad: The Sphynx of Damascus*, London, 1988, p.136.
44. Sergei Parkhomenko, *op. cit.*, p.17.
45. *Ibid.*
46. *Ibid.*
47. *Ibid.*
48. *RFE/RL Daily Report*, no.209, 3 November 1994, p.1.
49. *RFE/RL Daily Report*, no.81, 28 April 1994, p.2.
50. *RFE/RL Daily Report*, no.51, 15 March 1994, p.1.
51. *Ibid.*
52. *RFE/RL Daily Report*, no.85, 4 May 1994, p.1.
53. *Ibid.*
54. Mikhail Lantsman, 'Dumtsy vstali na zashitu Golanskikh vysot' (Duma deputies rise to the defence of the Golan Heights), *Segodnia*, 21 June 1994, p.2.
55. *Ibid.*
56. *Ibid.*
57. Sergei Medvedko, 'Rossiia-Siriia: Zolotaia svad'ba' (Russia-Syria: a golden wedding), *Literaturnaia gazeta*, 27 July 1994, p.9.
58. *Ibid.*
59. *Ibid.*
60. Aleksandr Sychev, 'Moskva eshche ne reshila, poshchat' li Sirii dolgi' (Moscow still hasn't decided to remit Syrian debts), *Izvestiia*, 12 May 1994, p.3.
61. *Interfax* (30 March 1995), *SWB*, SU/2268, 3 April 1995, B/7.
62. Dmitrii Osipov, 'Political Guarantees Won't Work without Money', *Kom-*

mersant Daily (March 31, p.4) in *Current Digest of the Post-Soviet Press*, vol.XLVII, no.14, 3 May 1995, p.26.
63. *Ibid.*
64. Vladimir Grande, 'Nevostrebovannyi potentsial' (Unused potential), *Nezavisimaia gazeta*, 16 October 1996, p.4.
65. *Ibid.*
66. Houda Husseini interviewing Viktor Posuvaliuk, *Al-Hayat*, 5 July 1996, p.16.
67. Vladimir Abarinov, 'Evgenii Primakov vozvestil o razriadke napriazhennosti mezhdu Siriei i Izrailem' (Evgenii Primakov announces *détente* between Syria and Israel), *Segodnia*, 5 November 1996, p.2.
68. *Ibid.*
69. Interview with Vitaly Naumkin, deputy director of Institute of Oriental Studies, Russian Academy of Sciences, conducted in Moscow, October 1996.
70. Ibrahim Himaidi, 'koziref: al-salam al'adel wal shamel min maslahitna' (Kozyrev: a fair and comprehensive peace is in our interest), *Al-Hayat*, 1 April 1995, p.5.
71. *Ibid.*
72. *Ibid.*
73. *Ibid.*
74. Interview with Naumkin.
75. Interview with Kepechenko.
76. A. Vavilov, 'Rossiia–Siriia i Livan: polveka druzhby i plodotvornogo sotrudnichestva' (Russia, Syria and Lebanon: half a century of friendship and of fruitful collaboration'), *Aziia i Afrika Segodnia*, no.1, 1995, p.28.
77. *Ibid.*
78. Interview with President Elias Hrawi, *Observer* (Supplement), 22 December 1996, p.10.
79. Himaidi, *Al-Hayat*, 1 April 1996, *op. cit.*
80. *Interfax* (21.4.96), *SWB* (part 1), SU/2592, 22 April 1996, B/11.
81. *Ibid.*
82. *Ibid.*
83. Special article by Denis Perkin in *Itar-Tass* (23 Apr. 1996), *SWB* (part 1), 26 April 1996, B/10.
84. Mikhail Gorelik, '16 Dnei gnev' (16 days of wrath), *Novoe vremia*, no.18–19, May 1996, p.32.
85. *Ibid.*
86. *Ibid.*
87. *Ibid.*
88. *Itar-Tass* (29 Apr. 1996), *SWB* (part 1), SU/2600, 1 May 1996, B/15.
89. 'Primakof yetaleb bitatbeek alkarar 425' (Primakov demands implementation of Resolution 425), *Asharq Al-Awsat*, 23 April 1996, p.2.
90. Interview with Major-General Yossi Ginossar of Shabak, the Israeli intelligence in *Moskovskie novosti*, 4–11 February 1996, p.13.
91. Elena Suponina, 'Net mira nod kedrom' (No peace under the cedar), *Novoe vremia*, no.4, January 1996, p.27.
92. *Ibid.*

93. *Ibid.*
94. Leonid Gankin, 'Repetitsia orkestra' (Orchestra rehearsal), *Moskovskie novosti*, no.44, 3-10 November 1996, p.5.
95. *Agence France Press*, 'Russian Envoy Discusses Israel-Hezbollah Prisoner Swap', Beirut, 5 December 1997.
96. Saleem Nassar, 'Ikhtiar Olbright wa Kohen Tahmish Ameriki li qadiat al-sharq al-awsat' (Nominations of Albright and Cohen an American obstacle to the Middle East peace cause), *Al-Hayat*, 7 December 1996, p.17.
97. Konstantin Eggert, 'Den'gi rozhdaiout Vliianie' (Money creates influence), *Izvestiia*, 30 October 1996, p.3.
98. Aleksander Shumilin, 'Po sledam Shiraka ediet primakov' (Primakov follows in Chirac's footsteps), *Nezavisimaia gazeta*, 23 November 1996, p.4.
99. Abarinov, *op. cit.*, p.2.
100. *Ibid.*
101. Medvedko, *op. cit.*, p.9.
102. Interview with Lebanese ambassador to London Mahmoud Hamoud, February 1997. Hamoud was ambassador to Moscow during the period of Gorbachev's New Thinking.

7

SAUDI ARABIA AND IRAQ: RUSSIA BETWEEN NEW FRIENDS AND OLD ALLIES

Rivalry between Moscow and the Western powers for a dominant position in and around the warm waters of the Gulf dated back to the nineteenth century. Since the 1960s the USSR looked to Iraq as a bridge towards this objective. In the post-Khrushchev era, ideology had become superseded by more practical and material considerations; thus the oil factor took on a greater priority. The Gulf region was treated as a separate geographical entity from the rest of the Middle East because it had not been directly affected by the Arab-Israeli conflict. For the superpowers, a strong position in the Gulf was in effect a means of controlling a substantial share of the world's energy supplies. But the complexities of the Middle East and the unpredictability of local actors (President Saddam Hussein in this case) resulted in financial and political losses for the Soviet Union which undermined the argument for the need for involvement in the Gulf. As a consequence of the Gulf War of 1991, some estimates put Russian financial losses at $18 billion in Iraqi debts and contract losses. The UN Security Council-imposed sanctions on Iraq not only resulted in material losses for Russia; the sanctions were a blow to the Kremlin's prestige and standing since Moscow had completely failed to provide any useful backing to the co-signatory of the Treaty of Friendship and Co-operation (1972) which was regarded as a strategic ally.

By contrast, Saudi Arabia had been an important wedge used by the West to restrict Soviet influence in the Gulf. Riyadh ranked second to none in its support for Islamic militants in Afghanistan during the 1980s, and the Soviet Union was dragged into a war that became more obviously unwinnable as the conflict became more prolonged. If the Afghanistan war played an important part in the disintegration of the Soviet Union then it was Saudi oil money which fuelled that event. The vast oil resources of

Saudi Arabia and Iraq offered enormous economic prospects. Saudi Arabia was wealthier in terms of a higher oil output and per capita income but Iraq was more advanced, boasting an educated workforce, a large and professional middle class and relatively diverse and modern industrial output, making it potentially among the world's most lucrative markets. The challenge for Russia's post-Soviet leaders was to avoid being excluded from both markets, with the United States virtually monopolising the Saudi market while maintaining an international embargo against Iraq.

A positive development for Yeltsin was that his country inherited from the Gorbachev era a breakthrough with regard to relations with Saudi Arabia and its little-brother sheikhdoms of the Gulf Co-operation Council (Kuwait, United Arab Emirates, Qatar, Oman and Bahrain). For the radical and pragmatic pro-Westerners, Saudi Arabia was seen as offering much better tangible rewards than the crippled economy led by the Iraqi regime. Pragmatic and extreme nationalists believed that Iraq offered a guaranteed return to the Gulf region, because of the strong ties developed in the Soviet era. The challenge for the leadership was to find a balance between these two forces and articulate a policy that would be fruitful on both fronts.

Saudi Arabia and the USSR

The Hejaz, which holds Islam's most holy centres, was recognised by the USSR in 1924, though at the time they were actually under the rule of the Hashemite ancestors of King Hussein of Jordan. When in 1932 King Abdul Aziz of the Najd area of central Arabia annexed the Hejaz and joined it with other conquered territories to form the Saudi kingdom, Moscow was among the first to grant him recognition. In fact, these were the first such relations between the Soviet Union and an Arab country. In August 1931 King Abdul Aziz signed an agreement with Soviet officials in which, again rather ironically, the Soviet Union was to provide shipments of 100,000 crates of petrol and kerosene.[1]

In the post-Second-World-War era, relations between the two countries gradually worsened until the very last few years of the existence of the Soviet Union. The rise of Nasser's pan-Arabism in the 1950s threatened the tribal-based monarchy and Soviet support for Egypt during that period naturally placed a great strain on Saudi relations with Moscow. Egypt's involvement in the Yemen war and the establishment of a 'Marxist South Yemen (PRSY – 1967-70) with Soviet support was perceived by the Saudi rulers as a threat to their own survival. This fear was compounded by the 1963 revolution in Iraq which moved Baghdad into the Soviet camp, later to be joined by Algeria, Syria and Libya in 1969 when Qaddafi's revolution displaced the British-Italian-backed monarch there. The Saudi response was to align itself more closely to the West, but the leadership faced a dilemma with regard to the Arab-Israeli conflict. Ostensibly, Riyadh supported the Arab line of not recognising the Israeli state by providing financial funding to the PLO and Egypt in order to allay criticisms. But it also endeavoured not to be drawn into direct confrontation with Israel, nor to provide sufficient backing to the front-line states to enhance the chances of an actual Arab victory. This was because Saudi Arabia's ruling family believed that its survival would be undermined if its policies ran counter to those of the West, or if the radical Arab regimes became too powerful.

Khrushchev's attempt to improve relations with Saudi Arabia in 1964 upon the coronation of King Faisal failed because of the monarch's personal antipathy towards communism. Khrushchev harboured similar prejudice towards the Gulf's rulers. In the same year that Kuwait established relations with the Soviet Union, Khrushchev made one of his typically undiplomatic remarks: 'Kuwait! there is some little ruler sitting there... He is given bribes, he lives the life of the rich, but he trades in the riches of his people. He has never had any conscience and he will not ever have one.'[2] The Kuwaitis grudgingly endured such attitudes because they hoped relations with Moscow would serve as a further check to Iraqi designs on the emirate. With Egypt's increasing financial dependence on Saudi Arabia and the West in the 1970s, Iraq became the greatest destabilising force to the monarchies.

The assassination of King Faisal in 1975 had no positive effect for the USSR, since his successors were equally committed to driving out communist influence from the Muslim world. In the late 1970s Riyadh was confronted, however, with several dilemmas which almost led to the resumption of relations with the USSR. Fearing a hostile reaction from the Arab masses, including their own, the Saudi government went along with the Arab League position of condemning Egypt for signing a peace treaty with Israel and increased its criticisms of Tel Aviv and Washington. In effect, Saudi Arabia adopted the same position as the USSR, which joined the Arabs in condemning the treaty for the reason that it divided the Arab stance. The growing resistance by the Saudi royal élite to US pressure led to more tension in bilateral relations. Perhaps as a consequence, the Western media began to criticise the super-rich lifestyle of Saudi princes and sheikhs which included gambling, drinking and womanising while they imposed an Islamic system which was rigid even by Muslim standards. The Saudi monarchy, highly sensitive to such campaigns, felt increasingly isolated, particularly after the Soviet invasion of Afghanistan at the end of 1979. Added to this was Washington's unwillingness to provide the kingdom with modern defence systems to protect itself from its neighbours. To make matters worse, the USA furnished Israel with even more advanced weapons on a highly favourable financial basis, while Saudi Arabia was refused similar weapons at the full price.

The most important event in the Gulf in 1979 was the overthrow of the Shah and the establishment of a Shi'ite Muslim republic in Iran headed by Ayatollah Ruhollah Khomeini, who preached a distinctly radical Shi'ite brand of Islam that was anathema to the conservative Sunni Islam of the Gulf states. What particularly worried Saudi Arabia was the feeble US response to the Iranian hostage crisis which led Saudi Minister of Defence Prince Sultan to state that 'in the end, it turns out that the US is only a colossus with feet of clay'.[3] In May 1979 King Fahd underlined the shift in Saudi outlook towards Moscow: 'We are aware of the important role that the Soviet Union plays in international politics and we are anxious to ensure that this role supports the Arabs' just cause.'[4] Evgenii Primakov, then director of the Institute of Oriental Studies in the Soviet Union, was able to respond: 'Personally at present I see no insurmountable obstacles to the development of normal Saudi-Soviet relations.'[5] An agreement was signed that year between the two countries which allowed Soviet aircraft to fly to South Yemen over Saudi airspace.

The apparent thaw in Saudi-Soviet relations however was shattered in December 1979 when Soviet forces rolled into Afghanistan. Saudi Arabia was the first country to announce that it would boycott the Moscow Olympic games in 1980 and its press orchestrated a critical campaign of the Soviet action. Of course the Saudis immediately seized on the religious significance of the invasion too, pointing out that it was a battle between fellow Muslims and the atheists. But the anti-Soviet position following the Afghan invasion was a more subtle manoeuvre than the simple reasons provided. The argument from Riyadh that the communist system of the Soviet Union was incompatible with Islam did not suffice as Saudi Arabia's growing relations with China were no longer secret by the early 1980s. A better interpretation of the Saudi reaction to the Soviet invasion to Afghanistan was that Riyadh saw an opportunity to rally Arab support, repair its damaged relations with the United States and force the West to resume a greater interest in the Middle East, where Saudi Arabia was beginning to feel distinctly isolated.

Washington and its new anti-Soviet President Ronald Reagan began to see Saudi Arabia's value as an Arab ally that would check the expansion of communism in the Middle East and the rest of the Islamic world. In the early 1980s the Gulf Co-operation Council was formed and King Fahd changed his title from 'His Majesty' to the 'Custodian of the Two Holy Mosques' in 1986 to boost his Islamic credentials, and rally Arab support against the Soviet invasion, successfully bringing long-standing Soviet allies such as Iraq to criticise Moscow's action. Saudi Arabia's more assertive role was made possible by the sudden and sharp increase in oil revenue. In the 1972-3 fiscal year revenue amounted to $4 billion, rising to an all time high of $96 billion in the fiscal year 1980-1.[6] The Saudi kingdom, with a population of barely fourteen million, and sparsely developed, was essentially earning far more than it could consume. There were five-year plans to develop agriculture, its petro-chemicals industry and its financial sector, but there were still enough petro-dollars left to be used to give the kingdom a substantial say in Arab and international affairs.

While with reference to Afghanistan Moscow regarded Saudi Arabia's involvement as directly damaging to its interests, the Soviet Union did to some extent indirectly gain from the increased revenue to be found in the Middle East. Saudi 'aid' and donations were extended to Egypt, Syria, Iraq, Jordan and the PLO during the 1980s. Syria, Iraq and Jordan all purchased military hardware from the Soviet Union, effectively with the help of Saudi money. According to the Saudi monarch, aid extended to Iraq in the period 1980-8 comprised '$5.8 billion in cash grants; $9.2 billion in concessionary (long-term interest-free) loans; $6.8 billion in oil (to be repaid eventually by oil shipments from Iraq); and $3.7 billion in military equipment and other items'.[7] Saudi financial support to Iraq slowly moved the latter away from the Soviet camp and towards the West, particularly Europe. With regard to Syria, Saudi money moderated Damascus's stand in the Middle East and gave it some leverage in the Lebanese civil war. Likewise, support for the PLO ensured that the Palestinian cause would not be completely dominated by Moscow.

Gorbachev's quest to rethink Soviet foreign policy in the Middle East, and with regard to Afghanistan, had obviously to include Saudi Arabia in the equation. Abdul Aziz Muhiyaddin Khoja, Saudi ambassador in Moscow during the final Gorbachev months and the first five years of the Yeltsin presidency, had no doubts that Gorbachev's transformations were genuine: 'Under Gorbachev the Soviet Union introduced radical changes as far as its international relations are concerned. [...] Gorbachev worked for the establishment of relations with the Gulf states and especially Saudi Arabia.'[8] Riyadh, however, preferred not to respond immediately until there was a clear commitment of a Soviet withdrawal from Afghanistan. The eventual withdrawal of the Red Army from Afghanistan in 1989 led to contacts between Saudi and Soviet officials but the establishment of full relations was undertaken with caution out of fear of offending the Saudi clerics, who posed the most serious political challenge to the ruling family.

It was the Iraqi invasion of Kuwait which facilitated the rapid normalisation of relations between Saudi Arabia and the USSR. Saudi suspicions about Soviet intentions in the Gulf were effectively evaporated by Moscow's co-operation with the US-led stance in the war. Saudi Arabia needed Soviet co-operation at the Security Council, which was received and then rewarded with the promise of improved diplomatic and economic relations. Ambassador Khoja confirmed this by saying that Riyadh was able to move closer to Moscow

[....] when the Soviet Union supported the Security Council's resolutions against Iraq and maintained its neutrality during the war. Moreover, the domestic policies under Gorbachev, which aimed at achieving reforms and liberalisation, particularly the right to worship, contributed to the consolidation of Saudi-Soviet relations and the speeding up of their development.[9]

On 17 September 1990 diplomatic relations between the USSR and Saudi Arabia were officially restored. In August 1991 Saudi Arabia offered the Soviet Union an aid package worth $1.5 billion in credits as a reward for Gorbachev's stance in the Gulf War. It was primarily aimed at easing Soviet debts to Arab countries, worth about $5 billion. The establishment of full relations with the rest of the GCC states took place subsequently. This was essentially what Gorbachev had hoped would be the consequence of his New Thinking, from which relations offered tangible rewards rather than claims to ideological superiority.

Russia and Saudi Arabia: failed expectations

Yeltsin's government needed hardly any time to take advantage of the door opened to them by Gorbachev. Ambassador Khoja's view was that 'President Yeltsin continued during 1992 the policies initiated by Gorbachev and even enhanced them'.[10] Russian government officials began arriving in the Gulf that year, eagerly seeking to establish markets at a time when the fledgling capitalist economy was seemingly close to collapse. In the words of the Saudi ambassador, 'the Yeltsin administration had pinned great hopes on receiving economic aid from the Gulf states as well as encouraging their investments in the Russian economy'.[11]

In May 1992 Kozyrev embarked on a major tour of the GCC states during which he indirectly acknowledged that there was little hope of securing large financial gains from the oil-rich states. 'I didn't come here for credits. A policy oriented solely toward financial assistance is worthless.'[12] Kozyrev (as head of the Russian delegation in the Gulf) also made it clear, however, that 'our visit is part of a drive for markets, including arms markets. [...] In the past our country relied on just a handful of states in the region – Iran, Iraq, Libya etc. But that was an extremely unfortunate choice. Now we prefer to deal with stable, moderate regimes, and these are the ones with which we are trying to develop military cooperation.'[13] These comments were a telling example of the way Gorbachev's New Thinking was extended into the early phase of post-Soviet foreign policy. It was also indicative of the dominant position of the radical and pragmatic pro-Western position in the first year after the demise of the Soviet Union, particularly in that Kozyrev described the formerly close relations with Iran and Iraq as an 'unfortunate choice'. Riyadh had declared its chief interest at the time to be in aiding the development of the Muslim republics of the former USSR. Nonetheless, the Saudi leadership did not underestimate the potential dangers that could arise from antagonising Moscow, despite the dominant position of the pro-Western radicals at the time. During Kozyrev's visit in 1992, King Fahd told the visiting minister with regard to Chechnia, which was then threatening to secede: 'Tell your president that we will never interfere in the internal affairs of other states. No matter what the religious convictions of a person living in Russia are, for us he is first and foremost a citizen of the Russian federation, and he should be loyal to his motherland.'[14] Most of the Saudi aid to Muslims in the Russian Federation and other CIS states took the form of religious and cultural material and projects such as the building of mosques and schools.

In November 1994 Prime Minister Viktor Chernomyrdin made a tour of the GCC states in an effort to achieve better results than his compatriot. Agreements were made with the UAE and Oman due to what Chernomyrdin described as Russia's 'rich experience in the oil and gas industries', and he invited businessmen from the latter country to go to Russia to study opportunities for investment.[15] Russia also proposed to the UAE the offer of participating in the development of a new multi-purpose fighter plane, the Su-37, and hoped that the UAE government would be interested in purchasing Russian air defence systems and T-80 tanks. Relations with Saudi Arabia appeared to develop more slowly after 1993, particularly in financial and economic terms.

After Chernomyrdin's 1994 visit to Saudi Arabia there were efforts by Moscow to sound upbeat about the results that had been achieved. An agreement signed by the two countries on 20 November was described as a turning point in their bilateral relations by Russia's prime minister. It had been reported that Saudi Arabia agreed to grant Russia a deferment on the 'repayment of the $250 million debt incurred by the former USSR. As a result Russia will be allowed not to repay the overdue amount of $100 million', according to vice-premier Oleg Davydov.[16] He also suggested that a substantial part of the rest of the Russian debt could be repaid by arms supplies to the Saudi kingdom. This was a dubious claim because the United States would have opposed any such possibility. In fact, Russian claims were refuted by the Saudi minister of finance, who pointed out that Russia had no debts to the Saudi government but to two Saudi banks which had extended loans to the Soviet Union in 1991. Since Russia had undertaken responsibility for loans signed by the Soviet Union the Saudi banks were demanding full repayment of the total, amounting to $250 million. The Saudi finance minister said that in order to 'help the two banks in their demand, the issue was raised at a meeting with the deputy premier' on his visit to the kingdom.[17] He also added that discussions about a joint investment bank were held but only on the understanding that the Saudi government would not be party to it; rather it would be through the private sector. In effect the Saudi government was distancing itself from economic ties on the inter-governmental level, while the stake of the ruling élite in Saudi financial institutions was fairly widespread and highly influential. Political commentators in Moscow were sceptical that the visit by the Russian prime minister had achieved anything substantial. One report bluntly stated that the visit 'did not fully meet expectations, especially in the economic sphere'.[18] The fact that the visit was made by Chernomyrdin, and not the defence minister or foreign minister, revealed that the purpose of the visit was to make a break through in the economic sphere and not the military or diplomatic spheres.

There appeared to be similar rigidity in the development of bilateral diplomatic relations up to 1998. Stumbling blocks which had arisen since 1991 included the ever-improving ties between Russia and Iran. Saudi Arabia and the other GCC states feared that Iran was developing a nuclear programme which posed a direct threat to their security; and suspicions that Moscow was aiding the nuclear project led to widespread Arab concern about Russia's role in the Middle East. Ambassador Khoja deliberately noted the Saudi concern regarding Russian support to Iran. He pointed out that between 1993 and 1996 'Russia strengthened its ties with Iran, particularly in the exports of arms. Iran bought three submarines as well as armoured vehicles and anti-tank missiles.'[19] The influential Saudi diplomat also noted Russia's role in helping the Persian state build a nuclear-powered reactor for energy generation.

Saudi Arabia and Kuwait in particular were also unhappy about the more active role adopted by Russia in attempting to ease the sanctions against Iraq and the seeming support that Moscow gave to the Ba'athist government in Baghdad after the Gulf War. A commentator for *Nezavisimaia gazeta* ('Moscow's actions puzzle Arabs') pointed out that Russia's overtly pro-Iraqi position at the UN, in which 'specifically, Moscow urged the Security Council members to consider establishing a mechanism for gradually lifting the sanctions against Iraq in response to its "positive steps" to accommodate the UN',[20] had become a source of friction with Saudi Arabia. At the Damascus Declaration Summit (GCC plus Syria and Egypt) in 1994 the Saudis made it clear, in a direct response to Moscow, that it was too early to 'ease sanctions against Iraq, as Russia proposes, let alone lift them'.[21] Another political observer in Moscow, in explaining the nature of relations between Russia and Saudi Arabia with regard to the Iraq issue in the post-Soviet era, reached the conclusion that 'Russian diplomacy's subsequent steps at the UN left no doubt that present-day Moscow intends to be friends with present-day Baghdad'.[22]

Russia and Saudi Arabia had more general differences over issues concerning the Islamic world. In Chechnia, while Riyadh supported the integrity of the Russian Federation, it preferred to distance itself from the whole affair. The Saudi attitude was perhaps best summed up by Ambassador Khoja: 'The Islamic countries, including Saudi Arabia, expressed their hopes for a peaceful solution of the Chechen crisis. They stressed, however, that it was an internal issue.'[23] Likewise, Russian support for the Serbs in the war in Bosnia-Herzegovina against the Muslim-dominated Bosnian government was severely criticised by the Saudi clergy, who placed considerable pressure on their government to be more critical of Moscow. When asked if Russia's policies could be interpreted by some as being anti-Islamic, Ambassador Khoja provided the typically diplomatic response of the official Saudi position:

I do not accept that Russian policies in Chechnia or in Bosnia were anti-Islamic because it is not in the Russian interest to be against Islam. [There are] 20 million Russian Muslims spread over ten entities of the Russian Federation. [...] The Russian leadership is keen to safeguard their religious freedoms. Russia is also committed to the implementation of the Dayton peace accord in Bosnia, and is now doing its best to solve the Chechen crisis through negotiations.[24]

Russia's media also veered toward a greater understanding of the unique Saudi system during the first five years of Russian foreign policy and moved away from the Soviet simplification of branding it a feudal monarchy. The media commented regularly on Saudi affairs in a more objective and, sometimes, sympathetic way than in the past. One event that attracted the attention of the Russian press was the announcement in January 1996 by the Saudi king that he would temporarily relinquish his throne for health reasons. One Russian weekly, commenting on the ailing king, wrote: 'The government of King Fahd was an era of stability for Saudi Arabia, one of the first to give a positive influence in the whole of the Middle East.'[25] But the article also provided a sound analysis of possible problems facing the political system of the kingdom, particularly as the crown prince and potential successor to King Fahd had little popularity even within the royal court.

There were remnants from the Soviet era of a cynical attitude among some Russian commentators. One article in *Novoe vremia* assessed the Islamic punitive system in which breaking the law could result in having an arm or a nose or even your head chopped off. In particular, the report looked at punishment handed out to suspected drug smugglers. 'In the last ten years', the article informed us, 'the number of drug-traders who have been beheaded were twenty Saudi citizens, eighty-two Pakistanis, seventeen Nigerians, nine Afghans and five Syrians', as well as others from a wide range of Asian and African countries.[26] The commentary's description was of a backward and hypocritical state, where no Westerners had been executed because of fear of upsetting their governments. Moreover, the article pointed out that drug money was used in large quantities to arm the Mujahedeen during the Soviet occupation of Afghanistan. The attitude of the Russian government towards such 'non-political' issues was that of benign indifference. When Moscow had to comment on specific events, such as the bomb blast in north-east Saudi Arabia in late June 1996 which killed nineteen US servicemen, it did so firmly in support of Riyadh. 'The Russian Federation strongly condemns the terrorist act which was carried out at the US military base...'

the official statement from the government said.[27] But then even the author of the press-release could not resist an indirect reference to Washington's bid to exclude Moscow from the kingdom: 'We (the Russian government) know from experience that terrorism cannot be stopped without fair international cooperation.'[28]

The task of improving relations with Saudi Arabia fell increasingly under the responsibility of Deputy Foreign Minister Viktor Posuvaliuk. His style was to promote the impression of great strides being made, noting that 'the two sides, which originally took a negative view of each other and looked at each other with suspicion, have managed to strengthen mutual trust' since the demise of the Soviet Union.[29] Saudi Ambassador Khoja also attempted to paint a rose-tinted picture of bilateral relations by saying that 'since Russia is a major power and as it is one of the permanent members of the UN Security Council there is no doubt that its relationship with the states of the region is expected to develop and flourish'.[30]

However, despite the rhetoric there were many obstacles which prevented a tangible improvement in bilateral relations. With the relationship between Saudi Arabia and the United States appearing to be closer than ever during the early 1990s, Washington became more determined that neither Russia nor any other country should move in on its most valuable prize in the Gulf. Moreover, there was recognition from Posuvaliuk himself by 1995 that relations with the Saudi kingdom were not as flourishing as he had hoped they would be. Writing in a Saudi-financed Arab daily, Posuvaliuk reflected on his visit to the Arab Gulf countries in early 1995. He noted the desire in Moscow 'to move away from declarations and promises towards the practical implementation of the trade-economic and military-technological fields'.[31] While Russia was happy with the progress being made with the smaller GCC countries, Posuvaliuk suggested that more could have been achieved with Saudi Arabia, which 'occupies a special place in which the exchange of political views carries a weighty position' in Moscow.[32] In particular, Russia was concerned about Saudi Arabia's role in the Islamic world, and its potential influence in Central Asia and the Caucasus. The deputy foreign minister sought to refute charges that Russia's policies were anti-Islamic by claiming to have a 'deep respect for Islam' and added that 'Orthodoxy and Islam co-exist in brotherly alliance within the Russian family'.[33] That

Posuvaliuk dedicated most of his article regarding his trip to Saudi Arabia to the rise of Islamic extremism in the CIS and to insist that there was no hostility between Russia and Saudi Arabia in itself revealed a deficiency in deep and flourishing bilateral ties.

In 1996 there was a noticeable freeze in Saudi–Russian relations, with Moscow expressing particular disappointment at the lack of progress in the trade-economic aspect of bilateral ties. In 1995 the volume of trade did not far exceed $50 million, a very small sum considering the size and wealth of the two national economies.[34] A leading Russian adviser to the Foreign Ministry sounded distinctly pessimistic in his assessment of bilateral relations during an interview in Moscow in late 1996: 'Nothing turned out with our relations with Saudi Arabia. The Saudis were not interested in developing relations, they are quite comfortable with the United States. [...] They don't see in Russia any kind of important player.'[35] Senior officials from the Foreign Ministry were equally downbeat. While saying that the existence of dialogue and diplomatic relations between the two countries was better than nothing, one such official reflected that 'it seems the break between us was too long and its impact was strong. We need to be patient.'[36] The narrowing of the Saudi avenue had arguably convinced Moscow that it should concentrate on another long-established partner, Iraq, for access to the Gulf.

Writing for *Al-Hayat* in April 1997, Posuvaliuk attempted to highlight some positive features of bilateral relations, following his meeting with the new Saudi ambassador in Moscow, Fawzi Shabokshi. But he was again forced to admit that 'some aspects of relations have not fulfilled earlier expectations'.[37] For the first time, it was openly admitted that despite earlier rhetoric, 'we must say frankly that events in Chechnia were part of the reason for the delay. Now that there is peace we can say that we understand the feelings of Muslims outside but that cannot detract from our firm need for the principle of the unity of the Russian Federation.'[38] The deputy foreign minister also bluntly pointed out that 'the exchange in trade between us remains a drop in the ocean'.[39]

Radical and pragmatic pro-Westerners had hoped, until 1993, that Saudi Arabia would be a good example of a new friendship which would provide tangible financial rewards for a democratic Russia. They believed, perhaps rather naïvely, that a new democratic Russia would be accepted by Saudi Arabia as part of the Western world and that the United States would encourage Moscow's participation in Gulf security. In fact, Washington made it clear to its Saudi client state (and Moscow) that Russian entry into the region was not welcome. Moreover, regional security issues such as the Iranian-Russian and the Iraqi-Russian relationships, and wider Islamic issues such as the Chechen war, all prevented the successful development of bilateral relations.

Iraq: an old friend with many enemies

The starting point in relations between the Soviet Union and Iraq was July 1958 when a military coup overthrew the Western-backed monarchy in Baghdad. After the Iraqi revolution Moscow provided Iraq with large-scale economic and military aid, similar to the way it had done with Egypt and Syria earlier. The Ba'athist regime of Hassan al-Bakr which took power in July 1968 attempted to heal many of the differences with Moscow that had surfaced in the preceding period, by signing a long-term oil agreement in 1969. The Soviet Union was to be repaid for its role in Iraqi oil field development with Iraqi crude oil. On 13 August 1970 a trade and economic agreement was signed between Iraq and the USSR which granted a $34 million loan to Iraq as part of the deal. The flourishing relationship led to over sixteen agreements being signed by mid-1971 between Iraq and the Soviet Union, which spanned the military, economic, technological and cultural fields. The culmination of this rapidly developing relationship was the signing of the Treaty of Friendship and Co-operation in April 1972. This coincided with the growing domination of Saddam Hussein within the Ba'ath Party and in Iraq. At the same time Moscow recognised that President Hussein was a political opportunist who was not prepared to share power with anyone else, including the Iraqi Communist Party (ICP).

Government persecution of Iraqi communists threatened to cause serious damage to relations between Baghdad and Moscow, particularly as there were rumours that KGB agents were behind attempts to create cells in the Iraqi army with the intention of overthrowing the Ba'athist regime. Hussein's antipathy towards communists was apparent in the statements he made, in which he described them as a 'rotten, atheistic, yellow storm which has plagued Iraq'.[40] The Soviet media saw other reasons for the anti-

Communist Party actions by the Ba'ath leadership. 'It may well be that Moscow saw more than just a domestic problem in Iraq's persecution of the ICP... Iraq, in leading the opposition to the Egyptian-Israeli treaty, was seeking to project itself as the leader of the Arab world.'[41] At that time Baghdad improved relations with its historic foe Syria and the PLO and, more important, it was clearly seeking to improve relations with Saudi Arabia. Therefore, the anti-communist propaganda campaign by Baghdad was intended to show Riyadh and other Arab capitals that Iraq was not a Soviet client state but an independent actor. The Treaty of Friendship signed by Baghdad in 1972 was in effect the limit of Baghdad's willingness to co-operate with the USSR.

On 29 May 1976 Prime Minister Kosygin went to Iraq to discuss the possibility of further harmonising relations between the two countries. His failure to secure changes in Iraq's policies which were more favourable to Moscow were only balanced by the realisation that there was no better alternative for Moscow. The most the Baghdad regime would concede to the USSR in the military sphere was 'the use of some Soviet-built bases or other facilities under Iraqi control and supervision'.[42] There were also many reports of the arrest and dismissal of Iraqi officers who opposed their president's policy of diversifying weapons purchases to avoid complete dependence on the Soviet Union.

But the arms trade remained the most significant aspect of bilateral ties between Iraq and the Soviet Union. In October 1976 the USSR promised to deliver $300 million worth of T-62 tanks and additional Scud missiles. In 1977 the Soviet Union announced it would supply Il-76 long-range military transport planes and upgrade its air force by sending more MiG-21s and MiG-23s, and in 1979, before the outbreak of the Iran-Iraq war, the USSR supplied Baghdad with MI-8 helicopters, MiG-23 and MiG-27 fighters, and MiG-25 fighter-reconnaissance aircraft. For Iraqi ground forces, SP-73 and SP-74 self-propelled howitzers were purchased.[43] The fact that Iraq, unlike Syria or South Yemen, could purchase such weaponry with hard currency made it a valuable market for the Soviet Union. Between 1964 and 1973 Iraq ranked fifth in the world behind Egypt, North Vietnam, India and Syria as a customer for Soviet arms supplies. However, between 1974 and 1978 Iraq moved into first place, not just in the Middle East, but in the world.[44]

Yet there is a more telling set of statistics which display the nature of Soviet-Iraqi relations in a different light. The percentage share of Soviet weapons bought by Iraq was to decrease as Baghdad looked increasingly to Western sources. 'Between 1964 and 1973, the USSR and its satellites supplied 90 per cent of Iraq's arms imports. The corresponding figure for 1974 through 1978 was 70 per cent, and the downward trend continued in 1979 and 1980.'[45]

IRAQI ARMS PURCHASES

(actual cash value in US$ millions)

	1964-73	1974-8
USSR (plus Czechoslovakia and Poland)	$843	$3,720
Total	$874	$5,300

The payments for arms that make up the latter total in the above table, other than a $10 million deal with China, went to Western suppliers and Yugoslavia. 'Of this amount $430 million went to France, $150 million to West Germany, $70 million to Italy', as well as deals struck with Brazil, Switzerland and Spain.[46] By the close of the 1970s France emerged as Iraq's second largest arms supplier, illustrating Iraqi diversification of sources for its military plans.

Perhaps the most enduring and complicated issue that all the Baghdad governments had to face had been the Kurdish question. The Soviet position on this issue had generally been sympathetic to the Kurds, which was a permanent source of friction in Iraqi-Soviet relations. Of Iraq, Syria, Iran and Turkey, only the first had officially recognised its Kurdish minority, roughly one fifth of the total population according to most estimates. The Kurds in Iraq were divided into two main strands and dominated by the leftist Jalal Talabani and the conservative tribal leader Mustafa Barazani, later succeeded by his son Massoud. The Soviet position in the 1960s was rather ironically supportive of the latter rather than the left-wing forces of Talabani.

In 1970 Barazani did come to an agreement with Baghdad in which the ruling Ba'ath allowed five Kurdish ministers to participate in government, released all Kurdish political prisoners, ceased all military operations against them, and introduced an economic plan to develop the areas of northern Iraq. This consensus was short-lived as by the mid-1970s hostilities resumed between the two parties. There were two main reasons for this and both were linked to Iran. First Barazani was promised that he could nominate a vice-president from his party (KDP), but his choice was turned down by Hussein because the nominee, the party's general secretary, was seen as being too closely associated with Iran. Secondly, friction increased between the two as Barazani's group began 'importing' Iranian Kurds, up to 100,000, according to Baghdad, into northern Iraqi cities, particularly Kirkuk which was a city of mixed ethnicity that was not recognised as part of Iraqi Kurdistan. This was part of Barazani's effort to take advantage of a promised census which would determine the limits of the Kurdish areas. As a result, there was growing strain on the Accords of 1970. *Pravda* correspondent E. Primakov (reflecting the official position) and other Soviet commentators were critical of Barazani's actions and expressed sympathy with the Ba'athist position. This trend continued so that by the 1990s, Moscow's position was that of fair arbitrator between Baghdad and the Kurds.

When Gorbachev came to power in 1985 Moscow was facing a major dilemma with regard to Iraq. Since 1980 Iran and Iraq had been fighting a bloody and costly war in which neither side appeared close to winning. In the early part of the war Moscow seemed to waver in favour of Iran, but when the Khomeini regime made it clear that it saw no distinction between the Western 'infidels' and the Communist 'infidels' then the Soviet leadership reverted to its support for Baghdad. Despite the increase in the number of Soviet military specialists in Iraq in the 1980s, from 1,300 in 1967 to 5,000 in 1990, Moscow could not prevent the Iraqi leadership from seeking military and economic support from the West. Nonetheless, Moscow continued to support Iraq up until 1990 for the reason that it had no other alternative in the Gulf and the Middle East in general. Syria and Libya were the only two Arab countries which sided with Iran in the Iran-Iraq war and, not uncoincidently, their relationship with the Soviet Union deteriorated in the late 1980s. With Iraq claiming victory over the much larger Iran in .1988, Saddam Hussein was hailed by most Arabs as a heroic figure defending their Arabhood. This leading role in the Arab world made him a valuable asset for Moscow.

In the light of this, many were surprised at the Soviet reaction to the Iraqi invasion of Kuwait in August 1990. Despite the New Thinking, 'accepting the deployment of American troops in Saudi Arabia went against the grain of all earlier Soviet policy in the region – to keep the Americans out'.[47] This was a particularly delicate situation considering the proximity of the region to Soviet borders. Yet under the banner of New Thinking there was a different interpretation to this event: that a new era of superpower co-operation had dawned, where the rule of international law and the quest for peace and stability would overshadow Cold War alliances. Gorbachev's position did improve the Soviet image in the West and, more important for him, it added to the credibility of his policies for Western leaders, though ultimately this was not enough to save his political life. The most relevant help the USSR provided was its support at the United Nations.

But Gorbachev's position led to substantial financial and economic losses for the Soviet Union. There was the delay of billions of dollars of unpaid debts, and the danger of forfeiting $6 billion worth of contracts as well as short-term losses. It was noted by Shevardnadze that $800 million worth of oil would be lost due to reduced shipments from Iraq.[48] Gorbachev's expectation that this position would result in Western rewards came under severe criticism by conservatives who argued that the USSR should look after its own interests. Conservative opponents of Gorbachev and Shevardnadze were also angered by what they regarded as a blow to Soviet prestige. By the autumn of 1990, criticisms of Gorbachev and Shevardnadze had become so severe that there was a noticeable retreat in the Soviet position. In October Gorbachev sent Primakov to Iraq to convince Saddam Hussein that his military action was doomed to fail since the West was determined to liberate Kuwait. But the move signalled a split between Gorbachev and the Foreign Ministry in the approach to the problem. Shevardnadze, unlike Gorbachev, 'did not believe his country could seriously affect Iraq more than any other. [...] He was more concerned about how Soviet behaviour in the crisis affected the USSR's standing in other parts of the world.'[49] By contrast, Primakov's efforts led to the illusion, shared by his president, that Soviet success in mediation in the crisis would enhance, rather than damage, Moscow's position in the Gulf and the world.

Such hopes were to be abruptly dashed as Western ground forces moved in to deal a crushing defeat for the Iraqi army.

Gorbachev did nothing to impede this; he faced up to conservative pressure at home (although he accepted the resignation of his friend Shevardnadze as Foreign Minister, thus deflecting criticism from himself) in order to maintain harmonious relations with Washington. Iraq's defeat was attributable in part to Hussein's inability to grasp the reality of a rapidly changing world-linked to the ending of the Cold War. For example, Soviet-US agreements to reduce conventional forces in Europe enabled US access to a larger number of troops that could be mobilised. 'More than half of the 540,000 US troops sent to the Gulf came from the central European front. [...] Together with British and French contingents they represented the cream of the army that NATO had been honing for combat for years.'[50] Moscow, as expected, distanced itself from the Iraqi military failure. The then Foreign Minister Bessmertnykh claimed that the ineffectual Soviet-built air defence system was 'not a reflection of a weakness of combat equipment. Ultimately equipment is good when it is in good hands.'[51] Without doubt 1991 marked a low-point in Soviet-Iraqi relations.

Russian-Iraqi relations: establishing a new framework

Indicating the importance of bilateral relations in the past, neither side gave up on the possibility of restoring the ties that had existed before 1992. Iraq, isolated and facing stiff international sanctions, needed all the allies it could get. Russia, on the other hand, was facing a more complicated situation. In 1992 President Yeltsin continued the policy of co-operation with the West, which remained a top priority under his leadership. But as Moscow gradually became more assertive in pursuing its national interests, the Iraqi factor took on a more prominent profile.

On 9 November 1992 a Russian parliamentary delegation headed by Sergei Baburin, leader of the Communist and Nationalist Unity Bloc, visited Baghdad. They were received by the Iraqi Speaker of parliament Sa'adi Mahdi Saleh, who announced that Baghdad wished to 'turn over a new leaf in its relations with Russia'.[52] Baburin was quoted by the Iraqi News Agency as saying that the 'continuation of the blockade on Iraq's children, elderly and women is a violation of international norms, charters and human rights', and attacked 'American piracy represented by seizing part of the Iraqi people's assets in foreign banks'.[53] Such visits appeared to lend weight to claims by the Ba'ath regime that it had an influence on members of Moscow's political élite. The Russian media was unrelenting about the financial losses as a consequence of the embargo against Iraq, and political opponents of Boris Yeltsin blamed this on the government's kow-towing to the West at the expense of national interests. Between 1992 to 1994 there was a growing wave of voices calling on the government not to ignore the potential gains to be made from enhancing relations with Iraq. An article in *Izvestiia* in August 1994 mentioned that Baghdad was 'proposing to repay its debt to Russia – about $7 billion – immediately after the sanctions are lifted or eased', and that payment would be made in oil.[54] There was also the attractive possibility of favourable contracts and arms sales which would benefit the Russian economy over its competitors.

Evidence that the decision-making élite was itself in accord with the view that relations with Iraq required serious consideration began to surface in 1994, when in November Moscow announced that it was 'ready to resume arms supplies to Iraq' once the UN sanctions were lifted.[55] It was also reported that as part of the deal, Russia would provide technical training to Iraqi officers in the field of communications. However, Moscow strenuously stressed that it would not act unilaterally in defiance of the United Nations sanctions. Moreover, Kozyrev stated that Russia's close relations with Iraq would not be at the expense of other Gulf states: 'Iraq and Kuwait are Russia's economic partners and that is why Moscow cannot take sides.'[56] When Tariq Aziz made an unexpected visit to Moscow on 6 December 1994, Russia's Foreign Ministry continued to emphasise this point. Yeltsin's envoy to the Middle East, Viktor Posuvaliuk, reaffirmed that 'we are not Iraq's advocates'.[57] Interestingly, he added that Russia was not seeking to improve links with Iraq for economic motives, and the interpretation that 'the Russian leadership is virtually possessed by the desire to recoup these seven billion dollars (in debt)' was incorrect because 'everything is much subtler'.[58]

Posuvaliuk seemed to suggest that strategic considerations held equal weight in Moscow. One indication of the growing importance of Iraq to Russia was an admission by a Russian diplomat that the frequent contacts between the two sides 'stem from the special significance of the "Iraqi component" in Russia's Middle East policy' in which stability in the Gulf was crucial.[59] Other

Foreign Ministry officials began pointing out in April 1994 that contentious issues such as Iraqi disarmament should not be used by the UN to delay the lifting of sanctions against Iraq. Although the Special Commission on the Disarmament of Iraq did not have a complete picture of the Iraqi programme of weapons of mass destruction, Russian officials noted that in the opinion of members of the commission, 'the remaining "gaps" are not fundamental in nature'.[60] This position was a direct accusation that the West's stubbornness on the issue was politically motivated rather than based on legal or technical factors.

Iraq hoped that it could utilise the historic links with Moscow in order to have a powerful ally on the UN Security Council. Tariq Aziz relayed a message from his president that Iraq 'trusts Russia' and added that Baghdad placed 'great hopes in Russia's objective and active role' with regard to the lifting of the international embargo against Iraq.[61] Russia's position since 1994 had been that the all or nothing position was harmful to the authority of the UN and Kozyrev urged the Security Council to be more flexible rather than act as a coercive tool. This interpretation was in fact a direct challenge to Washington's position on the sanctions, supported by Kuwait and Saudi Arabia, which argued that Saddam Hussein should be punished by the international community for his aggression. In what was clear criticism of the United States and Britain, Kozyrev said he regretted that certain members of the UN Security Council supported 'use of sanctions and tough pressure without applying political methods'.[62] Thus, over a two-year period Moscow had become bolder in highlighting the difference of opinion that existed between itself and Washington over the Iraqi issue. But Yeltsin's government had no intention of conceding to demands by certain sections of the domestic opposition, namely pragmatic and extreme nationalists, to unilaterally break the united international stance. In November 1994 Kozyrev retorted to the Communist-Nationalist Bloc: 'Over the past few years the opposition has persistently claimed that the sanctions have been unfair, that this is almost an imperialistic plot against Iraq and that we should lift them unilaterally...regardless of the situation. We did not and have not agreed with this.'[63] Official statements which understated growing links between Moscow and Baghdad were aimed at easing US concern and suspicion. In addition, the Russian leadership had to be careful not to unintentionally send a signal to the Iraqi regime which it could interpret as a green light for further acts of aggression. At the same time Kozyrev reflected that while 'Iraq itself is a very complicated partner...there are Western interests which, in this case, do not coincide with our interests, and we should simply take this fact into account clearly and soberly'. He noted that while comparisons with the Cold War were wrong, 'very deep differences stem from here'; specifically, that the West could get its petro-dollars from other Gulf states, while Moscow had lost $7 billion from Iraqi oil sales.[64]

In November 1994, Yeltsin dispatched Kozyrev to Baghdad to participate in Iraq's recognition of the sovereignty and boundaries of Kuwait in order to strengthen their case for ending the international sanctions. The Foreign Ministry could boast: 'For the first time in the history of Iraqi-Kuwaiti relations it has become possible, thanks to Russia's efforts, to achieve a clearly formulated recognition of Kuwait by Baghdad.'[65] The most surprising aspect of the Russian initiative was that support was not only directed towards Iraq, but also towards the Iraqi leader Saddam Hussein. Kozyrev told the Iraqi parliament on 10th November that he was 'delighted at the political wisdom of Saddam Hussein' in recognising Kuwait's sovereignty.[66] For the liberal Kozyrev to comment on Hussein's 'wisdom' was a rather ironic situation, considering the Iraqi leader's record on human rights and the huge blunders he had made in the Gulf War. Moscow could have concluded that the best way to the Iraqi dictator's heart and mind would be through his vanity, and so making complimentary remarks would have been a cost-effective way of recouping influence in Baghdad and the Middle East.

Kozyrev's mission was clearly intended to provide much needed legitimacy and support to the internationally isolated regime. Russia's Foreign Minister told the members of the puppet parliament in Baghdad that 'the future of the Iraqi people today is in your hands and in the hands of the Revolutionary Command Council' (Iraq's equivalent of the Soviet Union's Politburo).[67] On his return to Moscow, Kozyrev urged the United Nations to react positively to the Iraqi initiative and repeated his criticism of the all or nothing approach of the United States. His retort to increasing references to US-Russian differences was unambiguous: 'Is the United States a sacred cow with which we cannot have disagreements?'[68] Moscow's leadership denied that Kozyrev's efforts were part of a new move by Russia to revert to the Cold War era, arguing that the contrary was true. Posuvaliuk pointed out that Moscow's success in getting Iraq to recognise Kuwait 'is an achievement for which the Gulf countries should be grateful'.[69] Later that year, in September, Deputy Minister of Foreign Affairs Boris Kolokov firmly stated the case for taking a pragmatic attitude towards Baghdad. 'It's naïve to think that Saddam Hussein can be removed. He is a flesh-and-blood politician. His behaviour does not conform to generally accepted standards, but if he takes positive steps, why not say so publicly?'[70] Kolokov admitted that Moscow's approach was indeed different to that of Washington. In his words, 'in Washington it is considered that Hussein's unreliability excludes anything other than an extremely tough approach to him. We, on the other hand, think that pressure on Baghdad will be more effective if it is stated publicly that there have been changes for the better, but such-and-such demands will have to be met in order for such-and-such restrictions to be relaxed.'[71]

One commentator writing for *Izvestiia* argued that the reason for the growing quarrel with the United States was that Washington had become accustomed to the view Moscow no longer played a role in Middle Eastern affairs. In his view, Russia and the United States had strategic goals in the region which could not be reconciled. 'The Americans are irritated at their Russian partner because, by offering Baghdad a compromise instead of capitulation and to exchange recognition of Kuwait's sovereignty and borders for a gradual lifting of the oil embargo, Moscow, in Washington's opinion, threw the drowning dictator a life-belt.'[72] Indeed, what became clear from the whole episode was that the United States had overstepped the boundaries of seeking to uphold international law, and in many ways used such means as a vehicle to look after its own national interests. The dawning reality was that Washington had specific intentions in the region which it achieved with relative ease, and any talk of 'compromise' or 'co-operation', if it did not coincide with US aims, was largely ignored. This view, which was once reserved for Russian communists and nationalists, soon became prevalent among the mainstream as well. 'The new Russia has now reached this by no means novel conclusion, after first entertaining infantile illusions about the un-bounded altruism and disinterestedness of the "civilised world".[73] Despite this shift of Russian policy to accommodate a wider spectrum of political views, Kozyrev's critics remained vociferous. Vladimir Lukin, as chairman of the State Duma Committee on International Affairs, spoke out in October 1994 against what he described as a policy that sought to appease all and pleased no-one. 'Should we have kicked desert sand into the eyes of two American presidents [Bush and Clinton], and in such a way as to directly affect their prestige all to no particular purpose?' he asked.[74] His main concern was that Russian foreign policy had become so ill-defined that few in the international community could associate with it. Lukin's contention that the Ministry of Foreign Affairs had lost its direction, particularly in terms of long-term planning, was widely shared among Russia's political élite. With the debate over sanctions, Lukin cast similar doubt: 'If our national interest consists in getting Iraq to start paying off its debt as soon as possible while at the same time avoiding any worsening of relations with the West...then, as a result of the diplomatic measures we have conducted, the situation has become more difficult on both counts.'[75]

If emphasising the importance of maintaining dialogue with Iraq was kicking sand in the eyes of US presidents, then Moscow continued to do this in 1995 and 1996. Following a visit by Posuvaliuk to Baghdad at the beginning of January 1996, a Foreign Ministry statement said rather tersely that 'Moscow attaches great significance to political dialogue with Baghdad'.[76] When within days of that statement it was announced that the successor to Kozyrev would be the orientalist Primakov, supposedly well ac-quainted with Saddam Hussein since the 1960s, many Western observers began to wonder if Russia was heading towards open defiance of the United States. In reality, this was extremely unlikely because Russia was still too weak but perhaps it was an indication that the internal dynamics were driving the country well away from the position of the late 1980s and the early 1990s. At the extreme end of these internal dynamics was the leader of the Liberal Democratic Party of Russia, who in January of 1996 praised Hussein for the 'repulse of the Western aggression of Desert Storm' Vladimir Zhirinovskii added that 'the immense army, well-armed and equipped with modern weapons of thirty imperialist states headed by the United States, was defeated by Iraq's valiant sons and daughters headed by Saddam Hussein, a wise and noble son of the Iraqi people'.[77] Such an outlook was not widely shared by Russia's political élite, but the Zhirinovskii factor did have an effect on some at the very lowest end of society.

Although Primakov was quick to dampen down any speculation of a growing rift between Washington and Moscow, he did so in a style different to that of his predecessor. Most notably, Primakov promoted the idea of co-operation but without conceding that the two countries should follow separate paths towards seeking their own national interests. Primakov told reporters after his meeting with his US counterpart in Helsinki on 11 February 1996: 'We have differences and there will be differences, but all this must be [resolved] without confrontation. That would be extremely dangerous for our mutual relations and also for the whole world.'[78] However, standing by Iraq in its time of need was seen as an investment for the future, and in that same month of 1996, Russia and Iraq signed what the *Guardian* headlined as a '"Giant" Iraq-Russia Oil Deal'.[79] Most reports indicated that the agreement was worth $10 billion in industrial projects, which were put on hold until the sanctions were lifted. Other than helping to restore the Iraqi oil industry, Russia would also be involved in building a metallurgical combine and factories producing chemical and other heavy industrial projects. In return, Iraq stated its readiness to pay off its debts as soon as the sanctions were lifted. In the words of one Russian government source, Moscow believed that the sanctions issue had 'come to a head and the time has come for this to be resolved in favour of Iraq, which overall is fulfilling all the demands being made of it by the international community'.[80]

In July 1996 a Russian Foreign Ministry statement was published, openly urging 'Russian organisations and entrepreneurial structures to become actively involved in buying oil from Iraq and delivering humanitarian goods to that country', adding a promise by the ministry to provide them with 'needed assistance in this endeavour'.[81] This was in the light of the UN decision to ease the sanctions to allow Iraq to buy urgent medical equipment and food with the sale of some of its oil. Nonetheless, the implication was that Russia was expecting its leading economic institutions to establish firm foundations for future enterprises with relation to Iraq.

An article in *Nezavisimaia gazeta* by Aleksandr Lavrentev managed to capture the over-riding view in Moscow's decision-making inner circle that was in existence in the summer of 1996. The article was written to coincide with the anniversary of the signing of the Treaty of Friendship and Co-operation with Iraq in 1972, which, it was pointed out, was still in force. Beginning with an overview of the history of co-operation between the two countries, and in particular the level of Soviet aid in the 1960s and 1970s, the article then almost inevitably moved into the hard facts and figures of the relationship. 'Between 1980-1990 alone, the Soviet Union sold Iraq weapons worth more than $15 billion; 55 per cent of all Iraqi military deliveries for that period.'[82] These military deliveries were to become a major cause of the large debt that Iraq owed Russia, but the latter had seen none of that debt being repaid. The reason for this was that despite the Iraqi oil wealth, 'possibilities for its use had been considerably curtailed as a result of the war with Iran in the 1980s, and in the 1990s, after the Gulf War, this had generally been transformed to practically nothing'.[83]

Indeed, many Russian and non-Russian commentators expressed growing concern at the ease with which the United States had been able to exert its political and economic power over regions such as the Middle East. There was a kind of see-saw effect in which the greater the prestige for the United States the less the respect for Russia. The fear for Moscow was that this would contribute to the loss of international markets, such as Iraq, to which it would become impossible to return. In fact, there were also many other rivals to Russia than the United States, the most notable of which was France, which even in the Soviet era was claiming a growing share of the Iraqi market.

Thus, the author concluded with the following point: 'Returning the debts and the traditional market of sales products from the military-industrial complex, joint oil exploration, the closeness to our boundaries and an important position in the Middle East all but force Russia to begin immediate serious preparation towards "day X". That is when the sanctions are lifted.'[84] While stopping short of calling on Russia to act as accomplice to a nation breaching international law, what was being called upon from the Russian government was to do everything else in its power, even at the expense of upsetting the United States, to reassert its interests.

Moscow was highly aggrieved following the US cruise missile attacks on Iraq in early September 1996. There was a united view in Russia condemning the military actions which encompassed a broad range of the political spectrum. The pragmatic nationalist Aleksandr Lebed, then Security Council chief, compared Clinton's behaviour to a 'bull in a china shop'.[85] It was reported at the time that various agreements with Iraq, particularly relating to oil, were being jeopardised by Washington as a result of the anti-Iraqi policies of the Clinton administration. These included a deal 'on rebuilding Iraq's petroleum industry and increasing oil production to 60.8 million [metric] tons a year. [...] Zarubezhneft [foreign oil] and Mashinimport [machinery import] are each hoping to get a 15 per cent share in the project, while Lukoil hopes to obtain a 70 per cent stake. Various estimates put the value of the project between $2 billion to $7 billion.'[86] As well as preventing Russia from benefiting from such deals, US insistence on isolating Iraq delayed Baghdad's pledge to repay its $7 billion debt to Moscow. According to one view, following the cruise missile attacks, 'Washington will now do everything in its power to prevent an easing of the embargo.'[87]

Washington's justification for the attack was related to Iraqi army involvement in inter-Kurdish fighting in northern Iraq. The Russian media was equally scathing about such motives:

> If one is to follow this logic of relations, which hardly favours Moscow, one can even imagine the following…in the final analysis, Saddam sent troops to battle separatists who are threatening the integrity of his country. [...] If one applies the standards the US has set for Saddam Hussein to Russian-Chechen relations, one can surmise that analogous UN resolutions would be adopted on Chechnia…and if one continues this reasoning even further, one should not rule out the possibility that the US could very well allow itself, in the future, to speak to Moscow in the language of Tomahawks too.[88]

Foreign Ministry spokesman Mikhail Demurin reflected Moscow's dismay regarding the US military strikes and added that his government wanted the resolution of the Kurdish problem to be 'guided by a political character'[89] – in other words, through dialogue and negotiations rather than through fighting. In a separate Foreign Ministry statement, a much more critical assessment of

Washington's actions, which included the extension of the 'no-fly zone' over Iraq, was presented:

> Serious concern is prompted by the fact that Washington is essentially laying claim to the role of supreme arbiter, trying, in effect, to supplant the Security Council, which in accordance with the UN Charter, possesses an exclusive right to authorise the use of force. The decision adopted unilaterally by the United States and Britain to expand the 'no-fly zone' in southern Iraq should also be viewed in this context. These actions, which set a dangerous precedent, are at variance with international law and are unacceptable. The military actions in and around Iraq must be stopped.[90]

These were some of the most severe criticisms of the United States in the first five years after the demise of the Soviet Union. What was even more indicative of the transformation that had taken place was that the comments were supported by the leading reformers in government, including the Presidential Chief of Staff Anatolii Chubais. Yeltsin's chief administrator said that he backed the Foreign Ministry criticisms and added that 'if our viewpoint had been taken into account, the bombardment would not have happened'.[91] Primakov's main objection, which met with agreement from a wide spectrum in Russia, was that the unilateral actions of one power were against the spirit of co-operation in a new world order. 'No one accepts diktats of any one power, be it the United States, Russia or another state.'[92]

Primakov met with Aziz in November 1996 to discuss the implementation of Resolution 986, authorising Iraq to export $2 billion of its oil over a six-month period in order to buy food and medicine. The two men also discussed the latest developments in northern Iraq, where the two main Kurdish factions of Barazani and Talabani continued to fight each other. Ostensibly, Primakov expressed non-interference from Russia and fully supported Baghdad's peace initiatives. However, it was also reported that 'according to information from confidential sources, Moscow is not only carefully following the development of events in northern Iraq, but also receiving emissaries from the parties to the conflict'.[93] In effect, such vigour and interest in the affairs of Iraq were significant in that they were indicative of a new approach by Moscow compared with five years earlier, when involvement in such matters was seen as costly and of little strategic value. In addition, this episode added credence to the argument that Moscow was deliberately downplaying its aims in the Middle East in order not to antagonise the West and some of the regional players, which continued to be wary of Russian intentions in the light of the Soviet past.

A senior official at the Foreign Ministry underlined Russia's contribution during fighting in Iraqi Kurdistan in late 1996 by saying that 'because of our influence and our political dialogue with Baghdad, we were able to calm the situation in the north and to reduce tension between Baghdad and Washington'.[94] The general thread of the argument was that Russia had the potential to play a positive and constructive role in the Iraq crisis which would also defuse tension in the Gulf. What was tacitly recognised in Moscow was that there was a lack of trust between the United States and Russia which prevented this from leading to co-operation over the issue. Washington's neglect of Moscow's efforts to resolve the Iraqi crisis was highly resented by the Russian leadership and opposition parties alike.

It was in this context that Moscow was quick to act during the Iraqi crisis which blew up towards the end of 1997 when Saddam Hussein decided on 29 October to expel US members of the UN Special Commission (UNSCOM), which was responsible for disarming his country. The decision appeared to be heading to a military confrontation between the United States and Iraq with both sides appearing uncompromising on the dispute.

As US warships gathered in the Gulf, Russia took the initiative by acting as honest-broker between Washington and Baghdad, sensing that neither side was fully commited to a new military adventure. On 19 November after talks with Iraqi Deputy Prime Minister Tariq Aziz, Primakov met his British and US counterparts in Geneva. Russia's Foreign Minister was widely praised for succeeding in convincing Iraq to reverse its decision and convincing the United States not to use the military option.[95] However, both Britain and the United States were critical of Russia's actions because it became clear that Moscow had made an agreement with Iraq that it would undermine the UN-imposed sanctions by supporting recommendations at the United Nations stating that Iraq's weapons of mass destruction programme was no longer a relevant issue.[96] The Russian Foreign Ministry also issued statements which seemed to apportion blame for the crisis to Washington by highlighting the 'constructive approach on the part of Baghdad [...and its] desire to cooperate with the international community'.[97]

With the tacit approval of the Russian Foreign Ministry, Communist leader Gennadii Ziuganov visited Baghdad on 27 November to show support for the Iraqi leader and to state that the 'Russian Communist Party, the State Duma lower chamber as well as the Russian people will continue to work for the lifting of the unfair embargo on the friendly Iraqi people'.[98] Earlier, President Yeltsin's spokesman Sergei Iastrzhembskii, clearly referring to the United States, noted that the Russian leadership was 'categorically against using the UN Security Council as cover for attacks on Iraq'.[99] This followed Primakov's self-praise for Russia's diplomatic efforts, which he contrasted with Washington's belligerence: 'What Russia achieved...without any use of violence, any use of weapons, without a show of force, was achieved through diplomatic means.'[100]

Conclusion: squaring the Gulf circle

The Iraqi example provides an excellent insight for understanding the objectives of post-Soviet Russia. This was a great power that would inevitably have to pursue its own interests, but only in the framework of international co-operation. According to Naumkin, there was a counter-reaction in Russia against Kozyrev's early policies of unquestioningly agreeing with Washington. 'Most political parties and activists in Moscow regarded the policy of Russia as being too closely linked to the United States, as if it did not have its own interests, nor its own view, and that it was giving up all its partners in the area.'[101] He noted that Iraq was one of the few countries in the world which could consume Russian products and had a history of buying arms. It was therefore inevitable that such economic necessities would lead to a policy which would encourage the ending of the sanctions.

But the dilemma facing Moscow was that upgrading its relations with Iraq would also negatively affect relations with Saudi Arabia. Moscow was seeking to raise the level of economic co-operation with the oil-rich kingdom in order to compensate for its losses with regard to Iraq. However, Riyadh's response to Russian endeavours was lethargic and slow. In part, US pressure had prevented the Saudi leadership from easing its overwhelming economic, political and military dependence on the government in Washington. The Saudis would have also wished to take advantage of a close relationship with Russia in order to have some form of ability to drive a wedge between Moscow's close relations with both Baghdad and Tehran. However, the constitution of the Saudi regime – its weak position internally and regionally, the threats facing it from both Iran and Iraq have made it very conservative by nature and prevent it from taking any risks which might antagonise the United States, its regional guardian. Nonetheless, Saudi Arabia had taken great care not to irritate Russia or pursue policies counter to Moscow's aims. The chief example was Riyadh's deliberate non-interference in the Chechen war and the toning down of its activities in the Muslim republics of Central Asia and the Caucasus. Saudi support for the Taliban in Afghanistan, which was criticised by Moscow, was not so much directed at Russia as it was an effort prevent Iran from extending its influence in the war-torn country.

Russia's adherence to the internationally imposed sanctions naturally provoked a negative reaction from Iraq, but it had been widely accepted as being a price worth paying for the sake of maintaining co-operation with the United States despite the loss of a profitable outlet. Nonetheless, after 1993 Russia embarked on a more energetic drive to remove Iraq from its position of international pariah through the United Nations Security Council as well as by more direct diplomatic channels. The problem for Russia, as one Russian commentator pointed out, was that Washington simply did not want to see the 'development of bilateral Iraqi-Russian economic relations. When Washington decides to remove the sanctions, it will be done easily and without us.'[102]

Primakov was attempting to steer a course through the stormy political waters of the Gulf which did not lead to a direct confrontation with Washington and which promoted relations with Saudi Arabia in the hope that they would result in high economic returns for Russia. This was a continuation of the policy initiated by Shevardnadze and maintained by his predecessor Kozyrev. However, as a centrist-nationalist, he believed that it was in Russia's interest to use the long-standing links with Baghdad to strengthen Moscow's position in the Gulf. Relations with Iraq were seen as promising large economic returns once the sanctions were lifted.

Moreover, the geo-strategic aspect of relations provided a balance to Washington's dominant position over the GCC countries, including Saudi Arabia. Riyadh had frustrated Moscow's efforts to further bilateral relations in order to gain entry into the highly sought-after economic market of the oil-rich kingdom. Preserving good relations with Iraq was also an indirect way of getting Saudi Arabia (as well as Iran, Turkey and other neighbouring states) to take account of Russia in regional equations. So, for example, if Riyadh was concerned about an Iraqi arms build-up, it would need the goodwill of Russia to use its influence in Baghdad to moderate the Iraqi position. As one commentator noticed, Moscow's foreign policy under Primakov 'is pursuing a low-cost and relatively risk-free strategy of stepping into regional disputes as peacemaker and bolstering its influence through successful mediation and conciliation, often at the expense of a "bellicose" U.S.'[103] Relations with Iraq also have an important bearing on relations with Iran, which in turn is important for Moscow in term of relations with Central Asian and Caucasian countries in the CIS. Primakov's realism, which characterises his foreign policy style, made it logical to preserve relations with Baghdad, but that same quality had led him to reiterate to both Washington and Riyadh that such a policy would take particular care not to undermine their interests. With Primakov as Prime Minister, such an approach is likely to be further consolidated.

NOTES

1. A. Yodfat and M. Abir, *In the Direction of the Gulf*, London, 1977, p.29.
2. *Ibid.*, p.53.
3. Robert O. Freedman, *Moscow in the Middle East*, London and Cambridge, 1991, p.83.
4. Yodfat, *The Soviet Union and the Arabian Peninsula*, London, 1983, p.97.
5. *Ibid.*
6. Eliyahu Kanovsky, *The Economic Consequences of the Persian Gulf War: Accelerating OPEC's Demise*, Washington, DC, 1992, p.6.
7. *Ibid.*, p.8.
8. Interview with Muhiyaddin Khoja, Saudi ambassador to Moscow 1991-6. The interview took place in London in the summer of 1996, just before he took up a new posting. The ambassador kindly answered a wide range of questions on the subject of Saudi-Russian/Soviet relations. He had been closely involved with many of the developments, including the establishment of relations between the two countries.
9. Interview with Ambassador Khoja.

10. *Ibid.*
11. *Ibid.*
12. Maksim Iusin, 'Our Visit is a Drive for Markets, Including Arms Markets', *Izvestiia*, in *Current Digest of the Post-Soviet Press*, vol.XLIV, no.18, 3 June 1992, p.15.
13. *Ibid.*, p.16.
14. Iusin, *op. cit.*, p.16.
15. Gennadii Ezhov and Viacheslav Anchikov (interview with V. Chernomyrdin), *Itar-Tass, Foreign Broadcast Information Service* (Central Eurasia), FBIS-Sov-94-227, 23 November 1994, pp.4–5.
16. *RIA news agency* (Moscow), 20 November 1994, *BBC SWB*, SU/2160, 23 November 1994, B/6.
17. *Kingdom of Saudi Arabia TV1,* 21 November 1994, *BBC SWB*, SU/2162, 25 November 1994 B/10.
18. Aleksandr Shumilin, 'Pochemu ne vyshlo proryva?' (Why no breakthrough?), *Moskovskie novosti,* no.60 (757), 27 November 1994, p.12.
19. Interview with Saudi Ambassador Khoja.
20. Aleksandr Ivanov, 'Deistviia Moskvy ozadachivaiut Arabov' (Moscow's actions puzzle Arabs), *Nezavisimaia gazeta,* 5 August 1994, p.4.
21. *Ibid.*
22. Shumilin, *op. cit.*
23. Interview with Ambassador Khoja.
24. *Ibid.*
25. Aleksandr Konstantinov, 'Prints nasleduet prestol' (Prince will inherit throne), *Novoe vremia,* no.3, January 1996, p.28.
26. Elena Suponina, 'The Punishing Sword Will Slice Your Neck Too!', *Novoe vremia,* no.23, June 1996, p.34.
27. *Itar-Tass,* 'Foreign Ministry Condemns Bomb Blast in Saudi Arabia', 26 June 1996, *BBC SWB* (part 1, former USSR), SU/2650, 28 June 1996, B/18.
28. *Ibid.*
29. *Itar-Tass,* 'Gulf Region a priority for Russian Foreign Policy, Deputy Minister Says', 1 March 1996, *BBC SWB* (part 1, former USSR), SU/2550, 2 March 1996, B/11.
30. Interview with Ambassador Khoja.
31. Viktor Posuvaliuk, 'Rihla fi al-khaleej' (A trip in the Gulf), *Al-Hayat,* no. 11726, 30 March 1995, p.15.
32. *Ibid.*
33. *Ibid.*
34. Elena Suponina, 'Musul' manie derzhat ramadan' (Muslims observe Ramadan), *Novoe vremia,* 26 February 1997, p.33.
35. Interview with Prof. V. Naumkin, Institute of Oriental Studies of the Russian Academy of Sciences, in Moscow, October 1996.
36. Interview with Sergei Kepechenko, deputy director of the Middle East Department of the Russian Ministry of Foreign Affairs, October 1996.
37. Viktor Posuvaliuk, 'Ta'amoulat ba'ed liqa' ma' safeer' (Hope after meeting an ambassador), *Al-Hayat,* no.12467, 17 April 1997, p.17.
38. *Ibid.*

39. *Ibid.*
40. Adeed and Karen Dawisha, 'Introduction' in Adeed and Karen Dawisha (eds), *The Soviet Union in the Middle East,* London, 1982, p.17.
41. Freedman, *op. cit.,* p.64.
42. Yodfat, *op. cit.,* p.63.
43. *Ibid.,* p.87.
44. Oleg Smolansky with Bettie Smolansky, *The USSR and Iraq,* London, 1991, p.28.
45. *Ibid.*
46. *Ibid.*
47. James Gow, *Iraq, the Gulf Conflict and the World Community,* London, 1993, p.124.
48. *Ibid.,* p.125.
49. *Ibid.,* p.127.
50. *Ibid.,* p.57.
51. William Perry, 'Desert Storm and Deterrence', *Foreign Affairs,* 1993.
52. *BBC SWB,* ME/1535, 11 November 1992, A/13.
53. *Ibid.*
54. El'mar Guseinov, 'Irak nadeetsia podkupit' Moskvu' (Iraq hopes to bribe Moscow), *Izvestiia,* 13 July 1994, p.24.
55. Adel Darwish, *The Independent,* 19 December 1994, *FBIS* (Central Asia), FBIS-Sov-94-243, 19 December 1994, p.11.
56. *Interfax,* 14 December 1994, *FBIS,* FBIS-Sov-94-241, 15 December 1994, p.6.
57. *Moscow NTV,* 6 December 1994, *FBIS,* FBIS-Sov-94-235, 7 December 1994, p.2.
58. *Ibid.*
59. *Ibid.,* p.3.
60. Irina Grudina, 'Mid, RF nastaivaet na smiagchenii rezhima aṇtiirakskikh sanktsii' (Russian Foreign Ministry insists on easing sanctions against Iraq), *Segodnia,* 29 April 1994, p.21.
61. *Itar-Tass* (World Service), 7 December 1994, *FBIS,* FBIS-Sov-94-236, 8 December 1994, p.3.
62. *Ibid.*
63. *Russia TV* (Moscow), 4 November 1994, *BBC SWB,* SU/2146, 7 November 1994, B/7.
64. *Ibid.*
65. *Itar-Tass* (World Service), 9 November 1994, *BBC SWB,* SU/2150, 11 November 1994, B/6.
66. Hosni Khashabah, 'Al-Iraq i'taraf bi al-Kuwait bi hudoudiha al-jadidah fi bayan waqa'ahu sadam wa shahada 'alayhi koziref' (Iraq recognises Kuwait's new borders in a declaration signed by Saddam and witnessed by Kozyrev), *Al-Sharq Al-Awsat,* 11 November 1994, p.3.
67. *Ibid.*
68. Jalal Al-Mashata, 'Tariq aziz sayoussalem olbrite watha'iq al-itiraf bilkuwait' (Tariq Aziz will give Albright documents recognising Kuwait), *Al-Hayat,* 12 November 1994, p.4.
69. Konstantin Eggert, 'MID Rossii predlagaet schitat' Saddama Khuseina dobrym

218   *Saudi Arabia and Iraq*

chelovekom' (Russian Foreign Ministry proposes that Saddam Hussein be considered a good man), *Izvestiia*, 9 August 1994, p.3.
70. *Ibid.*
71. *Ibid.*
72. Stanislav Kondrashov, 'Chto khotela dokazat' Rossiia v sluchae s Irakom' (What Russia wanted to prove in the Iraq affair), *Izvestiia*, 21 October 1994, p.4.
73. *Ibid.*
74. Vladimir Lukin, Chairman of the State Duma Committee on International Affairs, 'Bengal'skii ogon' v araviiskikh peskakh' (Bengal light in the Arabian sands), *Moskovskie novosti*, 23-30 October 1994, p.13.
75. *Ibid.*
76. *Itar-Tass*, 'Russian Foreign Ministry Statement on Deputy Minster's Baghdad Visit', 4 January 1994, *BBC SWB* (former USSR, part 1), SU/2502, 6 January 1996, B/7.
77. *Interfax*, 'Zhirinovskii Congratulates Iraqi President', 16 January 1996, *BBC SWB* (former USSR, part 1), SU/2512, 18 January 1996, B/14.
78. David Hearst, '"Giant" Iraq-Russia Oil Deal', *Guardian*, 12 February 1996, p.11.
79. *Ibid.*
80. *Interfax*, 'Russia "Ready to Implement" Industrial Projects in Iraq when Sanctions Lifted', 19 February 1996, *BBC SWB*, SU/2540, 20 February 1996, B/10.
81. *Kommersant-Daily*, 24 July 1996 (p.4), 'Russian Businessmen Advised to Buy Iraqi Oil', *Current Digest...*, 21 August 1996, p.22.
82. Alexander Lavrentiev, 'Segodniashniaia Rossiia i zavtrashnii Irak' (Today's Russia and Tomorrow's Iraq), *Nezavisimaia gazeta*, 16 August 1996, p.4.
83. *Ibid.*
84. *Ibid.*
85. Rossen Vassiliev, 'The Primakov Doctrine', *The Jamestown Foundation* (via internet), 24 October 1996.
86. *Kommersant-Daily*, 4 September 1996 (p.4), 'Tomahawk Blow to Russia's Interests', *Current Digest...*, 2 October 1996, p.7.
87. *Ibid.*
88. *Ibid.*
89. Dmitrii Gomostaev and Aleksandr Rontov, 'SShA vnov' nanesli udar po Irak' (USA again launches strikes on Iraq), *Nezavisimaia gazeta*, 4 September 1996, p.1.
90. Dmitrii Gomostaev and Aleksander Rontov, 'Vtoroi udar po Iraki podtverdil: SShA schitayiut, chto im pozvaleno vse' (Second strike on Iraq confirms that US thinks it can do anything it wants), *Nezavisimaia gazeta*, 5 September 1996, p.2.
91. Feliks Babitskii, 'Radikal Chubais predosteregaet ot krainostei' (Radical Chubais warns against extremes), *Rossiiskie vesti*, 5 September 1996, p.1.
92. Iuri Nikolaev, 'Nikto ne primiet diktata odnoi derzhavi' (No one accepts diktats of one power), *Rossiiskie vesti*, 5 September 1996, p.1.
93. Vladimir Abrinov, 'Moskvu "udovletvoriaet pozitsiia irakskikh vlastei"' (Mos-

cow 'satisfied with position of Iraqi authorities'), *Segodnia*, 11 November 1996, p.1.

94. Interview with Kepechenko.

95. 'Primakov Scores Victory in His Crusade for Russia', Reuters, 20 November 1997.

96. Evelyn Leopold, 'Russia Hold Out in UN Council on Iraqi Arms Probes', Reuters, 24 November 1997.

97. Adam Tanner, 'Russia Praises Iraq's "Constructive" Approach', Reuters, 27 November 1997.

98. Reuters, 'Russian Communist Chief Arrives in Baghdad', 27 November 1997.

99. *Itar-Tass*, 12 November 1997, *BBC SWB* (former USSR, part 1), SU/3074, 12 November 1997, B/3.

100. Judith Ingram, 'Russia Claims Diplomatic Victory in Iraq Crisis', Associated Press, November 1997.

101. Interview with Naumkin.

102. Lavrentiev, *op. cit.*, p.4.

103. Vassiliev, *op. cit.*

8

RUSSIA, TURKEY AND IRAN:
A REGIONAL POWER GAME

As regional powers in their own right, the influence of Turkey and Iran was not related just to the Middle East, but also to the vast area to the south and south-west of Russia's borders. The greatest fear that accompanied Moscow's diminishing influence was that the three powers would clash as a result of instability in the Caucasus. There was also discord over the delineation of the Caspian Sea and the Black Sea. Such differences were not new, but had existed for centuries. However, the post-Soviet era added a new equation to the formula: there was no longer a direct border between Russia the other two Muslim powers. Instead, a geo-political space was opened for the three historic rivals to reassert their own influence. In 1992 with the domination of the pro-Western radicals at its peak, Moscow focused its attention on relations with the West while seeking to avoid entanglement with the 'Muslim world' to its south. It was believed in that year that the biggest threat to its security from that region would come from Islamic fundamentalism, guided by Iran. But as pragmatism became the dominant feature of Russian foreign policy, many observers were surprised to find that Moscow was increasingly co-operating with Tehran in order to balance Ankara's more assertive role in the Eurasian land-mass stretching from Central Asia to the Balkans.

Bilateral relations with Turkey and Iran were another key component on which Russia placed greater significance from 1993 onwards. Arms sales to Iran, as well as industrial projects, were to have an important bearing on relations with the United States as well as other key states of the Middle East, particularly Turkey, Iraq, Saudi Arabia and Israel. Furthermore, co-operation with Iran promised Russia a more influential voice in the politics of the Gulf. Turkey was involved in a territorial and water dispute with Syria, which became more hostile towards Ankara after the latter began to raise the level of military co-operation with Israel. The Kurdish issue also forced Turkey to become more involved in Iraq and more hostile towards Syria for its support of extreme Kurdish factions. Thus it could be seen that relations with Iran and Turkey preoccupied Russia in a massive geo-strategic tangle which was of vital importance to Moscow's national security.

Post-Second World War relations with Iran and Turkey

Immediately after the Second World War, the Soviet Union had two basic objectives with regard to the Middle East: first, to ensure a Soviet presence in the region to the south of its border; second, to weaken or eliminate British and Western influence in the area. Stalin's obsession with the concept of creating a buffer zone around the USSR left Turkey and Iran particularly vulnerable to Soviet expansion. In October 1945 Moscow fortified its military position in northern Iran, contravening the internationally agreed agenda that foreign troops would pull out within six months. In December of that year uprisings and fighting broke out in Azeri regions of Iran which led to the establishment of the Autonomous Republic of Azerbaijan and a month later it was followed by the creation of the Autonomous Kurdish Republic of Azerbaijan. Moscow declared that these new areas would come under Soviet protection and Iranian government forces were prevented from entering. Such actions from Stalin caused alarm in the West and the matter was taken to the United Nations where British and US protests forced the withdrawal of all Soviet troops from Iran on 9 May 1946.

Stalin was equally careless with Turkish fears in the post-war years. Strategically, Turkey was more important to the Soviet Union not only because it bordered its south-westerly frontier but because it controlled the straits which allowed entry and exit to Soviet ships into and from the Black Sea. Added to this was a territorial dispute between the two countries over the Eastern Anatolian provinces of Kars and Ardahan, which were under Turkish control after 1920 as a result of an agreement between the Bolsheviks and the Ataturk revolutionaries. Stalin, not happy with the terms of the agreement, called in 1945 for the return of these territories. At Potsdam, Stalin also demanded joint control of the Dardanelles and Bosphorus Straits, 'specifically a naval base in the Sea of Marmara which connected the two straits'.[1] Both Britain and the United States rejected Soviet demands and gave total backing to unrivalled Turkish control of the Straits. As with Iran, Stalin sought to increase the pressure with intimidatory tactics by amassing Soviet troops on the Turkish border. Ankara responded by declaring martial law and suppressing all left-wing groups. Many observers subscribed to the view that 'by the spring of 1947 Ankara genuinely feared a Soviet invasion'.[2] Washington was concerned by these developments and announced the establishment of a naval presence in neighbouring Greece as part of the Truman Doctrine's aim of containing Soviet expansion. Stalin's Turkish bluff was called and he backed down as he was not seriously contemplating a direct conflict with the West. But his style and actions served to enhance the suspicions of the Turks who requested NATO membership in 1949, which was accepted in 1952. The consequence was that Turkey became a highly valued base for NATO and US forces, with direct proximity to the Soviet Union. In the Turkish case, as the Iranian example, Moscow's policy was clumsy and blundering, leaving Stalin's successors with the difficult task of winning back trust and co-operation from such important neighbours.

Khrushchev's energetic drive to improve the Soviet Union's international standing enabled Moscow to jump over the crescent of countries that seemed to be containing the Soviet bloc and build relations with key states of the Middle East such as Egypt and Iraq. But Moscow's policy makers were well aware that it was crucial to soften the hostility of Iran and Turkey: a difficult task considering that both regimes were inherently opposed to communism; Iran's conservative monarchy and the fiercely nationalist Turkish republic regarded socialism as a challenge to their values and, in effect, the legitimacy of their existence. Yet Khrushchev was fairly successful on both counts, particularly Iran, because of the Shah's strategy of playing both superpowers against each other. The fruit of such efforts was that in 1962 the Shah of Iran announced that his country would not deploy any foreign missiles, opening the way for the development of bilateral relations. In 1963 Leonid Brezhnev made an official visit to Tehran, the year that the USSR gave Iran a $38.9 million loan.[3]

Turkish rulers were less malleable. Although Khrushchev

renounced the territorial claims to Kars and Ardahan in July 1953, many differences remained. In 1957 bilateral relations suffered a further blow when the USSR threatened to attack Turkey if that country invaded Syria, which had become, with Egypt, a key Soviet ally. In February 1955 Turkey's signing of the Baghdad pact with Iraq was interpreted as a way of blocking Soviet entry into the region and of asserting Western influence on the Middle East. Turkey was thus portrayed as an agent of Western imperialism given the task of dividing and weakening the countries of the Middle East as well as threatening the security of the Soviet Union. As a beneficiary of the Truman Doctrine, Turkey received through the Marshall Plan $500 million by 1955. By 1967 this figure totalled $1.9 billion in US aid.[4]

Khrushchev's successor, Leonid Brezhnev, was able to build on the new course pursued by Moscow, particularly by improving economic relations. The first major deal was struck when Kosygin visited Ankara in September 1966, where a $200 million Soviet loan was provided to allow Moscow to construct a steel mill and several other industrial projects.[5] Turkey reciprocated by allowing freedom of movement for the USSR's newly developed Mediterranean fleet, intended to counter the US Sixth Fleet. Similar successes were being achieved with Iran, which was manifested in the visit by the Shah to the Soviet Union in July 1965, followed a year later by a $288.9 million loan. But of greater significance was the Soviet-Iranian agreement reached at the time, whereby the Russians would provide Iran with $110 million in military equipment, primarily small arms and transport equipment, in return for Iranian gas.[6] In the Cold War arena, it began to appear as if the Soviet Union was chipping away at spheres which had been under more or less complete US influence. By 1970, the Brezhnev-Kosygin leadership promised to provide $788.9 million in economic aid to the nations of the Northern Tier (Turkey and Iran), along with $110 million in military aid.[7]

Soviet relations with Iran (1970-91)

After 1970 relations between Iran and the Soviet Union gradually deteriorated and tension rather than *détente* characterised events. The Indian-Soviet Treaty of Friendship in 1971 was a potential threat from the east while a treaty with Iraq had the same effect on Iran's western border. But despite such concerns, there was little evidence to suggest that Moscow deliberately sought to undermine the Shah, who was perceived to be a stable and pragmatic leader capable of standing up to the United States in order to defend Iranian interests. In this context, it was not unusual that Moscow was among the last countries to withdraw political support for the Iranian monarch before he was replaced by the Ayatollah Khomeini. The initial Soviet view of the revolution was that it had been instigated by the United States because of the growing differences between the Shah and the administration in Washington. Eventually, the anti-Western rhetoric that accompanied the new order encouraged Moscow to believe that Iran could be convinced into joining the 'anti-imperialist' bloc under the leadership of the Soviet Union. However, the ageing Brezhnev leadership failed to understand that the anti-Western rhetoric of the Ayatollahs was directed not only at the Westernisation of values and culture introduced by the Shah, but also at the atheistic Soviet Union.

Relations with Iran were further complicated by the outbreak of the Iran-Iraq war. Sporadic fighting which had been taking place on the Iraqi-Iranian border escalated in September 1980 when Iranians began the heavy shelling of Iraqi border towns. The Iraqis reacted by launching a full-scale military invasion of the Iranian-held land in the Shatt Al-Arab. The war posed a dilemma for Moscow because while it was hoping to establish good relations with the Islamic regime in Iran, it already had a long-standing and profitable alliance with Iraq. The Soviet leadership initially portrayed Iran as a victim of US imperialism and Zionism and in further efforts to court the Islamic government in the first year of the war Moscow ordered back a naval convoy carrying weapons to Iraq and soon after 'imposed an actual embargo on new arms shipments to Iraq'.[8]

With the defeat of the Iranians imminent in the early phase of the war, as Iraqi successes multiplied, it was difficult to understand Moscow's tilt towards the besieged government in Tehran at the expense of old allies in Baghdad. According to Middle East specialist Dennis Ross:

> First, the Soviets saw Iran – twice as big as Iraq, with over three times its population – as the most important country in the region. It was the country that bordered the Soviet Union and physically separated it from the Gulf. [...] Second, the risk the

Soviets took in backing Islamic Iran was probably seen as minimal compared to the costs of seeing the United States re-emerge in Iran. [...] Third, in case they were wrong, they assumed they would in time be able to recoup their position with a victorious Iraq. [...][9]

Iran's success in the latter phase of the war made its government more belligerent, seeking to spread its influence throughout the Arab and Islamic world. As was later discovered, some of this newly-found confidence was due to substantial military supplies from the United States, in what became known as the Irangate scandal. Tehran also continued to criticise the Soviet Union and to persecute communists within Iran. Gorbachev put an end to the confused policies of his predecessors and adopted a consistent line which tilted towards Iraq but which encouraged an immediate end to the fighting. His main aim was to preserve the *status quo* in the Gulf and prevent direct interference from both superpowers. In February 1986 Gorbachev attempted to break the ice with Iran by dispatching First Deputy Foreign Minister Gregorii Kornienko, who was the highest-ranking Soviet official to visit that country since the Islamic revolution. The Iranian leadership praised the visit and expressed optimism to Moscow of an improvement in relations. However, it was more than coincidence that a week after the visit Iran launched a major military offensive, making major territorial gains. It quickly became clear to Moscow that Tehran 'had exploited the Kornienko visit' and the promise of better Soviet-Iranian relations to discourage Moscow from increasing military support to Iraq while it launched its own offensive. 'In case Moscow did not see the significance of the Iranian ploy in February, Iran was to repeat the manoeuvre again later that year.'[10] Indeed, Tehran deftly provided Moscow with tempting 'carrots' such as economic co-operation, the resumption of natural gas sales to the USSR, and the return to Iran of Soviet technicians who had been expelled the year before, in order to counter-balance Soviet-Iraqi ties.

By 1987 Gorbachev could no longer ignore the advantage gained by Iran from these tactics at the expense of Iraq. In January 1987 Moscow issued a severe criticism of the nature of the war and adopted a line similar to that of Iraq which effectively called for an end to the fighting. Iran tried to soften Soviet criticism by sending Foreign Minister Ali Akbar Velayati in that year, and his meeting with President Gromyko was reported to be tense. Gromyko bluntly told him that the USSR could not tolerate the Iranian action for much longer. The attack on a Soviet ship on 6 May 1987 added to the strain on bilateral relations. Soviet ships were then being used to help Kuwait and Saudi Arabia transport oil safely out of the Gulf.

The announcement of a Soviet withdrawal from Afghanistan in February 1988 removed a major barrier to the improvement of bilateral ties. However, a major blow occurred at the end of that month when Iraq launched a missile attack against Tehran. The Iranian leadership denounced the Soviet Union for supplying Iraq with the missiles, and Iranians angrily surrounded the Soviet embassy in Tehran shouting anti-Soviet slogans. At the end of July Iran finally accepted a cease-fire agreement with Iraq, largely due to the Iraqi army's successful reversal of an Iranian offensive. After the cease-fire, relations between Iran and the Soviet Union greatly improved, and in March 1989 Velayati went to the Soviet Union where the two countries announced a major new gas deal. The death of Khomeini in June 1989 did not impede the meeting between the new Iranian leader Hashemi Rafsanjani and Gorbachev in the same month. The meeting was accompanied by media reports that the Soviet Union had offered Iran 'sophisticated weaponry and advanced radar' in return for a more positive and helpful Iranian policy in the area.[11] As Gorbachev was to observe: 'Geography and history have determined that the USSR and Iran are "fated", one might say, to live peacefully as good neighbours and to co-operate with one another.'[12]

The Soviet Union and Turkey to 1991

After the military take-over on 27 May 1960, relations between the Soviet Union and Turkey began improving. The military government of Kemal Gürsel was quickly recognised by Moscow and a month later Khrushchev told its leaders that 'it is our deep conviction that the most sincere relations between our two countries would develop if Turkey embarked upon the road of neutrality', though he let it be known that neutrality was 'not a condition for beginning the improvement of our relations'.[13] Turkey played a vital part in the Western military bloc against the Soviet Union. According to one military analysis,

With Greece, Turkey can put approximately 25 divisions into the Balkans. As a result, the Warsaw Pact requires somewhere around 34 divisions to defend against them. [...] By the same token Turkey has 8 divisions in eastern Turkey near the Transcaucus which forces the Soviet Union to keep approximately 12 divisions forward deployed and in a fairly high state of readiness.[14]

Therefore, the necessity for keeping Soviet military resources and personnel on the southern flank undermined the Warsaw Pact's level of strength on the central arena.

Washington, in particular, placed a high value on Turkey because NATO bases to the east of the country (İnçirlik, Mus and Batman) made it possible to strike both the Transcaucus and, if necessary, the Persian Gulf. Turkey's control of the Bosphorus was another key asset to NATO. According to estimates, '60 per-cent of Soviet exports and 50 per-cent of Soviet imports' passed through the Bosphorus. In 1986 alone, there were over 18,000 Soviet ship transits through the Straits. In addition, 'an average of 150 Soviet merchant ships ply the Mediterranean on any given day...approximately a third of their combatants are in the Black Sea'.[15] Turkey was, in a geographical sense, also a barrier between the Soviet Union and the Arab world. Added to this, it was a base for AWACs and other air surveillance which seriously limited Soviet air power in the eastern Mediterranean and the Middle East. According to US Defense Department estimates Turkey provided as much as 25 per cent of NATO's hard intelligence.[16] Following the fall of the Shah in Iran, when US radar and surveillance installations were downgraded, Turkey's role became even more important.

These figures did not hinder Soviet persistence in courting Ankara until by 'the summer of 1978 its developing ties with Turkey were crowned by a political document on the principles of good neighbourliness and friendly co-operation'.[17] This included a Turkish pledge to uphold the Montreux Convention of 1936 regarding the Straits in which free navigation was assured during peacetime, and no ships which threatened the Soviet navy were permitted in the Black Sea.

Gorbachev continued to place a high priority on Turkey and his reforms were generally welcomed in Ankara. However, former US Ambassador to Turkey George McGhee seemed to suggest that Washington was unconcerned with these developments because the two countries were more likely to differ than to agree. McGhee concluded that despite closer relations with the Soviet Union, there was little 'evidence that Ankara was moving closer to Moscow, in the political sense'.[18] One incident in 1989 temporarily caused tension when a Soviet pilot assaulted a guard and commandeered a MiG-29 to Turkey on 20 May. Turkey agreed to return the plane on the same day but it refused to send back the pilot. On 14 June the Turkish ambassador was called to Moscow where he was warned that 'the actions of the Turkish side with regard to the criminal A.M. Zuyev can only be viewed by the Soviet Union as contrary to the spirit of good-neighbourliness in Soviet-Turkish relations and their current positive development'.[19] But bilateral relations were mutually recognised as being far more important than that single incident, which was quickly swept aside.

Soviet-Turkish relations under Gorbachev continued to improve until the very last year of the existence of the USSR. Turkish President Turgut Özal arrived on an official visit in Moscow on 11 March 1991 and met Gorbachev the following day. The outcome of the meeting was the signing of the Treaty of Friendship, Good-neighbourliness and Co-operation between the two countries. From the perspective of both countries, the significance of the treaty was raised in the light of the break-up of the Soviet Union.

Russia and Turkey: diplomacy and trade on separate tracks

Kozyrev's visit to Turkey in June 1994, as part of a NATO Conference on Partnership for Peace, resulted in meetings with Prime Minister Tansu Ciller and his Turkish counterpart Hikmet Cetin. In the Kozyrev-Cetin meeting the issue of the Straits was raised and Russia's displeasure with Ankara's plan to introduce new guidelines and restrictions was expressed. The Turkish side seemed as determined as ever to stand its ground. 'If necessary', Cetin said, 'we can clarify some of the issues again and explain that they do not violate the Montreux convention...but Turkey cannot allow a city of 10 million people to be threatened'.[20] The emergence of new Muslim republics and fears that Turkey was seeking to expand its reign of influence into these areas created added tension between the two countries.

Turkey's introduction of new procedures for seafaring through the Straits, implemented on 1 July 1994, led to criticisms from the Russian Foreign Ministry because the move was seen as an attempt to limit Russian merchant and military shipping out of the Black Sea. Deputy Foreign Minister Albert Chernishev complained that while Moscow accepted the need to update and improve rules and codes to improve seafaring, they should not have been made unilaterally. He accused the Ankara government of acting contrary to the spirit of the Geneva Conventions. 'The interests of all parties concerned and particularly those of the Black Sea region should also be taken into account', Chernisev maintained.[21] Foreign Ministry spokesman Grigorii Karasin echoed this point and added that freedom of navigation in the Black Sea was of primary importance for the Russian economy. 'In this connection the Russian side has repeatedly made clear that we are unable to recognise the introduction of procedures which essentially amount to having to ask for authorisation to cross the Straits and unilateral restrictions up to and including a *de facto* ban on such crossings for certain categories of vessels as legally binding.'[22]

Turkey had long been irritated by Moscow's unrelenting attention to the issue of the Straits because it believed that Russia's ultimate motive was some form of control over them. Ankara sought to counter Russian complaints by arguing that the changes it had introduced were intended to improve sea traffic, which had grown rapidly over the years, and for the sake of improving environmental and safety standards for the ten million citizens of Istanbul. The undercurrent of Turkish suspicions was expressed in extreme terms by the Turkish General Gueres in June 1994. He claimed that Russia posed a bigger threat to Turkey than it did during the Cold War, arguing that 'Moscow had expansionist desires towards the Caucasus region, Ukraine and even the Balkan states'.[23] The Russian Foreign Ministry was sufficiently concerned to make an immediate response in which it expressed its hope 'that the statements made by Gueres do not reflect the point of view of Turkey's political leadership...'.[24]

The Turkish political establishment had fears of its own, caused by the rise of Russian nationalism and the possibility that it could become uncontrollable to the existing leadership in Moscow. Both the government and media of Turkey paid much attention to the rise of Vladimir Zhirinovskii, the Russian ultra-nationalist whose comments were offensive to all of Russia's neighbours. The Turkish Foreign Ministry prevented Zhirinovskii from entering Turkey in February 1994, wrecking his plan to lead a fifteen-man delegation at the invitation of a Turkish newspaper.

Another major point of difference between the two countries which continued to affect bilateral relations was the traditional support shown by Moscow to the Kurdish movement and their quest for independence. Yeltsin's government had made clear its support and respect for the integrity of the Turkish Republic and attempted to distance itself from the terrorist PKK, the Kurdish Communist Party. However, the Turkish government did not contain its anger at Moscow for allowing Kurdish groups to hold a conference in the Russian capital in February 1994. The conference was sponsored by the Russian Ministry of Affairs of Nationalities and Regional Policy and was titled 'Kurdistan at a historical and political cross-roads'. Turkish President Suleiman Demeirel warned Moscow that 'our people are very sensitive to this issue. It is necessary that Russia provide additional explanations to prevent the impression that it supports terrorism.'[25] In fairness to the Russian government, the Turkish government's view that any form of Kurdish nationalist expression represented terrorism was not shared by most countries of the world community.

Yet the Turkish government did not view the special attention paid to the Kurdish issue by the Russian press and diplomatic officials with benign indifference. The Kurdish point of view was often reflected in the mainstream press, which implied that the fault lay with the Turkish leadership. One article, openly supporting Kurdish self-determination, asked: 'Is that really such a high price to end a thirteen-year-long war, which has already taken 25,000 lives and costs Ankara from $7 billion to $9 billion a year?'[26] The reader was reminded that the forty million Kurds scattered around the world were the largest ethnic group without a homeland. More significantly, it was noted that one million of them lived in Russia and other CIS states. Realistically, however, in the words of the Russian commentator, 'the Kurds recognise that Russia is not currently in a position to quarrel with Turkey, its largest trade partner outside the CIS'[27] Nonetheless, in October

1998, it became clear that Russia was host to PKK leader Abdullah Ojailan, after he fled Syria under Turkish pressure. The Duma voted in early November to reject Turkish demands that he should be extradited. Thus the Russian government was left in the embarrassing position of explaining itself to Ankard for allowing Ojailan to live in relative safety in a western suburb of Moscow. Clearly, the issue has negatively damaged Russian-Turkish relations as the 1990s come to a close.

Since 1995 Turkey had sought to moderate its relations with Russia. Observers noted that while Russia remained muted about Turkish operations against Kurds in northern Iraq, 'Ankara reciprocated on the Chechnia issue', and it was also pointed out that 'Russia has the lion's share of the $5.2 billion Turkish investments in the CIS'.[28] The trade links continued to flourish between the two countries to the extent that each side viewed the other as a vital economic partner. In December 1995 an agreement was signed between Oleg Davydov, Deputy Prime Minister and Minister of Foreign Economic Relations, and Bilgin Unan, the Turkish ambassador to Moscow, in which Turkey extended a $350 million credit to Russia and the two countries restructured the debt of the USSR.[29] The agreement was seen as a breakthrough in resolving the Soviet debt issue and allowing new investment to flow into Russia. The turnover of trade between the two countries stood at $3 billion in 1995. In addition the value of contracts for the construction of facilities by Turkish firms stood at $5 billion in that year. There were also other important factors such as the well-being of Turkish workers in Russia and the number of Russian tourists in Turkey that added to the value of economic interaction. Moreover, Turkey agreed to earmark $100 million of the $370 million Russian debt for the purchase of weapons for the Turkish army.[30]

The coming to power of Necmettin Erbakan in 1996 was not met with enthusiasm in Moscow. The Russian media compared his views to the militant leaders of Iran, and quoted him as saying that 'our goal is to liberate Bosnia, Azerbaijan, Chechnia and Jerusalem'.[31] The seventy-year-old Erbakan of the Welfare Party was averse to the growing Western influence in Turkey and wanted to restore traditional values in society. But a traditional Islamic outlook, as Moscow found so often in the past, was not necessarily sympathetic towards Russia because it was accompanied with many historic suspicions.

Toward the end of 1996, the niggling differences between Turkey and Russia had not subsided. Russia's dismay with Turkey's indirect support for the Chechens intensified when a Chechen mission was opened in Istanbul. This was the reaction in a statement by the Russian Foreign Ministry in early December 1996: 'Governments that allow Ichkeria's so-called missions to be turned into embassies will be taking a clearly unfriendly step toward Russia, attempting through such action to challenge the territorial integrity of the Russian Federation.'[32] According to Russia's Military Doctrine, any country threatening the unity of the Russian Federation was in effect making a declaration of war. The strong language from Moscow led to a counter-response from Ankara insisting that the mission would not be upgraded and that it considered 'Chechnia to be a member of the Russian Federation and [Turkey] respects Russia's territorial integrity'.[33]

Moscow also revealed some unease at Turkey's military build-up and its upgrading of naval power in the Black Sea. According to Russian defence sources quoted in the press, the Turkish fleet had a clear superiority over the Black Sea Fleet that was two to one in Turkey's favour. The Turkish navy continued to be augmented 'not only by American-built fighting ships, but also by small craft produced in Turkey'.[34] The 700,000-strong Turkish army was the second largest in NATO and Ankara's plan to modernise it was a clear-cut challenge to Moscow's military strategists to utilise and upgrade resources for securing the defence of that region.

The visit to Russia by Deputy Prime Minister and Foreign Minister Tansu Ciller in mid-December 1996 was accompanied with a list of complaints brought to Moscow which included matters such as 'the sale of Russian weapons to the government of Cyprus and the activities of Kurdish organisations' on Russian territory.[35] The first point was a reference to Russian plans to sell Cyprus several S-300 surface-to-air missile systems for around $660 million. Russia had also been supplying the small Mediterranean island T-80U tanks in 1996.[36] In return, the Russian government delivered its own misgivings, which included the 'restrictions that Ankara has imposed on the passage of tankers through the Bosphorus

and the activities of numerous organisations that have been providing support to the Chechen separatists'.[37]

On 15 December 1997 Prime Minister Chernomyrdin visited
Turkey in an effort to resolve some of the political differences
between the two countries. In reference to Russian misgivings
about Turkish involvement in the Caucasus and the latter country's
concern about Moscow's proposed sale of arms to Cyprus, Mesut
Yilmaz, Chernomyrdin's counterpart, said that it had been 'agreed
to refrain from acts that would pose threat to each other's security
or territorial integrity'.[38] The two sides also highlighted the need
to resolve differences over other issues, including sea-traffic through
the Straits and the routing of gas and oil piplines through the
region. However, these issues continued to be separated from
bilateral economic relations as a $20 billion gas deal was signed
between the two countries and further measures were proposed
to facilitate trade between the two countries. Reports suggested
that the volume of trade between the two countries at the beginning
of 1998 had reached $12 billion a year.[39]

Russian officials happily pointed towards the ever-growing trade
links with Turkey but there was a more forthright tendency to
discuss the political differences by 1998. A senior diplomat in the
Foreign Ministry, discussing Ankara's ambitions and potential threat
to Russia's regional domination, rather sarcastically commented
that 'Turkey exaggerated its own capabilities and pictured itself
without an objective base'.[40] In other words, Turkey's leaders did
not quite have their feet on the ground when considering their
country's role in the regional context. Primakov continued the
Soviet policy of seeking to co-operate with Ankara, despite the
various bilateral issues which left them in disagreement. Although
many of these differences were not resolved by early 1999, the
growing economic dependency of the two countries on each
other was a positive counterweight to the political problems.

Russia and Iran

Russia found a similarly mixed relationship with Iran. In the past
Iran had had a long-standing policy of 'negative equilibrium' with
regard to foreign policy, which was based on rivalling Russo-British
interests in the nineteenth and early twentieth centuries. This
took on a revised form in the Khomeini era with the slogan

'neither East nor West' characterising the country's foreign policy. In the post-Soviet era Iran was internationally isolated while Russia was left greatly weakened. Both shared similar worries about instability in Central Asia and the Caucasus. Although many experts predicted in 1991 that there would be inevitable conflict between the two countries because of rivalry over the Central Asian republics, the opposite actually seemed to take place, with co-operation being the dominant characteristic.

Well before the December 1993 elections which brought Zhirinovskii to world attention, Russia's policies in the former Soviet republics had already become more assertive. In the early years following the demise of the Soviet Union, 'Russian policymakers expressed great scepticism about Tehran's intentions in these predominantly Muslim areas' of Central Asia and the Caucasus.[41] Moscow's new democratic leadership expected Turkey to be the more favoured partner in promoting moderation in the region. But the pragmatic influence of President Rafsanjani enabled a rapid *rapprochement* between Iran and Russia in the early 1990s, to the extent that the United States began to show growing agitation at this development. Both Iran and Russia refrained from criticising the other on a variety of issues ranging from the war in Bosnia to events in the Gulf. For example, when Russia announced that it planned to sell a number of advanced weapons to Kuwait, Iranian news reports were uncharacteristically neutral, pointing out that the $800 million deal was vital for the Russian economy.

The most controversial development in Russian-Iranian relations was the announcement that Russia would complete the Bushehr nuclear plant in southern Iran by 1999. Reza Amrollahi, head of the Iranian Nuclear Energy organisation, pointed out that Germany, which carried out 85 per cent of construction, had refused to complete the deal following pressure from the United States. The Iranians were angered by the German withdrawal and the claims made by Washington that the plant was a cover for an Iranian military nuclear project. Tehran argued that the allegations were intended to divert attention from Israeli refusals to sign the Nuclear Non-Proliferation Treaty (NPT) which was up for renewal at the time. But this did not lessen genuine concern by the United States, and Iran's neighbours, about Tehran's motives and the development of Russo-Iranian ties. Yeltsin attempted to answer

US worries during his visit in late September 1994 when he said that 'this co-operation is not extensive, nor does it threaten regional stability'.[42] But the following month Chernishev met with an Iranian Foreign Ministry delegation to 'examine all aspects of bilateral relations', with Kozyrev characterising existing ties as good and stable at the end of the two-day meeting.[43] Deputy Foreign Minister Mahmoud Va'ezi, who led the Iranian delegation, announced that Iran and Russia had signed thirteen documents relating to bilateral co-operation encompassing commercial, scientific, technical and cultural ties.

On 8 January 1995 the two countries officially signed the contract for the completion of the Bushehr Atomic Energy Station. Under extreme criticism from the United States and other countries in the Middle East concerned about Iran's nuclear potential, Tehran found it necessary to make a defence of the project. The Iranian government argued that while the West had hundreds of similar plants, it had 'repeatedly tried to deny Iran the right to have its own power plant'. The statement added that 'it was natural that Iran would turn to Russia to finish the construction of the power plant in Bushehr'.[44] Tehran announced that 500 Russian engineers and inspectors would be working on the site, though 'the Russians say they will send 3,000' and about 150 of them began arriving in the early months of 1995.[45]

Russia's leadership must have been aware that such a deal would result in a strain in relations with many key countries in the Middle East as well as the United States. Iraq and Israel had most to fear from a nuclear-armed Iran. Israel's government and media strongly attacked Moscow's support for Iran and expressed concern about the potential to transform the use of nuclear power for military purposes. Russian-Iranian co-operation resumed the old dilemma regarding the latter's bitter enemy Iraq. However, Primakov appeared to have deftly convinced both sides that Russia supported them both in their shared aim of ending US domination of the Gulf region. Moscow also criticised Washington for imposing sanctions on the two countries and for its large-scale military sales to the GCC states, particularly Saudi Arabia. Primakov was subtly downplaying the differences between Iraq and Iran and highlighting their shared interests, which Moscow supported. At the same time, perhaps with a forked tongue, Primakov sought to assure Iran's enemies, such as Israel and Saudi Arabia, that Moscow's co-operation with Tehran was to their benefit because it would have a moderating effect on the region.[46]

Despite this atmosphere of criticism, further exchange in the nuclear field between Russia and Iran was announced on 18 February. But there was added concern that the internal instability in Russia and the organised crime factor would allow the possibility of the smuggling of equipment and material which could enable countries such as Iran to develop their own nuclear programmes. Israeli television reported that Turkish security forces in Istanbul arrested several Iranians smuggling 'plutonium and osmium'. The report said that the arrested men had been under surveillance and that they had been in regular contact with the Iranian deputy defence minister. On 20 February 1995 Israeli Foreign Minister Shimon Peres said that 'according to information he received in Paris, Iran will be able to produce its first nuclear bomb within three years'.[47] The report also added, without giving any sources, that 'a senior Moscow official claimed that the Russian decision to supply four nuclear reactors to Iran will help the Iranians manufacture a nuclear bomb within a few years'.[48] The factual basis of such allegations was very difficult to prove, but Russian Minister of Atomic Energy Viktor Mikhailov stressed that 'the nuclear reactors which are to be delivered to Iran are not capable of producing plutonium used in nuclear weapons'.[49] He did not believe that Iran would be capable of developing its nuclear power for military use.

The Russian Foreign Ministry journal *Mezhdunarodnaia zhizn'* contained articles on a regular basis defending Moscow's right to co-operate with whom it chose. In one such article, Iu. Melnikov and V. Frolov wrote that the United States continued to stubbornly ignore 'the right of Russia to provide nuclear reactors, under the control of the NPT, to Iran for peaceful aims, and Russia's interest in supporting and developing the friendly and business ties with its neighbours'.[50] In their view, Russia could not neglect the development of 'normal bilateral relations with its influential southern neighbour, regardless of outside pressure on [Moscow] to do so by using the issue of the nuclear reactors'.[51] They stressed that Washington had neglected to take into account the fact that 'the issue here is not only about financial interests but also about the geo-political interests of the Russian Federation and considerations of the national security on the southern borders of the CIS'.[52]

The construction of the nuclear reactor represented only one side of the multifaceted nature of Iranian-Russian relations. Bilateral trade, ranging from raw energy to foodstuffs, led Moscow to be highly optimistic about the future to the extent that it was prepared to face such international pressure at a time when Russia needed Western support as an emerging democracy. In 1995 President Bill Clinton had made it clear that he wished to limit the influence of Iran by imposing a trade ban and calling on other countries to do so. Washington's view of Iran was that it was a destabilising factor in the Gulf and the rest of the Middle East. For example, its support for Hezbollah in Lebanon had greatly undermined the peace negotiations on the Syrian/Lebanese-Israeli tracks. Its support for militant groups in countries ranging from Algeria to Afghanistan was a contributory factor to war and bloodshed in those regions. Hence Russia's nuclear and other economic deals with Iran were perceived by Washington as enabling Tehran to escape international efforts to squeeze the Islamic regime into refraining from its adventures outside its own borders.

Moscow reacted angrily to Washington's position by claiming, first, that the United States had exploited the lucrative Arab Gulf markets without taking into account the poor human rights record and the lack of democracy in those countries. Russia believed that as the United States had seen it justifiable to overlook such matters for the sake of profit with regard to Saudi Arabia it had little right to criticise Russo-Iranian economic co-operation. Russian officials such as Deputy Foreign Minister Gregorii Mamedov insisted that Russia would continue to seek ties with Iran. He reflected the growing view among Russians in general that 'Russia is not a colony. It is an independent state and its decisions will be on the basis of its national interests.'[53] This sentiment was reported by the Iranian media during Mamedov's visit to Tehran on 26 February 1995. However, Russia's press agency Itar-Tass reported a different angle to the meeting, saying that there were differences between the two sides regarding the Non-Proliferation Treaty. The report commented that Iran wanted 'further participation in the said treaty only for a limited period and on several conditions' while Russia favoured 'unlimited and unconditional prolongation of this international document'.[54] From this statement cynics claimed that Moscow was seeking to deflect international criticisms. However, in the Soviet era Moscow was meticulous in preventing the spread of nuclear weapons; indeed, that was a major factor in the split with China. Russia's leaders were without doubt unlikely to stray from this path, because it was not in the national interest to have small unpredictable regimes controlling nuclear missiles on its own doorstep.

There were other problems affecting Russian-Iranian relations, in both the economic and political spheres. Despite Russia's participation in Iran's large-scale economic projects, the Tehran government had been lax in paying Russian companies for the services provided. In the past, the Soviet government sometimes turned a blind eye for the sake of securing political and diplomatic gains but in the post-Soviet era, when capitalist values became dominant, it was more difficult to neglect the hard cash factor. Overdue debts by Iran amounted to $582 million by the end of July 1995 and the figure continued to grow. Of this sum there was '$383 million owed to the Rosvooruzhenie [Russian Arms] State Company'.[55] There were also complaints by Russian sources that the quality of supplies from Iran to Russia were often of a low standard and did not always meet deadlines. However, by the end of 1996, successes were achieved in resolving the economic problems between the two countries. Deputy Prime Minister Oleg Davydov, who for the first time had promoted the concept of a strategic alliance between Iran and Russia, participated in an agreement in which Tehran would pay back the $600 million debt to Moscow by the end of the year 2000 with oil. Moreover, it was aimed to increase the trade turnover between the two countries from $400 million in 1996 (the figure was $200 million in 1995), to $4 billion by the year 2000.[56]

Yet at times, it did appear as if Russian diplomatic efforts were deliberately attempting to understate the development of bilateral ties, in order to prevent close attention from the United States in particular and other Middle East states in general. During his visit to Iran in December 1996, Primakov complained that the media was 'trying to put a spurious accent on my stay. [...] We are not having talks here [in Tehran] which are directed against anyone else. [...] Evidently, someone is trying to use this visit to cause conflict with someone.'[57] Yet Primakov delivered a message from Yeltsin to Rafsanjani which stated 'the urgency of establishing greater co-operation between Russia and Iran to end instability in the region'.[58]

Primakov's deputy, Posuvaliuk, told journalists in a news conference on 25 December 1996 that there was no need for the West or anyone to worry about the improving ties with Iran. It was still somewhat indicative of Moscow's sensitivity regarding the issue that there was a need to continually justify the relationship. Posuvaliuk insisted that 'the US administration must understand that we have a sovereign right to build our relations with Iran so as to promote our interests'.[59] In the same breath he added that no country was more interested in peace and stability in the region than Russia. Posuvaliuk noted, with reason,'that as a neighbour of Iran, Russia had a far greater interest than the United States in keeping Iran nuclear-free and he reaffirmed that the Bushehr nuclear project was purely for peaceful purposes. Iran and Russia had signed a Memorandum of Understanding which defined export control and according to the deputy foreign minister this highlighted the positive nature of Russian foreign policy in the world community. He argued that the Memorandum was 'an important achievement in our efforts to draw Iran into the international non-proliferation regime' since it would 'help in having objects and technologies covered by export control to be used only for their intended purposes'.[60]

In an interview given to a Russian newspaper at the end of 1997, Primakov once more criticised US allegations that Moscow was supporting Iran's rocket technology programme. He pointed out that only a few weeks earlier Russian Security Service officials had caught and expelled Iranian agents attempting to smuggle parts necessary for such military purposes. Primakov asked the interviewer: 'Why should we arm a neighbouring country with rocket technology with a larger radius?'[61]

Primakov criticised both the United States and Israel for endeavouring to wreck the growing relations between Russia and Iran by exaggerating the threat they posed to international security. The Islamic Conference, held in Tehran in December 1997, merely heightened Israeli fears about a growing coalition of states, supported by Russia, which could undermine Israel's future security. Netanyahu warned that the more Iran 'arms itself, and in the absence of any effort to stop this process...more and more Arab leaders will flock to Iran'.[62] However, Primakov repeated that stable and positive Russian-Iranian relations would actually enhance Israel's security by keeping Iran within the fold of the international community.

Russia strongly encouraged the development of trade relations with Iran. In March 1996 Velayati went to Moscow at the end of an extensive trip through CIS territories. There was much discussion about developing and linking the infrastructures of Iran, Russia, Central Asia and Caucasia in order to create a large new economic zone. It was therefore odd that one Foreign Ministry official should state in October 1996, 'I can't say that Iran has a special priority for Russia', but he could not deny that it was 'a relationship of good neighbours and joint interests'.[63] When interviewed for this book, the Russian official was careful not to show excessive enthusiasm for the Tehran regime and the state of relations. But he reiterated the view in Moscow that 'the isolation of a country such as Iran is not in the interest of the area'.[64]

However, Primakov's visit to Iran at the end of 1996 underlined the eagerness to improve relations as Russia began to develop a foreign policy centred around geo-strategic interests which placed neighbouring areas as top priority. Primakov also sought to utilise the contacts he had developed with the leadership in Tehran to put forward Russian interests in the Gulf region. The Russian foreign minister said that the two countries had shared interest in 'preventing an increased military presence in the Persian Gulf' which effectively meant that the two countries were opposed to US policy in the oil-rich region.[65] Primakov's visit, and his subsequent comments, were clearly incompatible with Washington's wish to isolate Iran in the same way that Iraq was at that time. He insisted that 'Iran should be a fully-fledged participant in the international community', and described bilateral relations as 'developing along an ascending curve'.[66] His Iranian counterpart Velayati went so far as to describe relations as being 'at the highest point for the last two centuries'.[67]

A new dimension: Central Asia and the Caucasus

The new republics formed after the collapse of the Soviet Union in 1991 were home to large Muslim populations, making them prone to influence from Iran and Turkey. It became possible that

Russia would face a serious challenge to its dominance over these co-members of the Commonwealth of Independent States. However, by 1998 neither Iran nor Turkey had made substantial inroads into these areas, in terms of economic, political and cultural influence. Radical Iran proved to be rigidly pragmatic in its approach, co-operating closely with Russia in all regional matters ranging from the civil war in Tajikistan to resource-sharing in the Caspian Sea. Turkey was less willing to act harmoniously with Russia but it took care not to overstep the limit which Moscow deemed necessary for its national security. In other words, it did not pursue policies which threatened the integrity of the CIS or directly challenged Russia's position as a great power in the region.

Moscow's policy in 1992 of deliberately distancing Russia from the Muslim republics, partly as an effort to avoid offending the nationalist sentiments of other republics and partly because of a nationalist tide which sought to assert a separate Russian identity, provided a ray of opportunity for Turkey and Iran to make headway. But events in the Muslim republics brought them to the forefront of Moscow's concerns. The most immediate was the civil war in Tajikistan which led to the involvement of Russian troops. The more obvious attention of Turkey and Iran was then perceived to have an effect on the national security of Russia itself and posed the challenge that if Moscow did not devise a clear-cut policy in its own backyard then someone else would take its place. Observers began to warn that Muslim fundamentalism and radicalism, imported via Iran and Afghanistan, would quickly spread in the Caucasus and Central Asia and threaten the unity of Russia itself. A rather simplified view began to be espoused describing 'Central Asia as a key link in a Muslim fundamentalist "arc of instability" stretching from North Africa to western China'.[68]

When on 8 December 1991 Russia, Ukraine and Belarus met to form their own Slav Commonwealth the leaders of Central Asia felt greatly humiliated. Although later that month the Central Asian republics were included, there was a general feeling of betrayal and a loss of trust. Despite this, it was surprising that in the following years, the new Muslim republics did not move closer to Turkey and Iran. Initially, Turkey was perceived as the most welcome alternative and Ankara was quickest off the mark to exploit any potential economic benefits. Added to this was the surge of nationalist feeling both in Turkey and in the republics, where dreams of a great new Turkic world stretching from the Balkans to China suddenly appeared to be a distant reality. The Central Asian leaders responded to Turkish manoeuvres to show Russia that they could have a powerful alternative that was a NATO member and backed by the United States. In other words, Turkey could provide the Asian republics with more leverage in their dealings with Russia.

This early enthusiasm for Turkey was tempered by certain difficulties that could not be easily ignored. The most obvious one was that Turkey did not actually share a border with the Islamic republics and was geographically distant from the five Central Asian republics. The Pan-Turkic sentiments expressed in the first year of independence were looked upon with great suspicion in Iran, which attempted to consolidate its position with Persian-speaking Tajikistan. Critics of the Iranian regime accused Tehran of taking part in the civil war in Tajikistan and causing instability there. While there had been evidence of Iranian involvement, it was unlikely to have been encouraged by the pragmatic Rafsanjani or the Foreign Ministry, which tried to mediate a peace in that country.

The fighting between Azerbaijan and Armenia over the enclave of Nagorno-Karabakh initially pushed the Baku government closer to Iran which it hoped would be a powerful ally. However, to Baku's disappointment Iran's response was tame. There was no revolutionary language, nor a call for the resumption of the Crusades to win Muslim lands, nor even threats that there would be Iranian involvement. Rather, there was a call to find a peaceful solution that would not be detrimental to either side. When in January 1991, before the demise of the USSR, Azerbaijan's Deputy Prime Minister visited Tehran to seek support and co-operation, 'he was forthrightly informed that Tehran would reciprocate within the framework of existing co-operation between Tehran and Moscow'.[69] Turkey on the other hand was less coy about courting Baku. The growing links between Turkey and Azerbaijan were duly noted in the Russian press. On his first visit to Turkey, in 1994, President Gaidar Aliev signed a friendship agreement and Turkey promised to provide economic help. Aliev said that 'as a new chapter and new stage in bilateral relations between Azerbaijan and Turkey, I think that we have succeeded in laying the basis for their further, more successful development'.[70] Similar visits were made by the leaders of Turkmenistan, Uzbekistan, Kyrgyzstan and Kazakhstan who on achieving independence announced that Turkey would enjoy top priority in their foreign policy. In October 1992 a summit meeting of these Turkic states was held in Ankara with Turkey establishing an aid programme, the Turkish International Co-operation Administration (TICA), extending credits of up to $1 billion. But the main effort was in the cultural field, with Ankara attempting to convince the other Turkic republics to adopt a Latin alphabet instead of the Cyrillic. Moreover, thousands of university and educational scholarships were made available to the newly liberated people of Central Asia and the Caucasus. These attempts at cultural domination did not go unnoticed in Moscow. Adding to the mutual hostility was Ankara's support for the Azeri cause, clashing directly with Russia's tilt towards the Armenians.

In Central Asia, Kazakhstan was most important for Russia because of the nuclear arsenal on its territory and the large population of Russians living there. Throughout the Muslim republics there was the problem of inter-ethnic tensions: all had a substantial Russian population which threatened to lead to a violent backlash, with Kazakhstan inhabited by the largest percentage of Russians, as the table below shows:

THE POPULATION OF THE CENTRAL ASIAN REPUBLICS
AND AZERBAIJAN, 1989 CENSUS [71]

	Population (millions)	Russian minority (%)	Other minorities (%)
Azerbaijan	7.1	6	Armenian 6
Turkmenistan	3.6	10	Uzbek 9; Kazakh 3
Uzbekistan	20.3	8	Tajik 5; Kazkakh 4
Tajikistan	5.3	8	Uzbek 24
Kyrgyzstan	4.4	22	Uzbek 13; Ukraine 3
Kazakhstan	16.7	38	German 6; Ukraine 5

Of all the Muslim republics Kazakhstan had been the most eager to ensure more co-operation with Russia. A Treaty of Friendship, Collaboration and Mutual Aid was signed between

Russia and Kazakhstan on 25 May 1992. Articles 2 to 10 of the agreement stressed the importance of developing a joint foreign and defence policy. Article 2 focused on the need for the parties to 'carry out a co-ordinated foreign policy', while Article 3 stated that there should be 'joint deployment of military bases'. As if to make the message even more blunt to other regional powers, Article 6 stated that the two countries 'will not participate in any alliance or blocs directed against either of them'.[72]

The republics of Tajikistan, Kyrgyzstan, Turkmenistan and Uzbekistan were the poorest of the successor states of the Soviet Union. Largely for this reason, there was much talk about the possibility of a union to be created between these countries to form a new power based on the historic state of Turkestan. This idea quickly collapsed in the midst of allegations that this was an Uzbek ambition to dominate its much smaller neighbours. But this did not prevent the leaders of these countries from turing to history for ideas and they joined together in June 1992 alongside the leaderships of Iran, Turkey, Kazakhstan, Pakistan and Azerbaijan to discuss the possibility of opening up the Old Silk Road, an ancient route linking China with the Mediterranean. There were also aims to create a new Central Asian economic and cultural zone. Although this appeared to be a logical step which would fill a newly created geographic gap, there were far too many stumbling blocks for this to occur successfully.[73]

In the latter half of 1993 Russia began to re-impose its position in the areas between itself and Iran and Turkey. In an article written by Foreign Minister Kozyrev in September 1993, a new language was emanating from Moscow about the security of Russia and the CIS. Kozyrev wrote that because of the 'deep-rooted' ties with its neighbours Russia 'could not and did not have the moral right to remain indifferent' to events taking shape there.[74] Kozyrev defended Russia's 'peace-making' role in the various conflicts taking place in Central Asia and the Caucasus, arguing that they did not contradict UN principles. Further still, he suggested that Russia had a right to act as it deemed necessary in these areas in order to guarantee national security. Russia's knowledge and influence in the region enabled it to act quickly, Kozyrev argued. He cited the examples of Tajikistan and Abkhazia where the international reaction was slow and inadequate, hence leaving Russia with the most important role to play. Russia was evidently becoming more assertive in 1993, paying increasing attention to the region that was being described as the Near Abroad. As Kozyrev explained, 'this is not a "neo-imperial" but still a unique kind of geo-political space', in which only Russia can play the role of peace-maker and stabiliser of a potentially explosive region.[75]

Turkmenistan was the least receptive to Russian influence among the Central Asian states. Ashgabad looked more favourably towards Iran after 1993 because of the realisation that both shared an interest in the development of their oil and petro-chemicals industries. Iranian President Rafsanjani visited Turkmenistan in October 1993 and signed with President Niiazov valuable economic agreements, 'the most important being the construction of pipelines to carry Turkmen gas and oil through Iran to Turkey or to the Persian Gulf'.[76] Rafsanjani and the more moderate elements of the leadership in Tehran stressed that their interest in Central Asia was purely economic and cultural and that they did not have a political agenda.

Rafsanjani also travelled across the Caspian Sea to Azerbaijan where he met President Gaidar Aliev in Baku. Azerbaijan's war with Armenia prompted many to speculate that the religious élite in Tehran would force a policy change to give support for the Azeri cause. During his visit the Armenians had pushed deeper into Azeri territory yet the Iranian president's comments were noticeably controlled compared to the fiery religious language that the ruling clerics were better known for. Rafsanjani told reporters that Armenia's assault on 'the territory of the Republic of Azerbaijan is regrettable and a source of anxiety...the world of Islam will not allow such an event to create hostility and grudges between the nations of the region'.[77] These carefully chosen words were effectively saying that despite the fact that one Christian country had attacked a neighbouring Muslim one, Tehran did not encourage grudges against Armenia by Muslims.

The Armenian advance to reach Nagorno-Karabakh meant that 10 per cent of Azerbaijan's territory was under occupation. Some of the fighting had actually been taking place on the Iranian-Azeri border. Towards the end of the visit, on 27 October, it had been revealed that the Armenians were stepping up their military offensive yet Rafsanjani remained restrained in his language, saying only that he was 'deeply concerned about the aggravation of the situation'.[78] The Iranian president also offered that his country accept the burden of hundreds of thousands of refugees and called for political dialogue between the two countries. Turkey meanwhile had taken a far more pro-Azeri line saying that Nagorno-Karabakh must remain part of Azerbaijan.

Kazakhstan was by far the least susceptible to overtures from Turkey and Iran. When Kazakh nationalists began to publicly air their resentment against their former colonial masters Nazarbaev's response was distinct: 'The Russian people have suffered most of all. During the Great Patriotic War who suffered the heaviest losses? The Russians. And in the 1930s more Russians died from famine and repressions than any other nationality. That is why I say to my opponents: Do not identify the Russian people with the empire.'[79] China had a higher significance for Kazakhstan than Turkey and Iran. During his visit to China in October 1993, Nazarbaev said: 'Kazakhstan takes economic and trade co-operation with China very seriously, as China is our largest trading partner. We are very interested in the experience of economic reform in China, and we particularly hope to learn about China's experience in establishing a market economy.'[80]

As 1993 came to a close relations between Kazakhstan and Russia were strained, mainly as a consequence of Moscow calling for the other successor states to introduce dual citizenship to accommodate the Russians living outside Russia. In that year the proportion of Russians fell to 31 per cent. It was suggested that Russians were leaving because of ill-treatment and discrimination by the Kazakhs but Nazarbaev argued that part of the explanation for this drop was that many Russian servicemen had completed their duties and returned home. The Kazakh leader also attacked the attitude of Russian nationalists within Russia and pointed out that over one million Kazakhs resided in Russia. 'I do not shout from the rooftops about their fate', complained Nazarbaev. He criticised Kozyrev's singing the nationalist tune as being irresponsible: 'The politicians will stand aside when it is the ordinary people who become embroiled in bloodshed.'[81]

Alma Ata continued to seek close relations with Russia despite the fact that Kazakh pride was offended by Moscow. At the end of November 1994, the Kazakh Foreign Minister Kasymzhomat Tokaiev was reported to have told the Interfax news service that his country's relations with Russia were top priority and this would be so 'for many years, most likely forever'.[82] Perhaps with a tinge of sarcasm, Tokaiev added that the two countries 'are doomed to live together'.[83] Since the first year of its independence commentators had pointed out that Nazarbaev's interest in developing close allegiances even with Turkey was not great. For example when Turkey's President Özal visited Kazakhstan in 1992, at around the same time as a visit paid by German Foreign Minister Hans-Dietrich Genscher, one observer noted that while 'Özal's visit was greeted by nationalist-minded intellectuals. [...] Nazarbaev himself appeared to be more interested in developing ties with Germany'.[84] It was Uzbekistan which had the most enthusiasm for Pan-Turkism and it developed friendly ties with Turkey. President Karimov openly stated that 'my country will go forward by the Turkish route'.[85]

On 8 February 1994 Aliev visited Turkey to mark a 'qualitatively new phase in Turkish-Azerbaijani relations'.[86] The two countries signed a ten-year Treaty of Friendship and Co-operation and various economic, cultural and scientific agreements. The two countries also expressed support for the tripartite mediation effort regarding Karabakh launched in 1993, comprising the United States, Russia and Turkey. But both the Azeri leader and Turkish President Suleiman Demirel 'indirectly condemned Russian attempts to mediate a settlement of the conflict unilaterally'.[87] Iran on the other hand intelligently put Russia at ease throughout that period despite the continued improvement of Turkmeni-Iranian relations, with Niiazov describing Iran as an 'island of peace'.[88] This continued improvement of relations alerted the United States and on 4 November 1994 the US Special Representative to the CIS, James Collins, met Niiazov to discuss the possibility of Washington supporting the Ashgabad government. Collins suggested that the United States could help develop the country's oil and gas industry. But he also asked the Turkmeni government to postpone a Ukrainian debt of $600 million which was mainly arrears for payment of Turkmeni gas imports. This was nonetheless an important event for the Ashgabad government which had won US recognition and esteem despite its authoritarian rule and the personality cult that had developed around President Niiazov.

All sides appeared to agree that it was dangerous to allow the tense situation in the Caucasus to grow out of control. Andranik Migranian, adviser to President Yeltsin, warned in an article that any encouragement of the break-away of the Caucasus from the

CIS would lead to 'destabilisation of the northern Caucasus and to squeezing the Russian border to the line of the mouths of the Don and Volga, which would be catastrophic for Russia's future'.[89] He noted that the Caucasus region was 'traditionally a political frontier and object of conflict for spheres of influence between Turkey, Iran and Russia'.[90] He said that one of the consequences would be the encroachment of the Muslim world deeper into the Russian Federation. His attitude reflected the new sense of urgency adopted by Moscow: 'An active Russia policy in Transcaucasus and the integration of this entire region into the geo-political space of the CIS has first-rank significance for the stability of the entire Russian state',[91] adding that such a policy would have consequences for the long-term future.

While the Russian leadership and conservatives in the Russian political system had become vociferous regarding the need for their country to re-impose itself upon the Caucasus and Central Asia, there were initially voices which questioned the need for such a policy. The liberal Westerners had argued that to deepen links with the Asiatic states would be simply holding back the transformation of Russian society into a modern, democratic and Westernised system. Moscow's leadership should concentrate on protecting the border of the Russian Federation and seek to make it the last frontier of the Western world, a separate entity from the world of the East. By the end of 1996, such views were silenced in the Russian political elite, despite the continuing influence of reformers on the Russian president. Instead, Primakov's pro-integrationist views dominated Moscow's thinking and relations with its neighbours.[92]

Conclusion: balancing regional interests

In the cases of both Turkey and Iran, Russia sought a policy of promoting stability. It strove to gain the co-operation and goodwill of both countries mainly by increasing the level of economic interaction. Although differences existed with both countries, Moscow sought to resolve them through compromise and diplomatic channels rather than the tactics used by Stalin after the Second World War. This was not because it feared a Western backlash if it used more aggressive tactics, though there could have been a tough response, but because Stalin's failures and the experience of diplomacy since Khrushchev had taught Moscow that there was more to gain from co-operation.

Russian-Turkish relations had in some ways taken on the same characteristics as those that existed in the Soviet era, in which economic relations developed fruitfully while diplomatic relations were more tense. By the beginning of 1997, for example, while Turkish workers and businessmen were playing a very prominent part in rebuilding Russian cities, senior officials in Moscow were being blunt with the Ankara government over the missiles to Cyprus issue: 'Tansu Ciller can threaten to engage in aggression and Turkey can disregard international law, but we're going to fulfil the signed contract, and the use of methods involving force to pressure the Russian Federation will accomplish nothing.'[93]

Iran and Russia seemed to be moving ever closer as the West began to cut itself off from the Tehran regime. In April 1997 the European Union abandoned the policy of 'critical dialogue' with Iran, though the following year Britain resumed relations with Tehran after an agreement was reached on the fate of the writer Salman Rushdie, who was in hiding because of Iranian threats to kill him. Russia's dilemma was to continue on good terms with Iran, reaping the economic rewards as well, without this being at the expense of its very important relations with the West. In 1996 Primakov had been generally successful in balancing the two conflicting interests, by arguing to the Western governments that the effect of neglecting relations with Iran would be far more damaging to Russia than it would be for Europe or the United States because of the highly conspicuous geo-strategic factors. During his 1996 visit to Iran, the Russian foreign minister highlighted the significance of co-operation with Iran in order to stabilise the existing wars in Tajikistan and Chechnia and between Armenia and Azerbaijan. A letter from Yeltsin to his Iranian counterpart stressed the 'strategic importance' of Central Asia and the Caucasus and the 'urgency' for co-operation between Moscow and Tehran.[94]

A broad political consensus developed in Moscow by 1996, which began to take shape from 1993, that Russia could not afford to ignore this strategically vital area, even if it was at the price of antagonising the United States. The pro-Western radicals were forced on the defensive on this issue, particularly in the light of the various conflicts in that region and the potential for more serious threats from a broader coalitions of forces. However, the extreme and pragmatic nationalist views were skilfully prevented from dominating foreign policy-making by Primakov, who presented a more moderate stance. The Primakov policy insisted on the vital importance of relations with Iran on the one hand, as was evident from his visit to Tehran at the end of 1996, while on the other hand he attempted to justify the motive as not being directed towards the United States or any other power, but simply as a necessary response to possible threats to national interests. One Foreign Ministry view noted that the end of the Cold War did not necessarily mean the decline in value of the region for Moscow. In fact, 'the new geo-political and geo-economical reality' resulted in Turkey and Iran being 'more important for Russia than in the period of the Cold War'.[95]

NOTES

1. Galia Golan, *Soviet Policies in the Middle East from WWII to Gorbachev*, Cambridge, 1990, p.33.
2. *Ibid.*
3. Robert O. Freedman, *Moscow and the Middle East*, Cambridge, 1991, p.23.
4. Charles B. McLane, *Soviet-Middle East Relations*, London, 1973, p.104.
5. Freedman, *op. cit.*, p.31.
6. *Ibid.*, p.32.
7. *Ibid.*
8. James Clayton Moltz and Dennis Ross, 'The Soviet Union and the Iran-Iraq War, 1980-1988' in George Breslauer (ed.), *Soviet Strategy in the Middle East*, Boston, MA, 1990, p.128.
9. *Ibid.*
10. Robert O.Freedman, 'Gorbachev, Iran and the Iran-Iraq War' in Nikki R. Keddie and Mark J. Gasiorowski (eds), *Neither East nor West: Iran, the Soviet Union and the United States*, London, 1990, p.117.
11. Carol R. Saivetz, 'The Soviet Union and Iran: Changing Relations in the Gorbachev Era' in Miron Rezun (ed.), *Iran at the Crossroads: Global Relations in a Turbulent Decade*, San Francisco, 1990, p.196.
12. *Pravda*, 5 January 1989 (p.1), in *Current Digest of the Soviet Press*, vol.XLI, no.1, 1989, p.25.
13. Alvin Z. Rubenstein, *Soviet Policy Toward Turkey, Iran and Afghanistan*, New York, 1982, p.17.
14. Bruce Kuniholm, *United States Foreign Policy Regarding Greece, Turkey and Cyprus*, Columbus, OH, 1989, p.20.
15. *Ibid.*
16. *Ibid.*, p.23.
17. Malcolm Yapp, 'Soviet Relations with the Countries of the Northern Tier'

in Adeed and Karen Dawisha (eds), *The Soviet Union in the Middle East: Policies and Perspectives*, London, 1982, p.26.

18. George McGhee, *The US-Turkish-NATO Middle East Connection*, New York, 1990, p.175.
19. *Pravda*, 15 June 1989 (p.5), *Current Digest...*, *op. cit.*, vol.XLI, no.24, 1989, p.27.
20. *TRT TV* (Ankara), 9 June 1994, *BBC SWB*, SU/2020, 13 June 1994, B/12.
21. *Moscow Radio* (World Service), 27 June 1994, *Central Eurasia* (Daily Report), FBIS-Sov-94-124, 28 June 1994, p.16.
22. *Ibid.*, p.10.
23. *Itar-Tass*, 3 June 1994, *Central Eurasia* (Daily Report), FBIS-Sov-94-108, 6 June 1994, p.11.
24. *Ibid.*
25. *Anatolia News Agency* (Ankara), 23 February 1994, *BBC SWB*, SU/1933, 28 February 1994, B/16.
26. Leonid Gankin, 'Kurds Want Peace but are Prepared for All Out War', *Moscow News*, 8-22 January 1997, p.1.
27. *Ibid.*, p.11.
28. Stephanie Hoffman (ed.), *Commonwealth of Independent States and the Middle East*, vol.XX, nos 6-7, Jerusalem, 1995, p.12.
29. Elmer Murtazaev, 'Turkey Extends $350 million Credit to Russia', *Segodnia*, 16 December 1995, p.20.
30. *Ibid.*
31. Maksim Iusin, 'Novyi prem'er-ministr Turtsii mechtaet osvobodit' Chechniu i Erusalim' (New Turkish PM dreams of liberating Chechnia and Jerusalem), *Izvestiia*, 10 July 1996, p.3.
32. Gennadii Charodeev, 'Flag Ichkerii na Bosfore?' (Ichkeria's flag over the Bosphorus?), *Izvestiia*, 4 December 1996, p.3.
33. *Ibid.*
34. Leonid Terentev, 'Russian Fleet Doesn't Take Orders From Turkish Navy', *Kommersant-Daily*, 11 September 1996 (p.3), *Current Digest of the Post-Soviet Press*, 9 October 1996, p.26.
35. Konstantin Eggert, 'Vizit vzaimnykh prenzii' (Visit of mutual complaints), *Izvestiia*, 19 December 1996, p.3.
36. Sergei Riabinin, 'Kipr poka ne budet razmeshchat' rossiiskie raketi' (Cyprus will not deploy Russian rockets for the time being), *Segodnia*, 15 January 1997, p.6.
37. Eggert, *op. cit.*, 19 December 1996.
38. Selcan Hacaoglu, 'Russian Premier in Turkey to Sort Out Disputes', Associated Press, 15 December 1997.
39. *Ibid.*
40. Interview with Sergei Kepechenko, deputy director of the Middle East Department at the Russian Ministry of Foreign Affairs, conducted in October 1996.
41. John Hannah, 'Evolving Russian Attitudes Towards Iran' in Patrick Lawson (ed.), *Iran's Strategic Intentions and Capabilities*, Washington, DC, 1994, p.55.
42. *Interfax*, 29 September 1994, *BBC SWB*, SU/2115, 1 October 1994, B/6.

43. *Interfax*, 10 October 1994, *BBC SWB*, SU/2124, 12 October 1994, B/11.
44. *BBC SWB*, ME/2197, 10 January 1995, MED/1.
45. Elaine Sciolino, 'Iran's Nuclear Giant Stirs From its Slumber', *Guàrdian*, 20 May 1995, p.14.
46. Leonid Gankin, 'Primakov's Campaign Speech', *Moscow News*, 4-10 July 1996, p.6.
47. *BBC SWB*, ME/2234, 22 February 1995, MED/15.
48. *Ibid*.
49. *Ibid*.
50. Iu. Melnikov and V. Frolov, 'Iranskii vopros vo bzaimootnosheniiakh Moskvy i Vashingtona' (The Iranian issue in relations between Moscow and Washington), *Mezhdunarodnaia zhizn'*, no.7, 1995, p.16.
51. *Ibid*, p.19.
52. *Ibid*.
53. *BBC SWB*, ME/2239, 28 February 1995, MED/1.
54. *Ibid*., MED/2.
55. Sergei Strokan, 'Vremia otdavat' dolgi' (Time to repay debts), *Moskovskie novosti*, no.1 (816), 1-14 January 1996, p.13.
56. 'Brimakov ghadan fi iran' (Primakov will be in Iran tomorrow), *Al-Hayat*, 21 December 1996, p.6.
57. *Russian Public TV*, 23 Dec. 1996, 'Primakov Accuses Media of Misinterpreting Ties with Iran', *BBC SWB* (part 1 USSR), SU/2805, 31 December 1996, B/10.
58. 'Yeltsin: ta'aoun russi-irani yanhi "al-niza'at fi al-mantaka"' (Yeltsin: Russian-Iranian cooperation will end 'instability in the region'), *Al-Watan*, no.653, 24 December 1996, p.1.
59. *Interfax*, 25 December 1996, 'Russia's Links With Iran not Directed Against USA, Deputy Foreign Minister Says', *BBC SWB* (part 1 USSR), SU/2805, 31 December 1996, B/10.
60. *Ibid*.
61. Aleksei Pushkov, 'Evgennii Primakov: Ia Chuvstvuiu doverie prezidenta' (I feel the trust of the President), *Nezavisimaia gazeta*, no. 245 (1570), 30 December 1997, p.5.
62. Dafna Linzer, 'Israel Wary of Islamic Summit', Associated Press, Jerusalem, 10 December 1997.
63. Interview with Kepechenko, Moscow, October 1996.
64. *Ibid*.
65. Vladimir Abarinov, 'Evgenii Primakov protiv inostrannogo voennogo prisutstviia v persidskom zalive' (Evgenii Primakov opposes foreign military presence in the Persian Gulf), *Segodnia*, 24 December 1996, p.3.
66. *Ibid*.
67. *Itar-Tass*, 'Iran', 23 December 1996, *BBC SWB* (part 1 USSR), SU/2803, 24 December 1996, B/8.
68. Shirin Akiner, 'Whither Central Asia?' in Rosemary Hollis (ed.), *The Soviets, their Successors and the Middle East*, London, 1993, p.143.
69. Hafeez Malik, *Soviet-Pakistan Relations and Post-Soviet Dynamics*, London, 1994, p.329.

70. El'mira Akhundova, 'Pervyi vizit Alieva v Turtsiiu' (Aliev's first visit to Turkey), *Literaturnaia gazeta*, 16 February 1994, p.9.
71. *Ibid.*, p.330.
72. J.L. Black (ed.), *Russia and Eurasia Documents Annual 1992*, vol.2: *CIS and Successor States*, Gulf Breeze, FL, 1994, p.93.
73. Interview with Iranian Ambassador to Moscow Mehdi Safari, 'Kaspii ne dolzhen stat' Persidskim zalivom' (The Caspian need not be another Persian Gulf), *Segodnia*, no.53, 18 March 1997, p.3.
74. Black, *op. cit.*, vol.1, 1995, p.290.
75. *Ibid.*
76. *Ibid.*, p.167.
77. *Ibid.*, p.184.
78. *Ibid.*, p.185.
79. *Ibid.*, p.273.
80. *Ibid.*, p.297.
81. *Ibid.*, p.311.
82. *Interfax* (28 November 1994), *Central Eurasia*, FBIS-Sov-94-230, 30 November 1994, p.60.
83. *Ibid.*
84. Bess Brown, 'Central Asia Emerges on the World Stage', *RFE/RL Research Report*, vol.1, no.1, 3 January 1992, p.53.
85. Elizabeth Fuller, 'Nagorno-Karabakh: Can Turkey Remain Neutral?', *RFE...*, *op cit.*, vol.1, no.14, 3 April 1992, p.36.
86. Elizabeth Fuller, 'Russia, Turkey, Iran, and the Karabakh Mediation Process', *RFE...*, *op. cit.*, vol.3, no.8, 25 February 1994, p.35.
87. *Ibid.*, p.36.
88. *IRNA* (Iranian news agency), *Central Eurasia*, Daily Report, FBIS-Sov-94-111, 9 June 1994, p.60.
89. Andranik Migranian, 'Rossiia i blizhnee zarubezh'e (Russia and the Near Abroad), *Nezavisimaia gazeta*, 18 January 1994, pp.4, 5 and 8. The author was adviser to President Yeltsin and his views seemed to mark the end of influence for radical pro-Westerners in the Kremlin, with regard to foreign policy.
90. *Ibid.*
91. *Ibid.*
92. Mark Webber, *CIS Integration Trends: Russia and the Former Soviet Union*, London, RIIA, 1997.
93. Pavel Felgengauer, 'Rossiia napamnila Turtsii "kak sleduet sebia vesti"' (Russia reminds Turkey 'to behave itself'), *Segodnia*, 17 January 1997, p.1.
94. Ghassan bin Jadou, 'Brimakov yantaqid al-ada' al-ameriki li-iran wa rafsanjani yu'ayid ta'awunan iklimia ma 'rossia' (Primakov criticises US hostility towards Iran and Rafsanjani supports regional co-operation with Russia), *Al-Hayat*, 24 December 1996, p.4.
95. Melnikov and Frolov, *op. cit.*, p.56.

9

CONCLUSION

The following key conclusions regarding Russia's foreign policy in the period since 1991 can be drawn: 'national' interests were for the first time in the history of Russia being promoted as a legitimate and absolutely necessary framework for conducting foreign policy; there was no longer a bipolar world, but one based upon regions of priority and interests; the Middle East region was one which had geo-strategic and economic value for Russia on its own merit, not just associated with the East-West conflict during the Cold War. Generally, Russia attributed different levels of priority to the countries of the Middle East, with Turkey, Iran and Iraq being regarded as the most valuable. Syria, Israel and Saudi Arabia were considered as being highly useful though they ranked below the former list. The Palestinian National Authority, Lebanon and Jordan were considered the least important, though it was believed to be practical to maintain good relations with them, as it was with all the countries of the Middle East, and the opportunity to enhance and promote economic links was given keen attention. Until the early 1970s, Egypt was at the core of Soviet policy in the region. After President Sadat switched to the Western camp, Cairo was largely ignored by Moscow, particularly as Egypt became isolated in the Arab world after signing a peace treaty with Israel.

Comparing the Middle East to other regions or countries which were important for Russia, clearly the United States, China, Europe, and the CIS ranked higher. But what developed in the early years after the Soviet Union collapsed was a realisation that the Middle East was of great importance, and that the undervaluing of that region in the late 1980s and early 1990s was an erroneous course to adopt. By the time Primakov was appointed Foreign Minister in early 1996, there was a much more active policy in the Middle East.

Retrospective overview

Between 1945 and 1985, Soviet foreign policy was ostensibly guided by Marxist ideology but the dominant leaderships introduced differing nuances to Moscow's relations with the outside world. Stalin was set in the two-bloc world, where communism and capitalism could not be reconciled. Eastern Europe was vital for Stalin's strategic plans, but he sought to gain a foothold in both Turkey and Iran in the hope of securing the USSR's south-western flank. The United States under Truman refused to allow Moscow to fulfil its ambitions, in the light of the developing policy of 'containment' of communist expansion. Moscow's demands for joint control of the Straits, allowing entry into and exit from the Black Sea, were flatly rejected, as were demands for disputed territories. Likewise, Stalin sought to take advantage of the presence of Red Army troops in northern Iran to create Soviet puppet states. In both instances Moscow backed down simply because it did not have the resources or ability to become involved in another major war immediately after the Second World War. Stalin's bluffs were costly, leading to heightened suspicion and hostility from both Iran and Turkey. The latter was consequently to become a key member of the North Atlantic Treaty Organisation, an anti-Soviet military institution. Iran also became a loyal Western ally, for decades to come, as a direct result of fear of Soviet intentions following Stalin's actions. Beyond those countries, Stalin had little interest in the rest of the Middle East. He viewed the Arab monarchies as backward and semi-colonies of the British and French empires. Stalin recognised the State of Israel in 1948 but soon afterwards changed his mind and a strong anti-Zionist campaign become predominant in the Soviet media and in Foreign Ministry statements. Stalin's recognition of Israel angered the Arab masses, which was heightened when Czechoslovakia sent a military shipment which enabled Israel's survival in the face of a united Arab attack. In sum, Stalin's lack of understanding of the region and his clearly unplanned actions led to one blunder after another in the Middle East in the last years of his rule. Effectively, Stalin had managed to offend and antagonise every single country in the Middle East between 1945 and 1953.

Khrushchev was left with the task of rectifying the mistakes made by Stalin, and to a large extent his overall record in the Middle East was a success. He altered the whole concept of foreign policy-making so that it ceased to focus on a two-bloc world. Khrushchev sought to take advantage of the newly independent Arab states, which were emerging from European domination, as part of his vision of a third force of a bloc of non-aligned countries which he believed would be hostile towards the West. Egypt became the focus of Soviet attention, particularly after the Suez Crisis when the British, French and Israeli plan attempted to undermine the radical new leader in Cairo, Gamal Abdel Nasser, and maintain Western control over the Suez Canal. Moscow's strong support for Cairo made it an instant champion of the Arab cause and, symbolically, the protector of the weak states against the powerful 'imperialist' West. Billions of rubles of investment were poured into the Egyptian economy and a special relationship was founded between the élites of the two countries, reflected in the growing personal friendship between Khrushchev and Nasser. Yet there were serious problems beneath the surface. First and foremost was Nasser's ideological opposition to communism: he was an Arab nationalist and did not accept that class was the main basis of social development.

When Nasser died in 1970, Brezhnev had consolidated his supreme leadership within the Soviet system. Soviet foreign policy under his direction took a noticeably more pragmatic approach, due to the recognition that countries such as Egypt could not become compliant communist allies. Anwar Sadat, Nasser's successor, had by 1974 completely reoriented his country's allegiance by throwing out the thousands of Soviet technicians and advisers and made Cairo a key ally of the United States. Moscow had lost years of investment and substantial economic and financial resources because of the decision of one man. As Egyptian minutes of meetings between Sadat and the Soviet leadership revealed, mutual suspicions resulted in a tense relationship between 1971 and 1972. Egyptian demands for more weapons and a greater Soviet commitment were met with a cold response from the Brezhnev triumvirate, which did not wish to fuel the volatile regional situation at the time.[1]

This episode highlighted the need for Moscow to reassess its whole foreign policy approach which resulted in a new emphasis being placed on economic factors and tangible political returns. For this reason, countries such as Iraq became all the more valuable because of the oil factor. Baghdad replaced Cairo as the most important Middle East ally, despite the fact that it was ruled by the fiercely independent and unpredictable Saddam Hussein, who was bitterly opposed to communism. Nonetheless, the Soviet Union turned a blind eye to Ba'athist persecution of communists in Iraq for the sake of securing an ally in the Gulf. The significance of this shift was that the Arab-Israeli conflict, which was at the focus of Soviet foreign policy in the Middle East until the mid-1970s, became less important in the latter years of that decade. Indeed, there was only Syria which was ostensibly leading the Arab opposition to Israel, but it became clear to Soviet leaders that Syria was no more trustworthy as an ally than was Egypt. Damascus's involvement in the Lebanese civil war, against leftist and PLO forces, and growing contacts between Syrian and US officials, seemed to indicate that Syria was more concerned about its own interests, which included gaining a profitable foothold in Lebanon, rather than an alliance with the Soviet bloc.

In the late 1970s, there was a stalemate in the Arab-Israeli conflict which was increasingly to the detriment of the Soviet Union. By contrast, the Gulf region was becoming a highly valuable arena for the two superpowers. The United States held a clear advantage there, with Iran and Saudi Arabia being traditional allies, but Iraq allowed the Soviet Union to have a foothold in the oil-rich region where a large share of the world's energy reserves were deposited. However, the deepening relationship with Iraq created a new set of problems for Moscow which were never properly resolved. The most important of these was trying to reconcile the support for Baghdad with seeking to establish good relations with Iran, which bordered the Soviet Union and was a major regional player. The most serious complication for Moscow arose when Iraq and Iran went to war with each other in 1980. Moscow's hopes of gaining influence with the new Iranian regime were quickly dented·upon the realisation that the radical Shi'ite leadership was vehemently anti-communist.

For the last years under Brezhnev, and his two short-lived successors Andropov and Chernenko, Soviet foreign policy had stagnated in the Middle East. There were strained relations with all the major players, and no relations at all with either Israel or Saudi Arabia, the latter taking particular objection to the Soviet invasion of Afghanistan. Only Syria attempted to create an atmosphere of co-operation with the Soviet Union, but that was because it was isolated in the region and was being accused by the West of being a major sponsor of terrorism. The Syrian government played up its 'special relationship' with the Soviet Union and presented itself as a loyal client of the Soviet empire, signing the Treaty of Friendship and Co-operation in 1980. It was one of a few states in the region which did not condemn the Soviet invasion of Afghanistan. Yet in reality it was a friendship of convenience: the Soviet Union did not trust the Syrian leadership and the latter was well aware that the former could only provide a limited amount of help in its confrontation with Israel. From the Soviet viewpoint, it created a facade of continued influence and involvement in the region despite the reality being to the contrary.

Gorbachev's foreign policy overhaul

Although Gorbachev recognised the contradictions and weaknesses of Soviet foreign policy from early on, it took a few years before his New Thinking began to have a real effect on the Middle East. The appointment of Eduard Shevardnadze to the post of foreign minister was central to Gorbachev's plans. Although the main task and priority for Moscow was directed towards Europe and the United States, the impact of Shevardnadze's foreign policy directives was to be greatly felt in the Middle East.

As Moscow sought to avoid confrontation with Washington over the Middle East, it was therefore unsurprising when Syria was informed by the Soviet leadership that Damascus would not be supported in its aim of achieving strategic parity with Israel. President Hafez Asad was told that negotiations would be the only hope for Syria to reclaim the land it had lost in 1967. The Soviet Union also informed the PLO that it could only justify providing continued political support to the Palestinian cause on the basis that the leadership encourage the peace process and rejected terrorism as a means of achieving its nationalist aspirations. Concerning the Iran-Iraq conflict, Gorbachev ended the years of wavering by tilting in favour of Iraq. The motive behind this was the fact of Iraqi demands for a cease-fire while Iran was calling for 'victory until death'. The Khomeini regime had become so fanatical that thousands of volunteers, often children of fifteen and sixteen, were being used for mass suicide missions in order to achieve a military breakthrough. In the era of openness under Gorbachev, Moscow found it difficult to show support for such a regime which was closely associated with international terrorism, assassinations and hostage-taking. It was only after Khomeini's death and the succession of the more pragmatic Rafsanjani, in 1989, that it was possible for relations between the two countries to improve and eventually lead to genuine co-operation.

Parallel to the policy of distancing Moscow from the hard-line regimes, Gorbachev adopted the radical position of establishing relations with Israel and Saudi Arabia. Gorbachev tackled the main obstacle in Israeli-Soviet relations by allowing Soviet Jews to emigrate. Such a move predictably incurred the wrath of Arabs because of the arrival of tens of thousands of Soviet Jews to settlements being built on occupied territories. Moscow persisted with this policy for two main reasons: first, with the democratisation of Soviet society it became impossible to justify the refusal to allow ethnic and religious minorities the freedom to leave the country; secondly, the United States had placed among its conditions for better relations with the Soviet Union that Moscow soften the tone of its attacks on Israel at the United Nations and aid Israel in its programme to import Soviet Jews. But there was another dimension to Moscow's decision to resume ties with Israel: the Soviet Union's position as peace-broker was severely undermined by the absence of relations with one of the parties in the dispute. Such conclusions fitted well with the overall theoretical perspective of New Thinking which argued that negotiations were the only viable option towards solutions, because in an age where weapons of mass destruction were widespread, war had ceased to be an option.

The Soviet Union also sought to establish relations with Saudi Arabia, another long-time adversary of Moscow in the Middle East. The Soviet withdrawal from Afghanistan opened the way for negotiations but Iraq's invasion of Kuwait in August 1990 led to full relations being established because Riyadh needed Soviet support on the Security Council to condemn the actions of Saddam Hussein and allow the international community to create a military force to repel the aggression. From the Soviet viewpoint, establishing relations with Saudi Arabia was of great significance because it greatly increased Moscow's options in the Gulf region.

Gorbachev also improved relations with Turkey, another

important state in the region which played a key role in the coalition against Iraq, courtesy of the NATO bases there. Turgut Özal, then Turkish President, welcomed many of the reforms introduced by Gorbachev and promoted the idea, in conjunction with Gorbachev, that Turkish-Soviet relations could be elevated to a higher level. Gorbachev was particularly keen to win Turkish support in the light of Soviet disintegration and instability in the Caucasus. In turn, Özal hoped to open the way for Turkish investors to operate in the territories of the USSR, and to win Soviet backing over volatile issues in the Middle East, namely over the Kurdish issue and the long-running territorial dispute between Ankara and Damascus. As if that was not enough to Syria's detriment, Moscow sought to improve its bilateral relations with Lebanon and overstep Syrian interference there. This was a clear signal to Damascus that Moscow did not support the 40,000-strong Syrian occupation of Lebanon, and that it wished to see the small Mediterranean state independent of outside control and allowed to develop its democratic traditions. As a final blow to the Syrian dictatorship Moscow put more efforts into improving its relations with Jordan, another state hostile to the regime in Damascus. Thus, when the Gorbachev era came to a close, and the Soviet Union became defunct, Moscow had inherited relations with all the countries of the Middle East, opening up possibilities which had never before existed in the history of the country.

A new chapter in foreign policy making

The Yeltsin era can be best characterised as one of a new Russia setting out on a new course for itself. In a rapidly changing world, the first task was to be familiar with the terminology which could act as sign-posts for policy making. Deputy Prime Minister Viktor Posuvaliuk noted in one Arab daily that the Middle East was difficult to define, in the light of the geographic changes which were taking place in recent years. He pointed out that generally in Russia, the Middle East signified Turkey, Iran and Afghanistan, while the Near East encompassed all the countries from the Atlantic countries to the Gulf.[2] However, Posuvaliuk argued that this was based on a West European outlook, because Turkey, Iran and Afghanistan were further east than North Africa. Yet this was debatable, in his view, if one took Turkey as an example, because 'is it Near or Middle East and can it ignore its European link?'[3] The point being made by Posuvaliuk was that in the post-Soviet world, there were no longer clear-cut geographical divisions as had been the case in the Cold War era. In the first year under Yeltsin, Moscow was dominated by so-called Atlanticists (even though Russia did not have a direct link with the Atlantic), who wanted to see their country as part of a broad coalition of 'civilised nations' to the east and west of the Atlantic Ocean. A more accurate description of those who espoused such a policy, radical pro-Westerners, replaced the term Atlanticist. The 'Atlanticist-Eurasianist' debate[4] was too much of a simplification for the subtle differences and nuances between various groups and policies. Foreign Minister Kozyrev, who was at the vanguard of the pro-Western radicals in 1992, appeared to accept existing political realities both internally and in international affairs, and adopted the policies of pragmatic pro-Westerners. Between 1994 and 1995 this position appeared to reflect the general line of the government and its leader, Viktor Chernomyrdin. Co-operation with the West remained a top priority, but Russia became more explicit about its great power status and certain spheres of influence, namely the CIS, were seen as necessitating direct intervention.

In fact, the Russian leadership was far more subtle and pragmatic than it appeared to be. Although initially wavering, a steady course was mapped out, culminating in the appointment of Evgenii Primakov as Foreign Minister at the beginning of 1996. The final destination of this course of state was a pragmatic, national foreign policy as was normal for any great power to have. The idealism and messianism of the Gorbachev era and early period when Kozyrev was Foreign Minister were replaced by themes such as realism, stability and predictability. Primakov elucidated this policy by adopting a centrist-pragmatic-nationalist policy. He criticised those in his country who espoused a return to confrontation with the West, rejecting theorists who argued that Russia was an Eastern power whose needs were incompatible with Western interests. Yet at the same time he did not accept the arguments of the pro-Western radicals that Russia should cut all its losses in Asia and the Middle East for the sake of appeasing the West. Instead, Primakov proposed that Russia needed to look at each problem and each situation separately and act in accordance with Russian national interests. When interests collided, as they often do in politics as in life, a list of priorities was available to guide the country's foreign policy on a steady course towards achieving its goals. Relations with the United States remained as the top priority, in terms of avoiding a return to confrontation with its old adversary. China was also very high on the list of Russian interests, again because it was a potentially dangerous enemy. The Middle East was not as highly regarded as these two countries, but it was nonetheless important enough for Moscow not to ignore. From 1993 there was a discernible and increasing re-entry into the region, so that by 1998 there were distinct lines marking out the differences between Russia and the United States over various issues concerning the Middle East.

There were five strands of views characterising the foreign policy debate by the mid-1990s: the pro-Western radicals, pragmatic pro-Westerners, centrist-nationalists, pragmatic nationalists and extreme nationalists. By 1994 Russian foreign policy was still in a state of transition, shifting between the pragmatic pro-Western position and the centrist position. The centrists were typified by Primakov, then head of the SVR, who argued that in principle there was no reason for Russia not to co-operate with the West. At the same time, Primakov argued that Russia had a right to pursue its interests and defend its national security even if airing such concerns unsettled Western governments. The key, according to centrist-nationalists, was that such differences could be discussed and negotiated with the West so that acceptable compromises could be reached.

The centrist argument regarding relations with the West was fairly similar to the pragmatic pro-Westerners, but there was a difference in emphasis. The pragmatic pro-Westerners placed more value on the need to co-operate with the West, thus their bartering position appeared to be weakened as a result. Kozyrev and his ever-dwindling group of supporters became too closely associated with the Western position because they basically argued that there was no alternative for Russia other than to accept Western superiority in the bartering process, and that Moscow had simply to get the best available deal it was possible to attain. Whether such an assessment was correct or not, Russia's political élite could not accept such a premise for making foreign policy because it was incompatible with the national aspirations of any large state.

The pragmatic nationalist view was characterised by the chief opponents of the Yeltsin leadership, the Communist Party and its leader Gennadii Ziuganov. (Others, such as Margot Light, refer to this group as fundamentalist nationalists, implying a greater intransigence in their policies regarding relations with the West.)[5] They considered Russia to be a great power, and that it had the potential to resume its role as a joint superpower because it had all the resources it needed. Therefore, Moscow had to concentrate on its own interests which included the eventual reintegration of the former Soviet Union, a more assertive policy regarding Eastern Europe, and the restoration of alliances with Eastern powers such as China, India, Iran and Iraq. Moreover, the pragmatic nationalists argued that rather than wait in hope for Western handouts, Russia could have a sizeable income from arms sales and trade with countries such as Iraq and Iran, to which the United States was opposed. The extreme nationalists, represented by Zhirinovskii, believed that Russia should go to war in order to reclaim the Soviet empire and beyond. Such views, it must be emphasised, had zero influence with the Russian government, and they were not taken very seriously by the Russian population as a whole. But the Western media in particular seemed to relish the possibility of using such sensational headlines and there was a constant hint that should the democratic experiment fail in Russia, then Zhirinovskii was a dangerous alternative. To some extent, Yeltsin deviously manipulated Western and domestic fears by arguing the same thing.

Primakov's vision of the world in 1998, the year he was appointed Prime Minister, was that it had changed into something less clear-cut than the days of the superpower confrontation. There were no longer obvious enemies, and alliances were more likely to change according to different issues and situations. In this new multipolar world, Russia's opportunities could be greatly enhanced because of the possibility of joining with other powers to have a bearing on various situations. Primakov accepted that, on its own, Russia did not have the ability to change events in the Middle East, but working closely and co-operating with France, the EU in general, or China could serve as a strong counterbalance to US domination. France, in particular, was allied with Russia against the United

States in calling for the sanctions against Iraq to be eased. President Jacques Chirac also announced in late December 1996 that France would pull out its aircraft from the northern Iraqi no-fly zone.[6]

In terms of international relations theory, neo-realists argued that this fluid international situation could have led to new dangers which had been contained within the order of the bipolar world during the Cold War; Moscow's changing policy after 1991 was within this context of thinking. The latter years of the Kozyrev period rejected the idealism of 'interdependence' theories, and under Primakov foreign policy was made from the neo-realist premise that 'good fences make good neighbours'.[7] In the post-Gulf War period in the Middle East, the United States stamped its authority in the region without much resistance. From Moscow's perspective, the challenge was to re-establish its parameters of interests and influence without overtly challenging US boundaries in the region. In principle, Primakov did not object to the idea of co-operating with the United States in the Middle East, as was often the case regarding various issues such as the Palestinian-Israeli talks. However, Washington's policies in the Middle East became ever-more intransigent against Russian interests as well as Arab interests and increasingly supportive of Israeli policies. The situation was aggravated by the election of Benyamin Netanyahu as Prime Minister in the spring of 1996.

When Moscow criticised the Israeli government's undermining of the peace process, and Washington's unwillingness to condemn these actions, it was not because Russia had become more hard-line but because events on the ground ran contrary to its principles and interests. In reality, Russia's position was not too different from France or the rest of Europe. Primakov and his European counterparts believed that Israeli violation of international agreements and Washington's compliance would serve to undermine stability in the region, which was in the long term not in the interest of all the parties concerned. Likewise, on the issue of sanctions against Iraq, Russia and France were in agreement that the US position had gone beyond the UN mandate. The pragmatism of Russia's foreign policy dictated that the punishment must fit the crime, and where Iraq was adhering to what the international community was demanding, sanctions should be eased to show reward to the regime in Baghdad. Both France and Russia felt that the United States was deliberately blocking their chance of capitalising on multi-billion dollar reconstruction deals with Iraq once the sanctions were lifted.

National interests and the Middle East

Vladimir Lukin, chairman of the International Affairs Committee of the State Duma, wrote in 1995 on behalf of the generally pro-Western Yabloko Party:

> It is necessary not to become trapped in confrontation with the larger Islamic countries such as Iran and to look for possibilities for agreements and bilateral profits in inter-state relations. At the same time it is necessary to give a firm repulse to attempts to limit our economic, political and military interests from the side of Turkey, Pakistan and Afghanistan.[8]

It is perhaps interesting to compare the comments in the same Foreign Ministry journal by the spokesman for the Liberal Democratic Party: Aleksei Mitrofanov wrote that it was necessary to take into account 'the expansionist policy of Turkey in the Caucasus and Central Asia which puts Russian strategic interest under a serious threat'.[9]

It was thus natural that the Middle East was divided into three main categories. The first included Iran and Turkey, namely because they bordered the CIS, they were non-Arab, and they were seen as fairly serious risks to regional security. They also had a degree of influence over the leaderships of the Caucasus and Central Asia. Turkey was especially important because it controlled the straits which allowed entry into the Black Sea, a crucial factor for Russian trade and military security, and because it played a pivotal role in the NATO alliance. Russia's main aim was to limit the influence of its rivals and re-impose its influence over the so-called arc of instability, which ranged from the eastern borders of China to the Black Sea. Lukin argued that 'Russia is the largest Eurasian power with many years of experience with the Muslim and Eastern civilisations. It is in our interest to influence the global balance of power and turn it to our good...'.[10] The war in Chechnia served to underline the crucial importance of the Caucasus region, taking into consideration the huge financial and human losses incurred. Russian involvement in Tajikistan also showed that Central Asia was an area which Moscow would not allow to come under the domination of other powers.

In the first two years after the demise of the Soviet Union, it was widely believed that Iran would pose the most serious threat to Russian interests in the Muslim states while Turkey was expected to be more pragmatic and compliant. By 1998 the reverse seemed to be true, with Iran co-operating over a number of issues, including the Nagorno-Karabakh dispute, the status of the Caspian Sea and Tajikistan. Turkey, on the other hand, while not openly defying Russia was less co-operative on many issues than Moscow would have hoped. Those most opposed to Russian domination, whether they were in Chechnia, Azerbaijan or Uzbekistan, appeared to be getting more sympathy from Ankara than Moscow would have liked. There was a fear in Russia, which extreme nationalists stoked to paranoia, that Turkey was part of a NATO conspiracy to surround Russia with hostile forces to ensure that it would be permanently weakened and unable to expand its influence. This was in the context of the growing argument between Russia and the West about plans to expand NATO into Eastern Europe.

Iran's potential as a firm ally was thus raised, as one of a few neighbours of the former Soviet Union which was not Western oriented and which could provide Russia with an ally in the Gulf. But Russia's role in the construction of a nuclear power station in Bushehr was to cause friction with the United States, which claimed that certain components would allow the Iranians to convert the nuclear energy from peaceful purposes to more militaristic aims. The Russians and Iranians strongly denied this but the issue became a matter of principle as far as Moscow and Washington were concerned. The US government argued that if Russia wanted to be a part of the Western family, it had to refrain from large-scale economic and military aid to governments which were hostile to Western interests. Moscow retorted that Russia had a right to conduct its diplomatic and international economic policy independently of outside criticisms and that it alone knew where its best national interests lay. Moscow went ahead with the nuclear project, albeit after compromising on some aspects of the deal to ease Western fears. The consequence of the episode was to reconfirm that Russian interests were very often not likely to be compatible with Western interests, particularly in the Middle East, and that by 1998 new terms would have to be established which differed from those which existed in the first year when Kozyrev was foreign minister. When in April 1997 the European Union downgraded its links with Iran following further evidence of Iranian terrorist activities, the prospect of 'comprehensive co-operation' between Tehran and Moscow was being promoted on both sides.[11]

Relations with the Arabian Gulf countries were of great importance to Moscow, but these countries did not have a direct geo-strategic bearing on Russia in the way Iran and Turkey did. Iraq was a long-standing ally which was a major arms purchaser and which offered huge economic potential. President Yeltsin was throughout his years in office adamant that Russia would comply with the UN-imposed sanctions on Iraq. He stressed that Russia was a law-abiding country which respected decisions of international institutions such as the United Nations, despite the economic and diplomatic damage which was incurred. That in itself did not mean that Moscow would accept that the decision was fair, and from 1993 there was a deliberate effort to regain the trust of the regime in Baghdad and to try to convince Washington to ease the sanctions. Moscow's policy of seeking to end the sanctions was supported by a broad political spectrum, which included many reformers including Anatolii Chubais and Boris Nemtsov, who in July 1997 declared that Russia would propose the lifting of the embargo on Iraqi oil when the subject was to be raised at the UN Security Council in October 1997.[12] Russia did indeed become more direct in its calls for the lifting of sanctions by the end of 1997. Moreover, Moscow played a crucial role in preventing a US attack on Iraq in November of that year after the regime in Baghdad had expelled US inspectors from the UN team investigating Saddam Hussein's weapons of mass destruction programme. Moscow attempted to do the same thing during the US-Iraqi crisis which erupted in November 1998.

The Saudi case was equally frustrating to Russia but in a different way to that of Iraq. The oil-rich kingdom was presented as a symbol of Russia's new world outlook as it was one of the countries with which relations were established as a result of New Thinking. Yet Moscow was to discover that US influence over Riyadh was too great to be able to make a genuine breakthrough. The Saudis were committed to buying US arms and to giving the United States priority in trade, industrial and financial projects, and

Washington held the final word in regional matters as well. Although the Saudi government would have probably preferred a more influential Russia in local affairs to provide an alternative to their dependence on the United States, the government in Washington had discouraged Riyadh from attracting too much attention from Moscow. By 1998, the Russian government had to be content with accepting that there was only a limited potential to be gained from Saudi Arabia and grudgingly conceded the right of way to the United States.

The third and final category of Russian interests in the Middle East included Israel and its neighbours which were involved in the peace process opened at the Madrid Conference in 1991. Russia placed high value on relations with Israel because they symbolised the transformation from the Soviet era, when the Jewish state was high on the list of enemies. On the trade-economic level, Israel quickly rose to become one of the most important partners in the region. However, on the political level many difficulties remained. The complications arose not because of Moscow's intentions but rather as a result of various Israeli actions, such as the bombing of Lebanon, the building of settlements on occupied land, and the destruction of Arab homes. Russia's policy regarding the peace process was that Israel should negotiate all existing differences with its neighbours before making any decisions which might inflame the situation on the ground. Israel, in turn, had been blunt in telling Moscow not to interfere in affairs over which it had no real influence. This Israeli attitude led to growing resentment in Russian circles and a genuine popular rejection of what was perceived as an example of arrogance by the Jewish state towards Moscow. At the same time, relations with the Palestinians, Syrians, Jordanians and Lebanese steadily improved. In early 1997 Primakov declared that relations with the Arab states were 'strategic' and Moscow would play a bigger role in resolving regional problems.[13] Relations with the Palestinians, Jordanians and Lebanese were not of great importance to Russia, though for the sake of appearances, Moscow constantly issued statements giving its view on the progress (or lack of) made in the peace process. Syria was slightly more important because it had been a Soviet ally for many decades and it was highly dependent on Russian arms to replace and update its existing military machine. But Russia was keen to convince Damascus to repay the $9 billion debt that had been owed to the Soviet Union. Syria had been unhelpful on the issue of repayment, partly because it wanted guarantees that once Russia had received what it was owed, it would not abandon its long-time ally. This issue was believed to be high on the agenda of talks during the visit of Defence Minister Sergeev to Damascus in mid-November 1998. But Russia wanted more from relations with Syria than the repayment of debts: the Russian leadership wanted to play a meaningful role in the Syrian–Israeli negotiations over the Golan Heights, and Moscow believed that its influence in Damascus would allow it to do so. Success on this track would not only have restored national pride and international prestige, it was also seen as important in terms of balancing US domination in this strategically important region.

The grey lines of Russia's policy

Naturally, the divisions in priority listed above were not distinct and many dilemmas remained unresolved. The most complicated task for Moscow was one which haunted the Soviet Union throughout the 1980s, and it was how to create a harmonious policy relating to Iran and Iraq. The two countries were highly valued by Russia and were perceived as important allies with a growing importance for the future. Yet the two countries were vehemently antagonistic towards each other, and when Moscow became too close to Iraq, Iran became hostile and vice versa. It would have been in Russia's interest for Iran, Iraq and Syria to form an alliance in agreement with Moscow. In late June 1997 improved relations between the three Middle East countries forced Moscow to issue a denial that it had been actively working for this end, although it admitted that it did not discourage such a development.[14] This would have been a nightmare scenario for the United States and its two most important allies in the region, Israel and Saudi Arabia. Regarding Iran, Moscow endeavoured to strengthen its ties while the West was gradually distancing itself from the regime in Tehran. Moscow justified this by arguing that Iran was more important for Russia than it was for Europe and the United States because it bordered the territories of the CIS. But Russia's relations with Iran also had a negative effect on relations with Saudi Arabia, Turkey, Israel and to some extent Lebanon. All four countries perceived Iran to be a major threat to stability in the region because it was believed to be embarking on a nuclear weapons project which was near completion. Moscow's counter-argument was that it was not doing anything to help Iran prepare nuclear weapons as it was not in its interest to have a medium-sized yet unstable nuclear power on the doorstep of the CIS.

Russian policy in the Middle East centred around basic aims in the region: to ensure stability, to minimalise US influence, and to allow fair access to trade and general economic relations. From the point of view of national interests, such aims were rational and did not much differ in their competitiveness from the way that France, Britain or the United States pursued their interests in the region. It would have been naïve to expect a great power such as Russia to abandon the defence of its national interests. However, Moscow's top officials also stressed that this did not mean a return to the past. Writing in *Al-Hayat*, Deputy Foreign Minister Posuvaliuk responded to Arab critics who were suggesting that Russia was a mere shadow of the Soviet Union in terms of its commitment to the region. 'First of all', he retorted, 'Russia is not the Soviet Union'. It was necessary for those set in the old mentality to realise that 'we are completely unable and unwilling at this moment to export large quantities of weapons or provide easy credits knowing that they would not be repaid. It should be remembered that such actions represent direct "grabbing" from the pockets of the Russian people, who are enduring many hardships. These people will thus demand to know the purpose of such donations.'[15] At the same time, it was regularly emphasised by the Russian Foreign Ministry from as early as 1993 that while foreign policy had to be made and pursued responsibly, 'it is clear that it is not in Russia's interest to stay away from Middle East affairs and from participation in the day-to-day political and diplomatic events of the region'.[16]

A school of thought emerged in the West which interpreted the changes in Russian foreign policy since 1993 as heading down the path of assertive nationalism. This concept of Russia First 'acknowledges that Russia is a Eurasian entity and not merely European. [...] The honeymoon with the West and the period of close emulation dating back to Peter the Great, is over.'[17] However, indications point towards a new set of conclusions: primarily, that the debates as to whether Russia would revert to

Soviet/imperial aggressive policies, those over the pro-Western/ Eurasian schism, or concerning the danger of a new form of Russian ethno-nationalism[18] did not match the realities of the period 1991-8. The rise of nationalism, and the rise of a national foreign policy, did not automatically imply a threat to the world order. 'The national mission can be benign: it can be defensive toward outsiders and focused on improving collective welfare, maintaining the territorial status quo, and strengthening internal cohesion and unity.'[19] By using the Middle East as an example, this book has sought to show Russian foreign policy had clearly pursued its national interests in terms of countering the unipolarist ambitions of the United States and promoting multipolarism with the purpose of achieving a higher level of international harmony. This 'national' policy also drove Moscow to pursue with greater purpose the economic and geo-strategic challenges which the Middle East offered and posed.

NOTES

1. Classified Arabic transcripts of minutes of meetings between President Sadat and the Soviet leadership, including Brezhnev, Kosygin, Podgorny, Gromyko, Grechko (Defence Minister), and Ponomarev (head of the CC International Department).
2. Viktor Posuvaliuk, 'Al-sharqan al-Awsat wa al-Adna'...min nafizah fi mosko' (The Near and Middle Easts...from a window in Moscow), *Al-Hayat*, 27 February 1997, p.17.
3. *Ibid.*
4. See Francis Fukuyama, 'The Ambiguity of National Interests' and Sergei Stankevich, 'Toward a New National Idea' in Stephen Sestanovich (ed.), *Rethinking Russian's National Interests*, Washington, DC, 1994.
5. Margot Light, 'Foreign Policy Thinking' in Neil Malcolm, Margot Light, Alex Pravda and Roy Allison, *Internal Factors in Russian Foreign Policy*, Oxford, 1996, p.35.
6. Christopher Lockwood and Julian Nundy, 'France Pulls Aircraft from Iraq No-Fly Zone', *Daily Telegraph*, 28 December 1996, p.19.
7. Fred Halliday, *Rethinking International Relations*, London, 1994, p.15.
8. Vladimir Lukin, 'Vybory 1995: vneshnepoliticheskie vzgliady partii' (Elections 1995: the foreign policy views of the parties), *Mezhdunarodnaia Zhizn'*, nos 11-12, 1995, p.25.
9. Aleksei Mitrofanov, *Ibid.*, p.16.
10. Lukin, *op cit.*, p.25.
11. Ghassan bin Jdou, 'Tahran tass'od ma' oroba bi ta'aoun shamil' ma' rossiia' (Tehran increases level of closeness towards comprehensive co-operation with Russia), *Al-Hayat*, 14 April 1997, p.1.
12. Sami Amara, 'Mosko tu'akid iltizamaha al'amal min ajel al-ouquobat 'an

al-iraq' (Moscow confirms the urgency of its efforts for the lifting of sanctions against Iraq), *Al-Sharq Al-Awsat*, 3 July 1997, p.2.

13. Faleh Hamrani, 'Mosko: al-ilaqat ma' al-arab istratijiah wa nasa' litaswiah alqadaiah alsou'bah li-salam' (Moscow: relations with Arabs are strategic and we aim to resolve difficult issues for peace), *Al-Watan Al-Dowli*, 20 February 1997, p.4.

14. Jalal Mashata, 'Mosko tanfi ilaqataha bi-altaqarub al-souri-al-iraqi' (Moscow denies link with Syrian-Iraqi rapprochement), *Al-Hayat*, 25 June 1997, p.1.

15. Viktor Posuvaliuk, "Ta'amoulat ba'd liqa' ma' safir" (Hopes after meeting an ambassador), *Al-Hayat*, 17 April 1997, p.17.

16. A. Chistiakov (deputy director of Department of the Middle East), 'Peremeny na blizhnem vostoke i vneshnii mir' (Changes in the Middle East and the outside world), *Mezhdunarodnaia zhizn'*, no.2, 1994, p.137.

17. Peter Truscott, *Russia First: Breaking with the West*, London and New York, 1997, p.5.

18. Astrid Tuminez, 'Russian Nationalism and the National Interest in Russian Foreign Policy' in Celeste A. Wallander (ed.), *The Sources of Russian Foreign Policy after the Cold War*, Oxford, 1996, p.41.

19. *Ibid.*, p.43.

BIBLIOGRAPHY

Adomeit, Hannes, *Soviet Risk-Taking and Crisis Behaviour: a Theoretical and Empirical Analysis*, London, 1982.

Arnold, Anthony, *Afghanistan: the Soviet Invasion in Perspective*, Berkeley, CA, 1985.

Aron, Leon and Kenneth M. Jensen (eds), *The Emergence of Russian Foreign Policy*, Washington, DC, 1995.

Balkir, Ianon, and Allan M. Williams (eds), *Turkey and Europe*, London and New York, 1993.

Barzilai, Gad, Aharon Klieman and Gil Shidlo, *The Gulf Crisis and its Global Aftermath*, London and New York, 1993.

Beliaev, Igor and John Marks (eds), *Common Ground on Terrorism*, London, 1991.

Bialer, Seweryn (ed.), *The Domestic Context of Soviet Foreign Policy*, London, 1991.

Blum Douglas (ed.), *Russia's Future: Consolidation or Disintegration*, Boulder, CO, 1994.

Bradley, Bill *et al.*, *Implications of Soviet New Thinking*, London, 1990.

Bresheeth, Haim and Nira Yuval-Davis (eds), *The Gulf War and the New World Order*, London, 1991.

Breslauer, George (ed.), *Soviet Strategy in the Middle East*, Boston, MA, 1990.

Brown, James, *Delicately Poised Allies: Greece and Turkey*, London, 1994.

Campbell, Kurt, and S. Neil Macfarlane, *Gorbachev's Third World Dilemmas*, London, 1989.

Cobban, Helena, *The Superpowers and the Syrian-Israeli Conflict*, New York, 1991.

Cohen, Ariel, *Russian Imperialism: Development and Crisis*, London, 1996.

Colton, Timothy, and Robert Leguold (eds), *After the Soviet Union*, New York and London, 1992.

Confino, Michael, and Shimon Shamir (eds), *The USSR and the Middle East*, Jerusalem, 1973.

Cordesman, Anthony, *Western Strategic Interests in Saudi Arabia*, London, 1987.

Cross, Sharyl, and Marina Obortova (eds), *The New Chapter in United States-Russian Relations*, London, 1994.

Dagan, Avigdor, *Moscow and Jerusalem*, London, 1970.

Dain, Uriel, *King Hussein's Strategy of Survival*, Washington, DC, 1992.

Dallin, David J., *Soviet Foreign Policy after Stalin*, London, 1960.

Dawisha, Adeed and Karen Dawisha (eds), *The Soviet Union in the Middle East*, London, 1982.

Dibb, Paul, *The Soviet Union: the Incomplete Superpower*, Hong Kong, 1986.

Duncan, W. Raymond and Carolyn McGiffert Eredahl, *Moscow and the Third World under Gorbachev*, Boulder, CO, 1990.

Edmonds, Robin, *Soviet Foreign Policy: the Brezhnev Years*, Oxford, 1983.

Farid, Abdel Magid, *Nasser: the Final Years*, Reading, 1994.

Freedman, Robert O., *Soviet Policy Toward Israel under Gorbachev*, New York, 1991.

——, *Moscow and the Middle East: Soviet Policy Since the Invasion of Afghanistan*, New York, 1991.

——, *Moscow in the Middle East*, London, Cambridge, 1991.

Garthoff, Raymond, *The Great Transition: American-Soviet Relations and the End of the Cold War*, Washington, DC, 1994.

Golan, Galia, *The Soviet Union and the PLO: an Uneasy Alliance*, New York, 1980.

——, *Gorbachev's New Thinking on Terrorism*, New York, 1990.

——, *Soviet Policies in the Middle East: from World War II to Gorbachev*, Cambridge, 1990.

——, *Moscow and the Middle East: New Thinking on Regional Conflict*, London, 1992.

Goldberg, David H., and Paul Marantz (eds), *The Decline of the Soviet Union and the Transformation of the Middle East*, San Francisco and Oxford, 1994.

Goodby, James E., and Benoit Morel (eds), *The Limited Partnership: Building a Russian-US Security Community*, Oxford, 1993.

Gorbachev, Mikhail, *The Meaning of My Life*, Edinburgh, 1990.

Gorodetsky, Gabriel (ed.), *Soviet Foreign Policy 1917-1991: a Retrospective*, London, 1994.

Gow, James (ed.), *Iraq, the Gulf Conflict and the World Community*, London, 1993.

Halliday, Fred, *Rethinking International Relations*, Basingstoke and London, 1994.

——, *Al-Islam Wa Al-Gharb: Khurafat Al-Muwajaha* (Islam and the West: the Myth of Confrontation), London, 1997. First published as *Islam and the Myth of Confrontation: Religion and Politics in the Middle East*, London, 1995.

Hanak, Harry, *Soviet Foreign Policy Since the Death of Stalin*, London and Boston, MA, 1972.

Hart, Alan, *Arafat*, London, 1994.

Heller, Mark A., *The Dynamics of Soviet Policy in the Middle East: Between Old Thinking and New*, Tel Aviv, 1991.

Hemsley, John (ed.), *The Lost Empire: Perceptions of Soviet Policy Shifts in the 1990s*, London, 1991.

Hitti, Nassif, *The Foreign Policy of Lebanon*, Oxford, 1989.

Hoffman, Erik and Frederic J. Fleron, *The Conduct of Soviet Foreign Policy*, New York, 1980.

Hoffman, Stephanie (ed.), *CIS and the Middle East*, vol.XVII, no.3, 1992, Jerusalem, 1993.

Hollis, Rosemary (ed.), *The Soviets, their Successors and the Middle East*, London, 1993.

Hormer, Stephen, and Thomas Wolfe, *Soviet Policy and Practice toward Third World Conflicts*, Toronto, 1983.

Ja'far, Kassem Mohamad, *Souria wal itihad al-sofieti* (Syria and the Soviet Union), London, 1987.

Jervis, Robert, and Seweryn Bialer (eds), *Soviet-American Relations after the Cold War*, London, 1991.

Kanet, Roger E., Deborah Nutter Miner, Tamara J. Resler (eds), *Soviet Foreign Policy in Transition*, Cambridge, 1992.

Kanovsky, Eliyahu, *The Economic Consequences of the Persian Gulf War: Accelerating OPEC's Demise*, Washington, DC, 1992.

Karsh, Efraim, *The Cautious Bear: Soviet Military Engagement in Middle East Wars in the Post-1967 Era*, Jerusalem, 1985.

——, *The Soviet Union and Syria*, London, 1988.

——, *Soviet Policy Towards Syria Since 1970*, London, 1991.

——, and Inari Rautsi, *Saddam Hussein*, London, 1991.

Katz, Mark N., *The USSR and Marxist Revolutions in the Third World*, Cambridge, 1990.

Keddie, R., and Mark J. Gasiorowski (eds), *Neither East nor West; Iran, the Soviet Union and the United States*, London, 1990.

Kienle, Eberhard, *Ba'ath v. Ba'ath: the Conflict Between Syria and Iraq 1968-1989*, London, 1990.

Kuniholm, Bruce, *United States Foreign Policy Regarding Greece, Turkey and Cyprus,* American Hellenic Institute Conference, Columbus, Ohio, 1989.

Lawson, Patrick (ed.), *Iran's Strategic Intentions and Capabilities,* Washington, DC, 1994.

Lebow, Richard Ned, and Janice Gross Stein (eds), *We All Lost the Cold War,* Princeton, NJ, 1994.

Lederer, Ivo J. and Wayne S. Vucinich (eds), *The Soviet Union and the Middle East,* Berkeley, CA, 1974.

Light, Margot (ed.), *Troubled Friendships: Moscow's Third World Ventures,* London, 1993.

Little, Tom, *The Middle East and North Africa – EUROPA (40th edn),* London, 1994.

Luciani, Giacomo (ed.), *The Arab State,* London, 1990.

Lynch, Allen G., and Kenneth W. Thomson (eds), *Soviet and Post-Soviet Russia in a World in Change,* London, 1994.

MacKenzie, David, *From Messianism to Collapse: Soviet Foreign Policy 1917-1991,* Fort Worth, TX, 1994.

Madfai, Rashid, and Madiha Jordan, *The United States and the Middle East Peace Process, 1974-1991,* Cambridge, 1993.

Malcolm, Neil, Alex Pravda, Margot Light and Roy Allison, *Internal Factors in Russian Foreign Policy,* Oxford, 1996.

Malik, Hafeez (ed.), *Soviet-American Relations with Pakistan, Iran and Afghanistan,* New York, 1987.

Malik Hafeez (ed.), *Domestic Determinants of Soviet Foreign Policy towards South Asia and the Middle East,* London, 1990.

Malik Hafeez, *Soviet-Pakistan Relations and Post-Soviet Dynamics, 1947-92,* London, 1994.

Mandelbaum, Michael, and Strobe Talbott, *Reagan and Gorbachev,* New York, 1987.

Mango, Andrew, *Turkey: the Challenge of a New Role,* London, 1994.

Ma'oz, Moshe, *Asad: the Sphinx of Damascus,* London, 1988.

McCauley, Martin (ed.), *The Soviet Union under Gorbachev,* London, 1987.

McGhee, George, *The US-Turkish-NATO Middle East Connection,* New York, 1990.

McLane, Charles B., *Soviet-Middle East Relations,* London, 1973.

Mesbahi, Mohiaddin (ed.), *Russia and the Third World in the Post-Soviet Era,* Miami, FL, 1994.

Midlarsky, Manus, John Vasquez and Peter Gladkov (eds), *From Rivalry* to Co-operation: Russian and American Perspectives on the Post-Cold War Era, New York, 1994.

Mooney Peter J., The Soviet Superpower: the Soviet Union, 1945-1980, London, 1982.

Naumkin, Vitaly (ed.), State, Religion and Society in Central Asia: a Post-Soviet Critique, Reading, 1993.

Nevers, Renéee de, Russia's Strategic Renovation, Adelphi Papers (London), 1994.

Nir, Yeshayahu, The Israeli-Arab Conflict in Soviet Caricatures 1967-1973, Tel Aviv, 1976.

Nogee, Joseph L., and Robert H. Donaldson (eds), Soviet Policy Since World War II, New York, 1988.

Pankin, Boris, The Last Hundred Days of the Soviet Union, London, 1996.

Parsons, Anthony, Prospects for Peace and Stability in the Middle East, London, 1993.

Peres, Shimon, The New Middle East, Dorchester, 1993.

Petro, Nicolai and Alvin Z. Rubinstein, Russian Foreign Policy: From Empire to Nation State, New York, 1997.

The Policy of the Soviet Union in the Arab World, ed. and publ. by Progress Publishers, Moscow, 1975. Referred to in various notes as 'Gromyko'.

Porter, Bruce D., The USSR in Third World Conflicts: Soviet Arms and Diplomacy in Local Wars 1945-1980, Cambridge, 1984.

Pursglove, Michael (ed.), The New Russia, Oxford, 1995.

Ra'anan, Uri, and Kate Martin (eds), Russia: a Return to Imperialism?, London, 1996.

Ramet, Pedro, The Soviet-Syrian Relationship Since 1955, Oxford, 1990.

Rashid, Ahmed, The Resurgence of Central Asia, London, 1994.

Rezun, Miron (ed.), Iran at the Crossroads: Global Relations in a Turbulent Decade, San Francisco, 1990.

Ro'i, Yaacov (ed.), The USSR and the Muslim World, London, 1984.

Rubenstein, Alvin Z, Soviet Policy Toward Turkey, Iran and Afghanistan: the Dynamics of Influence, New York, 1982.

———, Moscow's Third World Strategy, Princeton, NJ, 1988.

Saikal, Amin and William Maley (eds), Russia in Search of its Future, Cambridge, 1995.

Saivetz, Carol R., The Soviet Union and the Gulf in the 1980s, Boulder, CO and London, 1989.

Sawyer, Herbert L., Soviet Perceptions of the Oil Factor in U.S. Foreign Policy, Boulder, CO, 1983.

Sella, Amnon, *Soviet Political and Military Conduct in the Middle East*, London, 1981.

Sestanovich, Stephen (ed.), *Rethinking Russia's National Interests*, Washington, 1994.

Shearman, Peter (ed.), *Russian Foreign Policy Since 1990*, Oxford, 1990.

Shevardnadze, Eduard, *The Future Belongs to Freedom*, London, 1991.

Smart, Christopher, *The Imagery of Soviet Foreign Policy and the Collapse of the Russian Empire*, London, 1995.

Smolansky, Oleg, with Bettie Smolansky, *The USSR and Iraq*, London, 1991.

Taylor, Alan K., *The Superpowers and the Middle East*, Syracuse, NY, 1991.

Triska, Jan F. and David D. Finley, *Soviet Foreign Policy*, London, 1968.

Truscott, Peter, *Russia First: Breaking with the West*, London and New York, 1997.

Valenta, Jiri and Frank Cibulka (eds), *Gorbachev's 'New Thinking' and Third World Conflicts*, London, 1990.

Vassiliev, Alexei, *Russian Policy in the Middle East: from Messianism to Pragmatism*, Reading, 1993.

Vinogradov, Vladimir and Nikolai Novikov, *Yomiat diplomassiya fi bilad al-arab* (Daily Diplomacy in Arab Countries), Cairo, 1990.

Wallander, Celeste (ed.), *The Sources of Russian Foreign Policy after the Cold War*, Oxford, 1996.

Webber, Mark, *The International Politics of Russia and the Successor States*, Manchester, 1996.

———, *CIS Integration Trends: Russia and the Former Soviet Union*, London, 1997.

Winrow, Gareth, *Turkey in Post-Soviet Central Asia*, London, 1995.

Yodfat, A. and M. Abir, *In the Direction of the Gulf*, London, 1977.

Yodfat, Y. Aryeh, *The Soviet Union and the Arabian Peninsula*, London, 1983.

———, *The Soviet Union and Revolutionary Iran*, London, 1984.

Zangeneh, Hamid (ed.), *Islam, Iran and World Stability*, New York, 1994.

Selected Periodicals and Journals

Associated Press (US news agency).

Aziia i Afrika Segodnia, Moscow.

BBC Summary of World Broadcasts, Part 1: *The Soviet Union and the*

Middle East, and Part 4: *Middle East, Africa, Latin America*, 3rd series.

Commonwealth of Independent States and the Middle East, University of Jerusalem.

Communist and Post-Communist Studies, Oxford.

Current Digest of the [Soviet and] Post-Soviet Press.

Daily Star (Beirut).

Daily Telegraph.

Diplomaticheskii vestnik (official monthly journal of the Russian Foreign Ministry).

Financial Times.

Foreign Affairs, Washington, DC.

Foreign Broadcast Information Service (Central Eurasia).

Guardian.

Gulf Cooperation Council Reports, published by the members of the GCC.

Al-Hayat (popular Arab daily newspaper published in London).

The Independent.

International Affairs.

International Herald Tribune.

Izvestiia.

Jane's Intelligence Review, London.

Journal of Communist Studies and Transition Politics.

Komsomol'skaia pravda.

Literaturnaia gazeta.

Al-Malaf, Beirut.

Mezhdunarodnaia zhizn'.

The Middle East Clipboard, Washington, DC.

The Military Balance (1987-8) (International Institute of Strategic Studies, London).

Mirovaia ekonomika i mezhdunarodnye otnosheniia (academic journal closely linked to Russian Foreign Ministry).

Moscow News (English-language weekly version of *Moskovkie novosti*).

Moskovskie novosti.

New Arabia (published in London till 1991).

Nezavisimaia gazeta.

Novoe vremia (Russian weekly magazine).

The Observer.

Obshchaia gazeta.

Political Science Quarterly.

Post-Soviet Affairs, Columbia.

Pravda.

Al-Quds (pro-PLO newspaper published in London).

Radio Free Europe/Radio Liberty Research Report on the USSR.

Reuters News Agency.

RFE/Radio Liberty Daily Reports.

Rossiiskie vesti.

RUSI Journal (Royal United Services Institute for Defence Studies, London).

Russia and Eurasia Documents Annual 1992, vol. 2: CIS and Successor States, J.L. Black (ed.), Gulf Breeze, FL.

Segodnia.

Al-Sharq Al-Awsat (pro-Saudi government daily newspaper based in London).

Soviet Jewish Affairs.

Soviet Military Review, Moscow.

The Soviet Union and the Middle East (published by Soviet and East European Research Centre, Hebrew University of Jerusalem).

Survey, London.

The Times.

Transition (post-Soviet evolution of *RFE Research Reports*).

United Press International, news agency based in Washington, DC.

USSR Documents (The Gorbachev Reforms).

Al-Wasat (weekly publication, London).

Washington Post.

Washington Times.

Al-Watan, Kuwaiti daily newspaper.

World Affairs Report, California Institute of International Studies.

The World Today (Royal Institute of International Affairs, London).

Key Articles and Documents

Abarinov, Vladimir, 'Evgenii Primakov protiv inostrannogo voennogo prisutstviia v persidskom zalive' (Evgenii Primakov opposes foreign military presence in the Persian Gulf), *Segodnia,* 24 December 1996.

Adomeit, Hannes, 'Russia as a "great power"', *International Affairs,* vol.71, no.1, Jan. 1995.

Bazhanov, Evgenii, 'Top Priorities of Russia's Foreign Policy', *New Times*, October 1995.

Brown, Bess, 'Central Asia Emerges on the World Stage', *RFE/RL Research Report*, vol.1, no.1, 3 January 1992.

Chistiakov, A. (deputy director of Department of the Middle East), 'Peremeny na blizhnem vostoke i vneshnii mir' (Changes in the Middle East and the outside world), *Mezhdunarodnaia zhizn'*, no.2, 1994.

Crow Suzanne, 'Why has Russian Foreign Policy Changed', *RFE/Radio Liberty Research Report*, vol.3, no.18, 6 May 1994.

Demchenko, Pavel, 'Mezhdunarodnoe obozrenie' (International survey), *Pravda*, 25 January 1987.

Dick, Charles, 'The Military Doctrine of the Russian Federation', *Jane's Intelligence Review*, Special Report no.1, January 1994.

Dunaev, Vladimir, 'V khode obstrela bazy OON v Livane pogibli bolee 100 bezhentsev' (More than 100 refugees killed as a result of bombing of UN base in Lebanon), *Segodnia*, 20 April 1996.

Dunaev, Vladimir, 'Mirovaia diplomatiia ishchet puti vykhoda iz livan-skogo krizisa' (Peace diplomacy seeks a way out from Lebanese crisis), *Segodnia*, 24 April 1996.

Eggert, Konstantin, 'MID Rossii predlagaet schitat' Saddama Khuseina dobrym chelovekom' (Russian Foreign Ministry proposes that Sad-dam Hussein be considered a good man), *Izvestiia*, 9 August 1994.

Fukuyama, Francis, 'The Ambiguity of "National Interests"' in Stephen Sestanovich (ed.), *Rethinking Russia's National Interests*, Washington, DC, 1994.

Galkin, A. A. (from the Gorbachev Foundation), 'Kontseptsiia natsional' nykh interesov: obshchie parametry i Rossiiskaia spetsifika' (The concept of national interests: general parameters and the Russian case), *Mirovaia ekonomika i mezhdunarodnye otnosheniia*, no.8, 1996.

Gorelik, Mikhail, '16 Dnei gnev' (16 days of wrath)', *Novoe vremia*, nos.18-19, May 1996.

Husseini, Houda, interview with Andrei Vdovnii (director of Middle East Department of Russian Ministry of Foreign Affairs), 'Al dor al-russi wal Fransi al-jadid fi al-sharq al-awsat az'aj Amrika' (The new Russian-French role in the Middle East irritates the US), *Al-Sharq Al-Awsat*, 19 June 1996.

Hyman, Anthony, 'Soviet-Iranian Relations: the End of Rapproche-ment?', *Report on the USSR*, vol.2, no.4, 26 Jan.1990.

Karaganov, Sergei, 'Problemy stoiashchie pered Primakovym' (Problems facing Primakov), *Nezavisimaia gazeta*, 18 January 1996.

Kondrashov, Stanislav, 'Rossiia ishchet novoe mesto v mire' (Russia searches for a new place in the world). Interview with Primakov, *Izvestiia*, 6 March 1996.

Kozyrev, Andrei and A. Shumikhin, 'Vostok i zapad v 'tret'em mire' (East and West in the 'Third' World), in *Mezhdunarodnaia zhizn'*, Moscow, Feb. 1989.

Kozyrev, Andrei, 'Peace with a Sword', *Moscow News*, 9-15 September 1994.

Lipski, Andrei, 'Ministr, Kotorogo ne rugaet oppositsiia' (The minister not cursed by the opposition), *Obshchaia gazeta*, 19-25 September 1996.

Lukin, Vladimir, 'Vybory 1995: vneshnepoliticheskie vzgliady partii' (Elections 1995: the foreign policy views of the parties), *Mezhdunarodnaia Zhizn'*, nos 11-12, 1995.

Malcolm, Neil and Alex Pravda, 'Democratisation and Russian Foreign Policy', *International Affairs* (RIIA), vol.72, no.3, July 1996.

Matsulenko, Major-General V.,'Lessons of Imperialist Local Wars', *Soviet Military Review*, no.1, January 1982.

Medvedko, Sergei, 'Rossiia-Siriia: Zolotaia svad'ba' (Russia-Syria: a golden wedding), *Literaturnaia gazeta*, 27 July 1994.

Melnikov, Iu. and V. Frolov, 'Iranskii vopros vo bzaimootnosheniiakh Moskvy i Vashingtona' (The Iranian issue in relations between Moscow and Washington), *Mezhdunardnaia zhizn'*, no.7, 1995.

Migranian, Andranik, 'Rossiia i blizhnee zarubezh'e'(Russia and the Near Abroad), *Nezavisimaia gazeta*, 18 January 1994, pp.4,5 and 8. The author was adviser to President Yeltsin and his views seemed to mark the end of the influence over foreign policy of radical pro-Westerners in the Kremlin.

Mlechin, Leonid, 'Temnye ochki meshaiut uvidyet' istinnoe litso ministra' (The dark glasses hide the true face of the minister), *Izvestiia*,15 May 1996.

Nassar, Saleem, 'Ikhtiar olbright wa kohen tahmish ameriki li qadiat al-sharq al-awsat' (The nominations of Albright and Cohen are an American obstacle to the Middle East peace cause), *Al-Hayat*, 7 December 1996.

Nikolaev, Iuri, 'Nikto ne primiet diktata odnoi derzhavi' (No one accepts diktats of one power), *Rossiiskie vesti*, no.167 (1088), 5 September 1996.

Parrish, Scott, 'Russia: Chaos in Foreign Policy Decision-making', *Transition*, 17 May 1996.

Portanskii, Aleksei, 'Moskva schitaet, chto Izrailiu izmeniaet chuvstvo mery' (Moscow considers Israel to have lost all sense of proportion), *Izvestiia*, 29 July 1993.

Posuvaliuk, Viktor, 'Mara ukhra...'an mowqa' russiya' (Once again on Russia's role), *Al-Hayat*, 12 June 1995.

———, 'Rihla fi al-khaleej' (A trip in the Gulf), *Al-Hayat*, 30 March 1995.

———, 'Ta'amoulat ba'ed liqa' ma' safeer' (Hope after meeting an ambassador), *Al-Hayat*, 17 April 1997.

Rabin, Yitzhak, 'Prospects for Peace and Security in the Middle East', in *Royal United Services Institute for Defence Studies Journal*, February 1993.

Rahr, Alexander, 'New Thinking Takes Hold in Foreign Policy Establishment', *RFE/RL Report on the USSR*, 6 January 1989.

Reich, Bernard, 'Israel in US Perspective' in Moshe Efrat and Jacob Bercovitch (eds), *Superpowers and Client States in the Middle East: the Imbalance of Influence*, London, 1991.

Rodionov, Igor (Defence Minister of Russian Federation, Col.–General), 'Russia and NATO: Life after Bergen', *Moscow News*, 9-15 October 1996.

Rurikov, Dmitri, 'How it all Began: An Essay on New Russia's Foreign Policy', in *Russian Security after the Cold War: Seven Views from Moscow*, Teresa Pelton Johnson and Steven E. Miller (eds), Cambridge, MA, 1994.

Shamir, Israel, 'Piat' protsentov pravosudiia (Five per cent justice), *Pravda*, 20 March 1996.

Sokirko, Viktor, 'Iordantsy bol'she ne prinimaiut ranenykh Chechentsev' (Jordan no longer taking part in Chechen crisis), *Komsomol'skaia pravda*, 16 March 1996.

Stankevich, Sergei, 'Towards a New Nationalist Idea' in Stephen Sestanovich (ed.), *Rethinking Russia's National Interests*, Washington, DC, 1994.

Ukraintsev, Vladimir, 'Tools of Provocations and Aggression', *Soviet Military Review*, no.11, November 1967.

Vassiliev, Alexei, 'Al-siassia al-sofietia fi al-sharq al-awsat' (Soviet policy in the Middle East), *Al-Hayat*, 26 July 1990.

Vavilov A., 'Rossiia-Siriia i Livan: polveka druzhby i plodotvornogo sotrudnichestva' (Russia, Syria and Lebanon: half a century of friendship and of fruitful collaboration), *Aziia i Afrika Segodnia*, no.1, 1995.

Weinberger, Caspar, 'Security Arrangements in the Gulf', *Gulf Cooperation Council Reports* no.3, 1988.

Personal Meetings

With Palestinian President *Yasser Arafat* (London, early June 1996). It is worth noting that part of the reason why he agreed to give the interview was because he valued Palestinian-Russian relations so highly. His visit to the UK was only a few days after the victory of the right-wing Likud in the Israeli elections and a few weeks before the presidential elections in Russia.

With *Sergei Kepechenko*, deputy director, Middle East Department, Russian Ministry of Foreign Affairs (Moscow, late October 1996).

With *Vitaly Naumkin*, deputy director, Institute of Oriental Studies, Russian Academy of Sciences (Moscow, mid-October 1996).

With *Mahmoud Hamoud*, Lebanese ambassador to London (London, February 1997). He was ambassador to Moscow during the period of Gorbachev's New Thinking.

With *Muhiyaddin Khoja*, former Saudi ambassador to Moscow for five years till 1996 (London, summer 1996). The interview took place just before the ambassador undertook a new posting. He kindly answered a wide range of questions on Saudi-Russian/Soviet relations. He had been closely involved with many of the developments, including the establishment of relations between the two countries.

With *Dr Abdel Magid Farid* (several occasions, 1994-7). Dr Farid currently heads the Arab Research Centre in London. In the 1960s he served in a number of postings under President Nasser, taking responsibility for the leader's, meetings with foreign guests and dealing with the international media. He regularly provided me with the latest cuttings of developments in Arab-Russian relations, and his help was invaluable.

With *Dr Ahmad Ashraf Marwan* (May 1995). Currently a successful businessman, he served under President Sadat of Egypt in the early 1970s as National Security Advisor and was married to a grand-daughter of President Nasser.

I owe him special thanks for providing me with top-secret Arabic transcripts made by the Egyptian Presidential Secretariat of Information of minutes of meetings between President Sadat and his foreign and defence ministers and members of the Soviet élite including Brezhnev, Kosygin, Podgorny, Gromyko, Grechko (Defence Minister) and Ponomarev. These meetings took place in October 1971 and April 1972, and there was a meeting at foreign minister level in July 1972.

Finally, there were many suggestions, corrections, advice and unarranged meetings with academics, diplomats, and journalists which taken together were of great help. A word of thanks to *Sami Amara*, Moscow bureau chief for the Egyptian newspaper *Al-Ahram* for twenty years: his exceptional knowledge of the press and diplomatic networks in Moscow greatly assisted my work while I was staying there.

INDEX